McDougal Littell Middle School

COURSE 1

Math

Larson Boswell Kanold Stiff

Notetaking Guide

The Notetaking Guide contains a lesson-by-lesson framework that allows students to take notes on and review the main concepts of each lesson in the textbook. Each Notetaking Guide lesson features worked-out examples and Your Turn Now exercises similar to those found in the textbook. Each example has a number of write-in boxes for students to complete, either in class as the example is discussed or at home as part of a review of the lesson. Each chapter concludes with a review of the main vocabulary of the chapter. Upon completion, each chapter of the Notetaking Guide can be used by students to help review for the test on that particular chapter.

McDougal Littell
A HOUGHTON MIFFLIN COMPANY
Evanston, Illinois • Boston • Dallas

Contributing Author

The authors wish to thank the following individual for her contributions to the Notetaking Guide.

Jessica Pflueger

ISBN: 0-618-25035-2

789–PBO–07 06 05 04

Contents

COURSE 1 Notetaking Guide

Contents

Contents

Contents

Whole Number Operations

Goal: Add, subtract, multiply, and divide whole numbers.

For Your Notebook

Vocabulary Review

Whole number:

Sum:

Difference:

Product:

Quotient:

Divisor:

Dividend:

Remainder:

EXAMPLE 1 Adding Whole Numbers

a. To find the sum 68 + 25, first you line up the numbers on the ______ place. Next you add the ______. Then you add the ______.

```
   1
  68
+ 25
 ____
```

8 + 5 = 13.
Regroup the ___ one(s) as ___ ten(s) and ___ one(s).

Review: If you need help with place value and regrouping, see pages 684 and 689 of your textbook.

b. To find the sum 867 + 54, you line up the numbers on the ______ place. Next you add the ______, then the ______, then the ______.

```
  11
 867
+ 54
 ____
```

___ + ___ = ___. Regroup the ___ one(s) as ___ ten(s) and ___ one(s).

___ + ___ + ___ = ___. Regroup ___ ten(s) as ___ hundred(s) and ___ ten(s).

EXAMPLE 2 Subtracting Whole Numbers

To find the difference of 342 and 58, you line up the numbers on the ______ place. Next you subtract the ______, then the ______, and so on.

```
 342
- 58
 ____
```

You need more ones to subtract ___, so ______.

342 = ___ + ___ + ___.

Check your answer to a subtraction problem by adding. In Example 2, if you add your answer to 58, you should get 342.

Your turn now **Find the sum or difference.**

1. 83 + 49	**2.** 226 + 75	**3.** 94 − 56	**4.** 800 − 136

EXAMPLE 3 Multiplying Whole Numbers

Car Rental It costs \$23 to rent a car for one day. How much does it cost to rent a car for 14 days?

Solution You need to find the product 23 × 14.

$$\begin{array}{r} 23 \\ \times\ 14 \\ \hline \square \\ \square\ \\ \hline \square \end{array}$$

First multiply ☐ by the ones' digit, ☐.

Then multiply ☐ by the tens' digit, ☐.

Add the partial products.

Answer: It will cost \$ ☐ to rent a car for 14 days.

EXAMPLE 4 Dividing Whole Numbers

To find the quotient of 481 and 9, you use long division. The dividend is ☐ and the divisor is ☐.

☐ R ☐

9)481

Divide ☐ by ☐, because ☐ is more than 4.

Multiply: ☐ × ☐ = ☐.

Subtract: ☐ − ☐ = ☐. Bring down the ☐.

Repeat the process.

The remainder is ☐.

Your turn now **Find the product or quotient.**

5. 35 × 28	**6.** 160 × 18	**7.** 835 ÷ 7	**8.** 523 ÷ 13

EXAMPLE 5 Finding Patterns

Video Games In your favorite video game, you pass Level 1 after earning 150 points, Level 2 after earning 250 points, Level 3 after earning 350 points, and Level 4 after earning 450 points. Describe the pattern. If this pattern continues, find the number of points needed to pass Levels 5 and 6.

Solution

Look to see how each number is related to the preceding number.

The number of points for each level is ______ more than the preceding level.

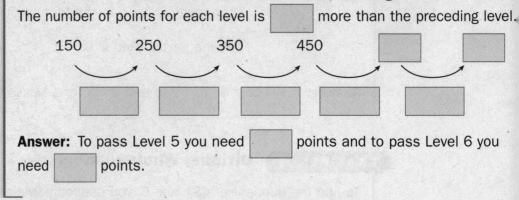

150 250 350 450 ______ ______

Answer: To pass Level 5 you need ______ points and to pass Level 6 you need ______ points.

Your turn now **Describe the pattern. Then find the next two numbers.**

9. 2, 7, 12, 17, ? , ?	**10.** 56, 52, 48, 44, ? , ?
11. 2, 6, 18, 54, ? , ?	**12.** 243, 81, 27, 9, ? , ?

Whole Number Estimation

Goal: Round to estimate with whole numbers.

For Your Notebook

Vocabulary

Leading digit:

Compatible numbers:

EXAMPLE 1 Estimating Sums

Comedy Club Tickets A comedy club sold 78 tickets for the 7 P.M. performance and 102 tickets for the 9 P.M. performance. Estimate how many tickets the club sold altogether.

By rounding to the nearest ten, you get a closer estimate of the actual sum than you would get if you rounded to the nearest hundred.

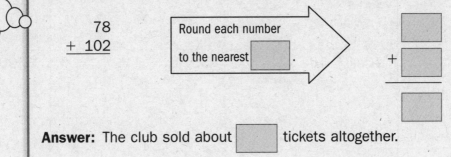

Solution

To estimate the total number of tickets sold, round the number of tickets sold for each performance to the same place value. Then add.

$$\begin{array}{r} 78 \\ +\ 102 \\ \hline \end{array}$$

Round each number to the nearest ____.

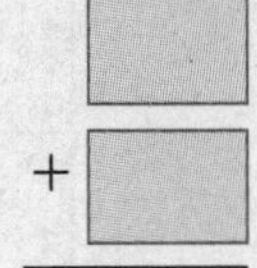

Answer: The club sold about ____ tickets altogether.

EXAMPLE 2 Estimating Differences

Printers A family is buying a new printer for their computer. They are considering a model that costs $225 and a faster model that costs $308. Estimate the difference of the costs of the printers.

Solution

To estimate the difference, round the costs to the same place value. Then subtract.

$$\begin{array}{r} 308 \\ -\ 225 \\ \hline \end{array}$$

Round each number to the nearest ______.

$$\begin{array}{r} \square \\ -\ \square \\ \hline \square \end{array}$$

Answer: The difference of the costs is about $ ______.

Your turn now **Estimate the sum or difference.**

1. 37 + 92	**2.** 43 + 279	**3.** 521 + 584
4. 41 − 16	**5.** 713 − 34	**6.** 907 − 244

EXAMPLE 3 Estimating Products

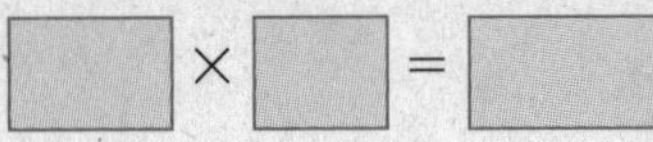

Estimate to tell whether the given answer is reasonable.

Use an estimate when you do not need an exact answer or when you need to check whether an answer is reasonable.

a. 134 × 16; 2144

☐ × ☐ = ☐ Round both numbers to ☐.

Answer: The answer ☐ reasonable because ☐.

b. 2361 × 6; 8266

☐ × ☐ = ☐ Round ☐ to its leading digit.

Answer: The answer ☐ reasonable because ☐.

EXAMPLE 4 Estimating Quotients

Estimate the quotient 635 ÷ 79.

The symbol ≈ can be read "is about equal to."

635 ÷ 79 ≈ ☐ ÷ ☐ Round the ☐ to its leading digit.

≈ ☐ ÷ ☐ Replace the ☐ with a close number that is compatible with ☐. Then divide.

= ☐ 635 ÷ 79 is about ☐.

Estimate the product or quotient.

7. 23 × 77	**8.** 784 × 42	**9.** 292 × 6
10. 133 ÷ 17	**11.** 311 ÷ 48	**12.** 896 ÷ 9

Powers and Exponents

Goal: Find values of powers.

Vocabulary

Factor:

Power:

Base:

Exponent:

Powers, Bases, and Exponents

The base of a power is the ______ and the exponent is the ______.

$9^4 = 9 \times 9 \times 9 \times 9$

There are ______ factors.

EXAMPLE 1 Writing a Power

Metric System In the metric system of measurement, there are 1,000,000 = 10 × 10 × 10 × 10 × 10 × 10 millimeters in one kilometer. Write the number of millimeters in one kilometer as a power.

1,000,000 = 10 × 10 × 10 × 10 × 10 × 10 There are ______ factors.

= ______

Answer: There are ______ millimeters in one kilometer.

Your turn now **Write the product as a power.**

1. $3 \times 3 \times 3 \times 3 \times 3 \times 3 \times 3$	2. $5 \times 5 \times 5 \times 5$	3. $40 \times 40 \times 40$

EXAMPLE 2 Finding the Value of a Power

a. Find the value of nine squared.

☐ = ☐ Write ☐ as a factor ☐ times.

= ☐ Multiply.

b. Find the value of three to the fourth power.

☐ = ☐ Write ☐ as a factor ☐ times.

= ☐ Multiply.

EXAMPLE 3 Powers in Real-World Problems

Movie Theaters A movie theater has 12 rows of seats. In each row there are 12 seats. How many seats are in the movie theater altogether?

In some cases, it may be helpful to draw a diagram so you can visualize the problem.

Solution

☐ × ☐ = ☐ = ☐

Number of seats in one row

Number of rows

Answer: There are ☐ seats in the movie theater.

Your turn now **Write the power as a product. Then find the value.**

4. 15^2 **5.** 7^3 **6.** 1^5

7. 10^4	**8.** 8 cubed
9. 2 to the sixth power	

Order of Operations

Goal: Evaluate expressions using the order of operations.

For Your Notebook

Vocabulary

Numerical expression:

Grouping symbols:

Evaluate:

Order of operations:

Order of Operations

1. Evaluate ______.
2. Evaluate ______.
3. ______ and ______ from left to right.
4. ______ and ______ from left to right.

EXAMPLE 1 Using the Order of Operations

WATCH OUT!
In part (a) of Example 1, divide *before* multiplying because the division is on the left. In part (b), subtract *before* adding because the subtraction is on the left.

a. $16 \div 8 \times 7 =$ ______ First ______.

$=$ ______ Then ______.

b. $21 - 13 + 4 =$ ______ First ______.

$=$ ______ Then ______.

c. $15 + 8 \div 4 - 9 =$ ______ First ______.

$=$ ______ Next ______.

$=$ ______ Then ______.

EXAMPLE 2 Powers and Grouping Symbols

a. $20 - 4^2 =$ ______ First ______.

$=$ ______ Then ______.

b. $(5 + 2) \times 6 =$ ______ First ______

$=$ ______ Then ______.

c. $\frac{3 + 9}{7 - 4} =$ ______ First evaluate ______

$=$ ______ Then ______.

Your turn now **Evaluate the expression.**

1. $6 + 4 - 7$	**2.** $14 - 2 \times 3$	**3.** $32 - 3 \times 5 + 8$
4. $42 - 5^2$	**5.** $10 \times (4 + 5)$	**6.** $(15 - 9) \times 4 + 3$
7. $8 + 2 \times 7^2$	**8.** $\frac{21 - 9}{4}$	**9.** $\frac{13 + 2}{10 - 7}$

EXAMPLE 3 Solving Multi-Step Problems

Ski Trip You and four of your family members are planning a ski vacation during an upcoming 3-day weekend. The ski rental is $14 each day for adult skis and $12 each day for junior skis. Your family needs to rent 3 pairs of junior skis and 2 pairs of adult skis. How much will the ski rental cost for the entire weekend?

Solution

1. ______ to find the cost of adult skis for three days.

   ___ adults ___ $ ___ per adult per day ___ ___ days = $ ___

2. ______ to find the cost of junior skis for three days.

   ___ juniors ___ $ ___ per junior per day ___ ___ days = $ ___

3. ______ the adult cost and the junior cost to find the total cost.

   $ ___ ___ $ ___ = $ ___

Answer: The total cost for ski rental is $ ___.

Your turn now **Use the situation in Example 3.**

10. If 3 more adults decide to go on the trip, what will be the new total cost for ski rental?

11. If the cost of a junior rental goes down by $1, what will be the new total cost for the original group?

LESSON 1.5

Variables and Expressions

Goal: Evaluate expressions that involve variables.

Vocabulary

Variable:

Variable expression:

EXAMPLE 1 Evaluating Expressions

a. Evaluate $12 - n$, when $n = 5$.

$12 - n =$ ____ Substitute ____ for ____.

$=$ ____ Subtract.

b. Evaluate $x \div 6$, when $x = 72$.

$x \div 6 =$ ____ Substitute ____ for ____.

$=$ ____ Divide.

Your turn now **Evaluate the expression.**

1. $t + 13$, when $t = 8$	**2.** $17 - a$, when $a = 12$
3. $y - 4$, when $y = 11$	**4.** $s \div 5$, when $s = 40$

EXAMPLE 2 Evaluating Multiplication Expressions

Bowling A bowling alley charges $1 for shoe rental and $4 for each game. The expression $4g + 1$ can be used to find the total cost of playing g games at the bowling alley. Find the total cost of playing 3, 4, and 5 games.

1. Choose values for g (number of games).

2. Substitute for g in the expression $4g + 1$.

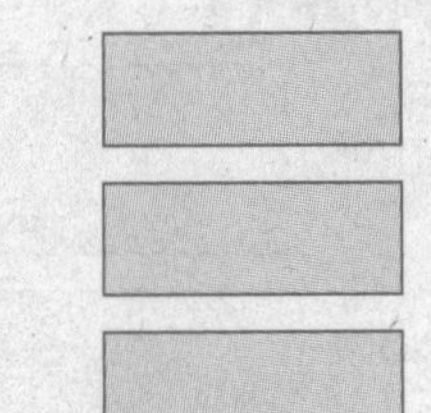

3. Evaluate the expressions to find the total costs of the games.

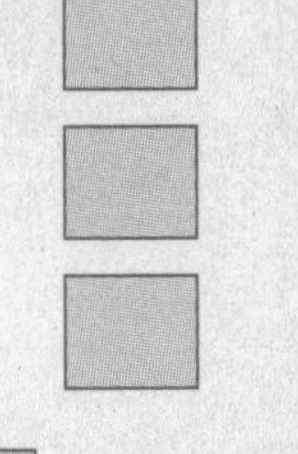

Answer: It costs $ ☐ to play three games. It costs $ ☐ to play four games. It costs $ ☐ to play five games.

EXAMPLE 3 Expressions with Two Variables

Evaluate the expression when $x = 3$ and $y = 7$.

a. $x + y =$ ☐   Substitute ☐ for ☐ and ☐ for ☐.

$=$ ☐   Add.

You may want to include part (b) in your notebook as a reminder to use the order of operations when evaluating a variable expression.

b. $x^2 - y =$ ☐   

$=$ ☐   Evaluate the power.

$=$ ☐   Subtract.

Your turn now **Evaluate the expression when $p = 12$ and $q = 5$.**

5. $4p$	**6.** $15q$	**7.** $3q + 2$	**8.** $38 - 2p$
9. $p - q$	**10.** $p + 6q$	**11.** $50 - q^2$	**12.** $p + 8 - q$

Equations and Mental Math

Goal: Solve equations using mental math.

For Your Notebook

Vocabulary

Equation:

Solution:

Solve:

EXAMPLE 1 **Guess, Check, and Revise**

Email You have a 4-digit password for your email account. The first three digits are 2, 3, and 7. The product of all the digits is 336. What is the last digit?

When using *guess*, *check*, and *revise*, use the information given in the problem to make an educated first guess.

Solution

To answer this question, you can use the problem solving strategy *guess*, *check*, and *revise*.

1. Try the digit 5, which is halfway between 1 and 9.

This product is ______ 336.

2. Try the digit 9, which is greater than 5.

This product is ______ 336.

3. Try the digit 8, which is less than 9.

This product is ______ 336.

Answer: The last digit is ___.

EXAMPLE 2 Checking a Possible Solution

Tell whether the given number is a solution of the equation.

a. $8m = 82; 9$

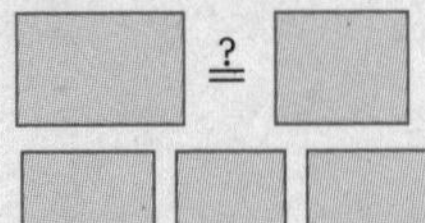

b. $x - 7 = 18; 25$

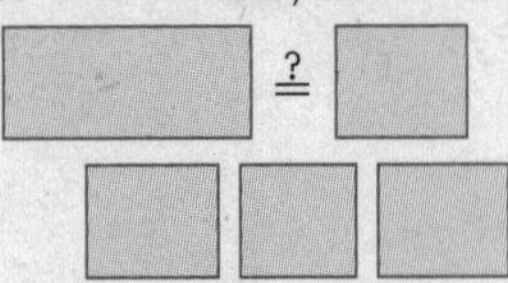

Answer: 9 ______ a solution.

Answer: 25 ______ a solution.

EXAMPLE 3 Using Mental Math to Solve Equations

In your notes for this lesson, you may want to include examples showing equations rewritten as questions.

Equation ⟶ **Question** ⟶ **Solution** ⟶ **Check**

a. $y - 6 = 14$ ______ minus ______ equals ______?

b. $15r = 45$ ______ times ______ equals ______?

c. $b \div 7 = 8$ ______ divided by ______ equals ______?

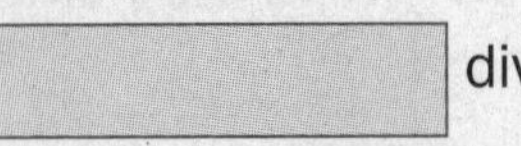

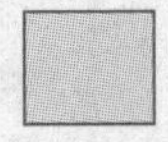

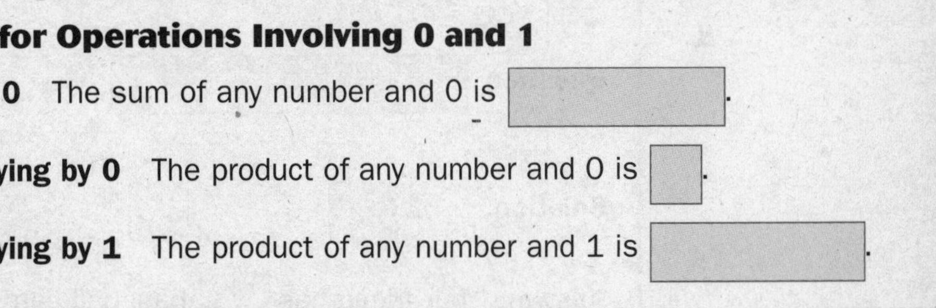

Rules for Operations Involving 0 and 1

Adding 0 The sum of any number and 0 is ______.

Multiplying by 0 The product of any number and 0 is ______.

Multiplying by 1 The product of any number and 1 is ______.

EXAMPLE 4 Mental Math with 0 and 1

Equation ⟶ **Question** ⟶ **Solution** ⟶ **Check**

a. $z + 9 = 9$

b. $12 \cdot c = 12$

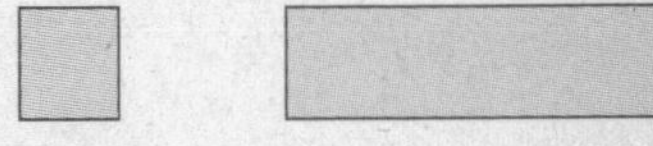

Your turn now **Solve the equation using mental math.**

1. $n + 13 = 22$	**2.** $17x = 17$	**3.** $t - 9 = 27$
4. $6p = 42$	**5.** $34 \div d = 2$	**6.** $3s = 0$

EXAMPLE 5 Solving Problems Using Mental Math

Baseball Cards Together, you and a friend have 250 baseball cards. You have 178 baseball cards. Use mental math to solve the equation $c + 178 = 250$ to find the number of cards c your friend has.

Solution

Think of the equation as a question.

Equation   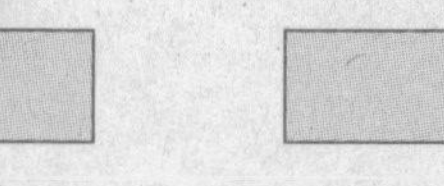

↓

Question  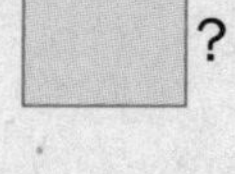 ?

↓

Solution  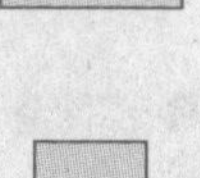   .

Answer: Your friend has ___ baseball cards.

A Problem Solving Plan

Goal: Use a problem solving plan.

For Your Notebook

Vocabulary

Verbal model:

EXAMPLE 1 Understanding and Planning

Book Sales A discount bookstore sells paperback books for $5 each and hardcover books for $9 each. At the end of the day, the store has sold 325 paperback books and 175 hardcover books. How much money did the bookstore make by the end of the day?

Solution

To solve the problem, first make sure you understand the problem. Then make a plan for solving the problem.

Read and Understand

What do you know?

What do you want to find out?

Make a Plan

How can you relate what you know to what you want to find out?
Write a *verbal model* to describe how the values in this problem are related.

= +

Your turn now **Use the information from Example 1.**

1. How can you figure out how much money was made from paperback books?

2. How can you figure out how much money was made from hardcover books?

EXAMPLE 2 Solving and Looking Back

Book Sales To solve the problem from Example 1 about bookstore sales, you need to carry out your plan from Example 1 and then check the answer.

Solve the Problem

Write a verbal model to relate the amount of money made by the end of the day to the amount of money made from selling each kind of book. Then substitute values into the verbal model.

[ ] = [ ] + [ ]

= [ ] + [ ]

= [ ] + [ ]

= [ ]

Answer: The bookstore made $ [ ] by the end of the day.

Look Back

Make sure your answer is reasonable. Estimate the amount of money made by the end of the day. This number should be close to your answer.

[ ] + [ ] ≈ [ ] + [ ]

= [ ] + [ ]

= [ ] ✓

Your turn now **Use Example 2 above.**

3. If hardcover books sold for $10 each instead of $9 each, how much would the store have made by the end of the day?

Problem Solving Plan

1. **Read and Understand**
2. **Make a Plan**
3. **Solve the Problem**
4. **Look Back**

EXAMPLE 3 **Draw a Diagram**

Tennis You and a friend are going to play tennis at the courts near your homes. You leave your house and walk 4 blocks north and then 2 blocks east to your friend's house. From your friend's house, you get to the courts by walking 1 block south and 3 blocks east. How many blocks do you have to walk to get back to your house from the tennis courts?

Here is a list of some common problem solving strategies.
Guess, Check, and Revise
Draw a Diagram
Perform an Experiment
Make a List
Work Backward
Look for a Pattern
Solve a Simpler Problem
Make a Model
Break into Parts
Use an Equation
Act It Out

Solution

Read and Understand

What do you know and what do you want to find out?

Make a Plan

Draw a diagram to show ________. Use the diagram to solve the problem.

Solve the Problem

Draw the path on a piece of graph paper.

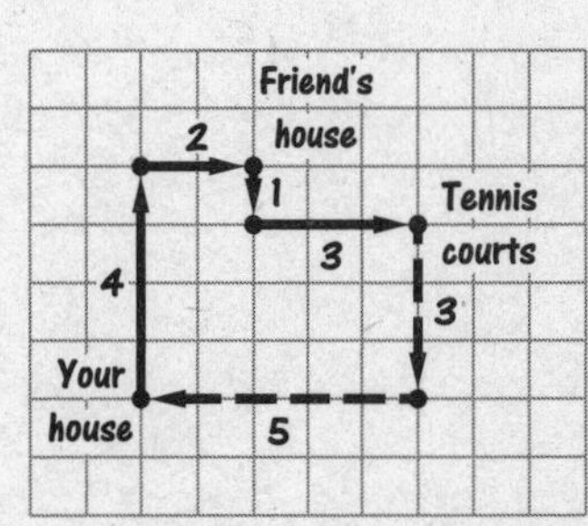

Answer: From the diagram, you can see that you will have to walk ____ blocks to get home.

Look Back

You walked ____ blocks to get to the tennis courts from your house via your friend's house. Because ________, the answer is reasonable.

Your turn now **The grid shows the locations of different places in your neighborhood.**

4. You leave home to drop off some books at the library, stop at the store for some items, and then return home. How many blocks do you walk during the trip?

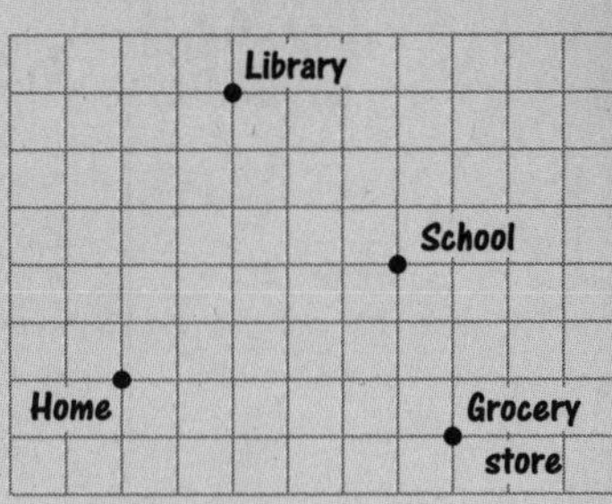

5. Write directions for your friend to get from school to your house.

6. If you walk to and from school every day, how many blocks do you walk between Monday and Friday?

Words to Review

Give an example of the vocabulary word.

Leading digit

Compatible numbers

Factor

Power

Base

Exponent

Numerical expression

Grouping symbols

Evaluate

Order of operations

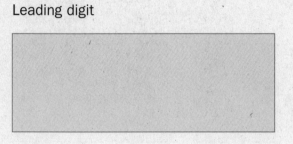

Variable

Variable expression

Equation

Solution

Solve

Verbal model

Review your notes and Chapter 1 by using the Chapter Review on pages 48–49 of your textbook.

Measuring Length

Goal: Measure length using customary and metric units.

For Your Notebook

Vocabulary

Inch:

Foot:

Yard:

Mile:

Millimeter:

Centimeter:

Meter:

Kilometer:

EXAMPLE 1 Using Customary Units of Length

Find the length of the leaf to the nearest inch.

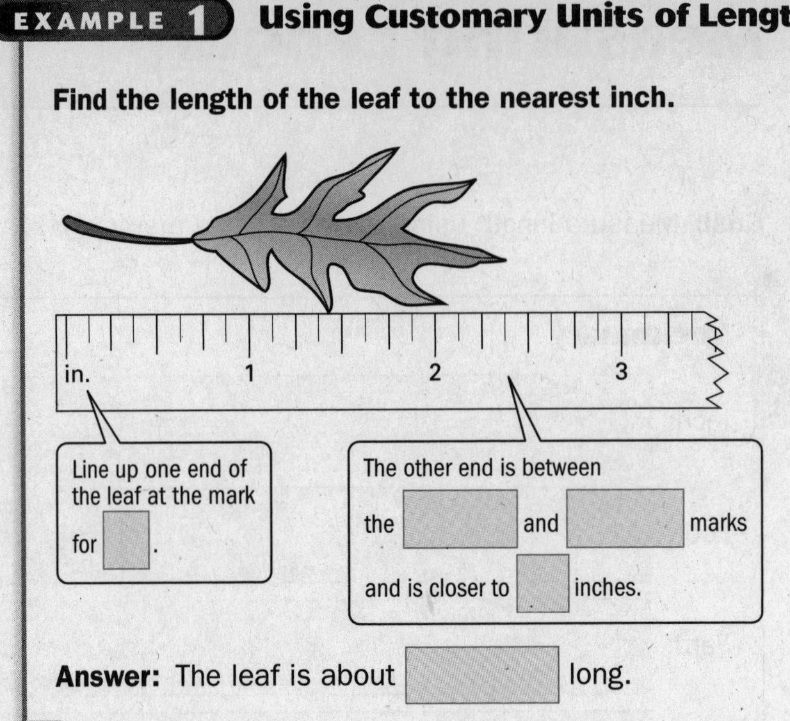
in.
1
2
3
Line up one end of the leaf at the mark for ___.
The other end is between the ___ and ___ marks and is closer to ___ inches.

Answer: The leaf is about ______ long.

EXAMPLE 2 Using Metric Units of Length

Find the length of the fish to the nearest millimeter.

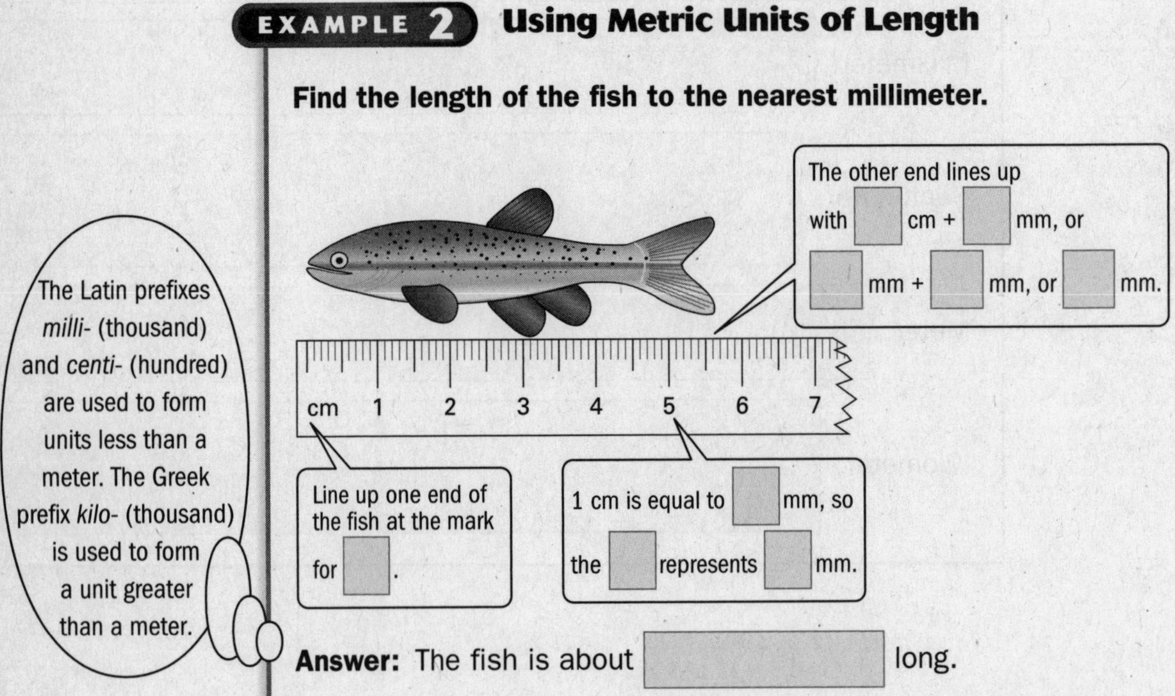
The other end lines up with ___ cm + ___ mm, or ___ mm + ___ mm, or ___ mm.
cm
1
2
3
4
5
6
7
Line up one end of the fish at the mark for ___.
1 cm is equal to ___ mm, so the ___ represents ___ mm.
The Latin prefixes *milli-* (thousand) and *centi-* (hundred) are used to form units less than a meter. The Greek prefix *kilo-* (thousand) is used to form a unit greater than a meter.

Answer: The fish is about ______ long.

EXAMPLE 3 Choosing Appropriate Units

Choose an appropriate customary unit and metric unit for the length.

a. height of a cell phone tower **b.** length of the Mississippi River

Solution

a. The height of a cell phone tower is much greater than ______ ______, and much less than ______. So, you should use ______.

b. The length of the Mississippi River is much greater than ______ ______. So, you should use ______.

Your turn now **Measure the object to the nearest whole unit.**

1. width of a CD case (millimeters)

2. width of a piece of letter-size paper (inches)

3. length of your shoe (centimeters)

Your turn now **Choose an appropriate customary unit and metric unit for the length.**

4. length of a ski	**5.** width of a milk carton

Benchmarks for Units of Length

A benchmark ______.

Customary Units

An **inch** is about the same as ______.

A **foot** is about the same as ______.

A **yard** is about the same as ______.

Metric Units

A **millimeter** is about the same as ______.

A **centimeter** is about the same as ______.

A **meter** is about the same as ______.

EXAMPLE 4 **Estimating Length Using Benchmarks**

Estimate the height of the volleyball net below in meters. Then measure to check your estimate.

Solution

You can use your own height as a benchmark when estimating.

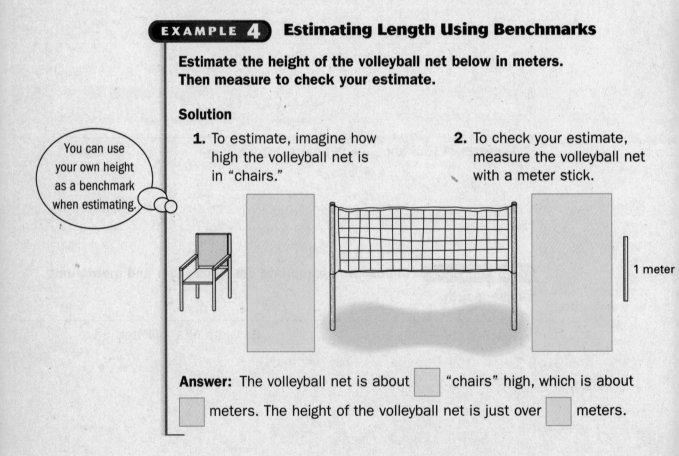

1. To estimate, imagine how high the volleyball net is in "chairs."

2. To check your estimate, measure the volleyball net with a meter stick.

1 meter

Answer: The volleyball net is about ___ "chairs" high, which is about ___ meters. The height of the volleyball net is just over ___ meters.

LESSON 2.2

Perimeter and Area

Goal: Use formulas to find perimeter and area.

For Your Notebook

Vocabulary

Perimeter: ______

Area: ______

Perimeter of a Rectangle

Words Perimeter = ______

Algebra $P =$ ______

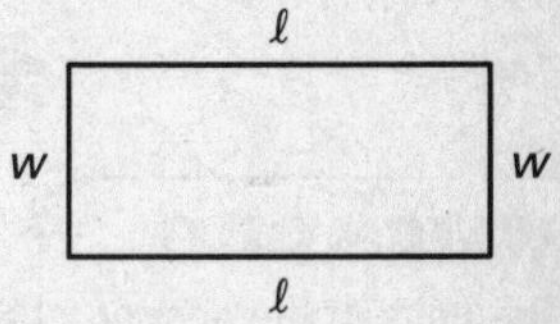

EXAMPLE 1 Finding the Perimeter of a Rectangle

Flower Box You are making a flower box using recycled railroad ties. The flower box will be 9 feet long and 4 feet wide. How many feet of railroad ties will you need to make the flower box?

Solution

To answer the question, find the perimeter.

$P =$ ______ Write the formula for perimeter of a rectangle.

$=$ ______ Substitute ___ for ___ and ___ for ___.

$=$ ______ Multiply.

$=$ ______ Add.

Answer: You need ______ of railroad ties to make the flower box.

Your turn now **Find the perimeter of the rectangle described.**

1. length = 4 yd, width = 7 yd	**2.** length = 17 cm, width = 12 cm

Area of a Rectangle

Words Area = ______

Algebra $A =$ ______

ℓ

w w

ℓ

EXAMPLE 2 Finding the Area of a Rectangle

WATCH OUT!
The units of the answer are square feet, not linear feet. To help you remember this, think of multiplying the units: $\ell w = \text{ft} \times \text{ft} = \text{ft}^2$.

Find the area of the flower box from Example 1.

$A =$ ______ Write the formula for the area of a rectangle.

$=$ ______ Substitute ______ for ______ and ______ for ______.

$=$ ______ Multiply.

Answer: The area of the flower box is ______.

EXAMPLE 3 Perimeter and Area of a Square

Find the perimeter and area of a 70-foot by 70-foot playground.

Perimeter = ______ Area = ______

= ______ = ______

= ______ = ______

Answer: The perimeter is ______. The area is ______.

Your turn now **Tell whether to find the *perimeter* or the *area* to help you decide how much of the item to buy. Then find the measurement.**

3. fabric for a 30-inch by 30-inch tablecloth

4. string to mark the outside border of an 18-meter by 9-meter volleyball court

EXAMPLE 4 Solving for an Unknown Dimension

Algebra Write and solve an equation to find the length of a rectangle whose area is 234 square millimeters and whose width is 13 millimeters.

Need help with thinking of a related equation? See page 687 of your textbook.

☐ = ☐ Write the formula for the ☐ of a rectangle.

☐ = ☐ Substitute ☐ for ☐ and ☐ for ☐.

☐ = ☐ Write the related ☐ equation.

☐ = ☐ ☐.

Answer: The length of the rectangle is ☐.

Your turn now **Write and solve an equation to find the length.**

5. Area of rectangle = 575 in.^{2}, width = __?__, length = 25 in.

6. Perimeter of square = 480 m, side length = __?__

Scale Drawings

Goal: Use scale drawings to find actual lengths.

Vocabulary

Scale drawing:

Scale:

EXAMPLE 1 **Interpreting Scale Drawings**

Floor Plan Find the actual lengths that correspond to 6 inches, 8 inches, and 13 inches on the scale drawing for the first floor of a house. What is the length and width of the first floor of the house?

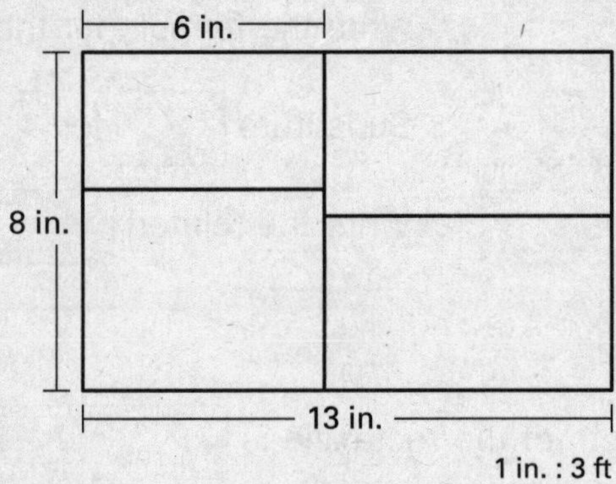

Solution

Make a table. The scale of the drawing is ______. Each inch on the drawing represents ______ of the house.

Scale drawing length (inches)	Dimension × ___	Actual length (feet)
6	___ × ___	18
8	___ × ___	24
13	___ × ___	39

Answer: The actual length and width of the first floor of the house are ______ and ______.

EXAMPLE 2 Using a Scale to Find Actual Lengths

Model Car A model car is 8 inches long. The scale used to create the car is 2 in. : 48 in. How long is the actual car?

The standard way to write a scale is *scale model : actual object.*

Solution

Find the relationship between the known length and the scale.

model : actual

[ ] : [ ] Write the scale.

× ?

[ ] : __?__ in. Ask, "[ ]"

Because [ ] × [ ] = [ ], you multiply by [ ] to find the actual length.

model : actual

[ ] : [ ] Write the scale.

[ ] : [ ] × [ ]

Answer: The actual car is [ ] long.

EXAMPLE 3 Finding Lengths for a Model

Model Bridge You are building a model of the George Washington Bridge using a scale of 1 in. : 500 ft. The actual bridge is 3500 feet long. How long do you make your model?

Solution

Find the relationship between the known length and the scale.

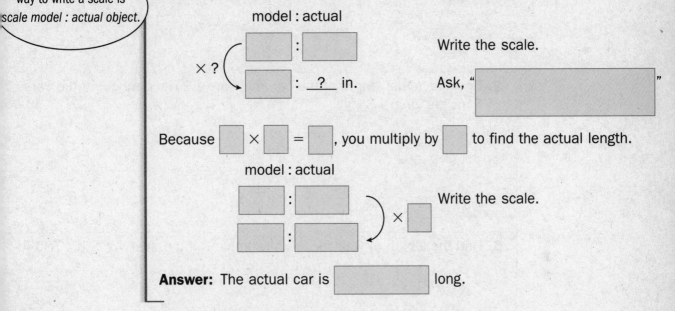

model : actual

[ ] : [ ] Write the scale.

× ?

__?__ in. : [ ] Ask, "[ ]"

Because [ ] × [ ] = [ ], you multiply by [ ] to find the length of the model: [ ] × [ ] = [ ]

Answer: You make your model [ ] long.

Your turn now **Refer to Examples 1–3.**

1. Find the length and width of the house in Example 1 using the scale 1 in. : 5 ft.

2. Find the actual length of the car in Example 2 if the model of the car is 6 inches long.

3. Find the length of your model in Example 3 if the scale is 1 in. : 700 ft.

Frequency Tables and Line Plots

Goal: Create and interpret frequency tables and line plots.

For Your Notebook

Vocabulary

Data:

Frequency table:

Line plot:

EXAMPLE 1 Making a Frequency Table

Family Vacation Students were asked to identify the month their family took a summer vacation. Make a frequency table of the data. In which month did most of the families take their vacation?

June, June, June, July, August, June, August, July, July, June, August, June, August, July, August

Solution

Month	Tally	Frequency
June		
July		
August		

Answer: Most of the families took their vacation in ______.

Your turn now

1. For a long list of data, explain why it is helpful to record the data as tally marks and then count the tally marks for the frequency.

2. Make a frequency table of the letters that occur in the word "Albuquerque." Which letter occurs most often?

EXAMPLE 2 Making a Line Plot

House Plants The frequency table shows the numbers of house plants people have in their house.

a. Make a line plot of the data.

b. Use the line plot to find the total number of people.

c. Use the line plot to find how many people have less than three plants.

Plants	Tally	Frequency
0	III	3
1	~~IIII~~ I	6
2	IIII	4
3	~~IIII~~	5
4	II	2
5	I	1

Solution

a.

The X marks above the number line show the ______.

Number of Plants

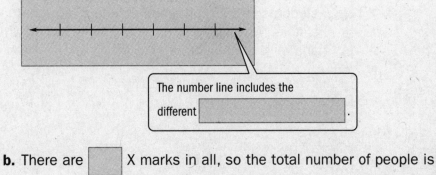

The number line includes the different ______.

Need help with number lines? See page 685 of your textbook.

b. There are ______ X marks in all, so the total number of people is ______.

c. The total number of X marks ______ the numbers ______ is ______, so ______ people have less than three plants.

Your turn now **The following data show the numbers of brothers and sisters in students' families. Use the data in Exercises 3–5.**

4, 0, 1, 1, 2, 0, 3, 3, 4, 5, 2, 2, 1, 0, 0, 0, 5, 2, 2, 4

3. Make a frequency table of the data.

4. Make a line plot of the data.

5. Choose one of the displays and use it to find out whether more students had 2 brothers and sisters or more than 3 brothers and sisters. Which display did you choose and how did you use it to answer the question?

Bar Graphs

Goal: Display data using bar graphs.

For Your Notebook

Vocabulary

Bar graph:

Double bar graph:

EXAMPLE 1 Making a Bar Graph

Speed Limits The numbers of states with a given speed limit on an urban interstate are shown in the table. Make a bar graph of the data.

Urban Interstates	
Speed Limit (miles per hour)	**States**
50	1
55	20
60	3
65	19
70	7

Solution

1. Choose a numerical scale. Start the scale at ____. The greatest data value is ____, so end the scale at a value greater than ____, such as ____. Use equal increments along the scale, such as increments of ____.

2. Draw and label the graph.

Need help with reading a bar graph? See page 704 of your textbook.

EXAMPLE 2 Making a Double Bar Graph

Radio Stations Make a double bar graph of the radio station data in the table.

Radio station format	Stations in 1999	Stations in 2001
Country	2305	2190
Rock	730	760
Top 40	401	468
R & B	278	301
Jazz	72	81

Solution

The greatest data value in the table is _____, so end the scale at _____.

Draw the first set of bars using the _____ data, leaving room for the _____ bars.

Then draw the _____ bars _____ the _____ bars and shade them a different color. Add a _____ and a _____.

Your turn now **Make a double bar graph of the data.**

1.

United States Crop Production (millions of metric tons)					
Crop	Corn	Soybeans	Wheat	Cotton	Milled Rice
1999	240	72	63	14	7
2000	253	75	61	17	6

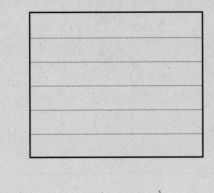

Coordinates and Line Graphs

Goal: Plot points on coordinate grids and make line graphs.

For Your Notebook

Vocabulary

Ordered pair:

Coordinates:

Line graph:

EXAMPLE 1 Graphing Points

a. Graph the point (2, 5) on a coordinate grid.

Start at ______. Move ______ units to the right and ______ units up.

b. Graph the point (4, 0) on a coordinate grid.

Start at ______. Move ______ units to the right and ______ units up.

Your turn now **Graph the points on the same coordinate grid.**

1. (0, 3)
2. (4, 1)
3. (5, 0)
4. (2, 2)

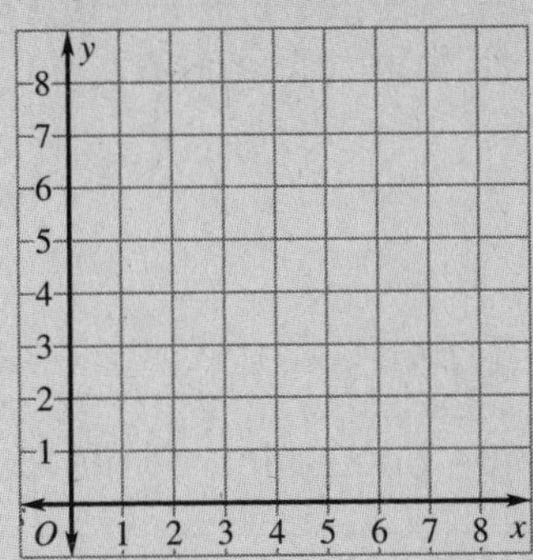

5. In Exercises 1–4, the first coordinate is the number of years a copier has been owned by a company. The second coordinate is the worth of the copier in hundreds of dollars. What is the copier worth after 4 years?

EXAMPLE 2 Making a Line Graph

Newspapers Make a line graph of the newspaper data below.

U.S. Weekly Newspapers						
Year	1975	1980	1985	1990	1995	2000
Newspapers	7612	7954	7704	7606	8453	7689

Solution

To make a line graph of the data, think of each column of the table as an ordered pair:

(______ , ______).

1. Choose a scale. Use a break in the scale for the population to focus on values between ______ and ______.

2. Graph ______.

3. Connect the points by ______.

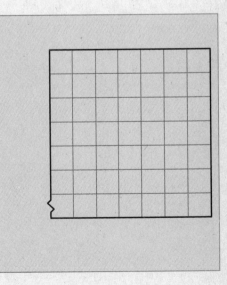

When choosing a scale for a graph with a break, make sure that the range of the scale can be divided into an even number of units.

Your turn now **In Exercise 6, use the graph in Example 2.**

6. During which years was the decrease in the number of newspapers the least? How can you tell from the graph?

7. Make a line graph of the population of the U.S. Virgin Islands.

Population of U.S. Virgin Islands					
Year	1960	1970	1980	1990	2000
Population (thousands)	33	63	100	104	121

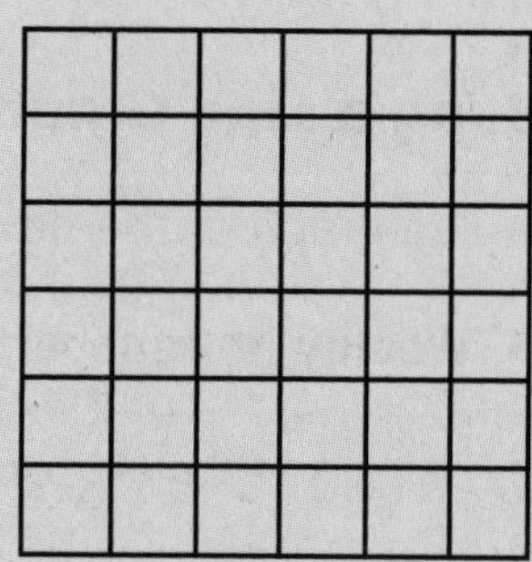

Circle Graphs

Goal: Interpret circle graphs and make predictions.

For Your Notebook

Vocabulary

Circle graph: ____________

EXAMPLE 1 Interpreting a Circle Graph

Paper A group of students are asked what kind of paper they use when taking notes in class. Their answers are shown in the circle graph.

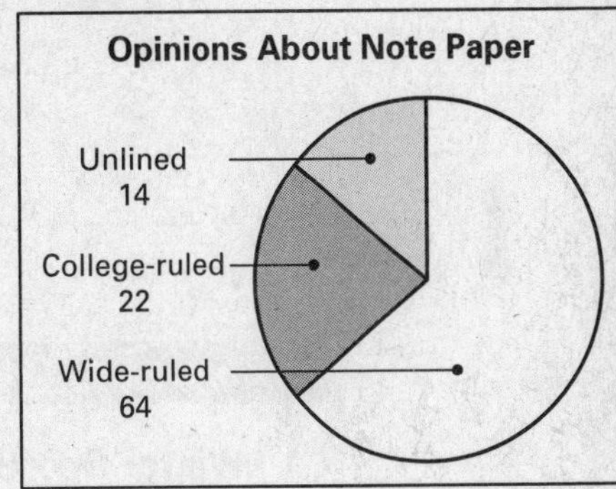

a. How many students prefer using wide-ruled paper?

b. How many students do not use wide-ruled paper?

Solution

a. To find out how many students prefer using wide-ruled paper, find the data value in the section labeled ____________

Answer: The number who prefer using wide-ruled paper is ____.

b. To find out how many students do not prefer using wide-ruled paper, add the values in the ____________ and ____________ sections:

____ + ____ = ____.

Answer: The number who do not prefer using wide-ruled paper is ____.

Your turn now **In Exercises 1–3, use the circle graph that shows how many teenagers out of 100 prefer using a bike, a scooter, a skateboard, or in-line skates.**

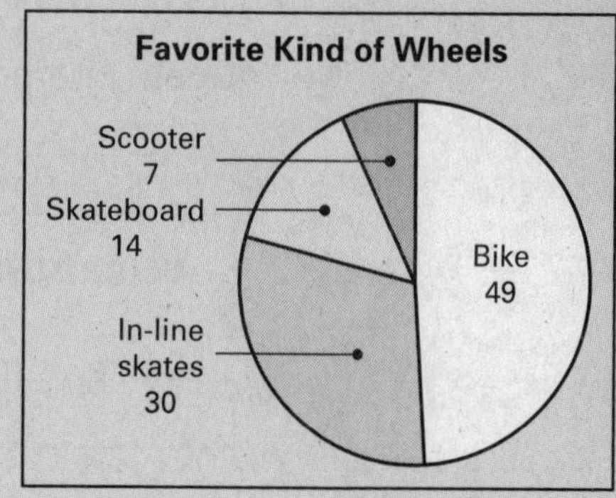

1. Which item is most popular?

2. How many teenagers do not prefer skateboards?

3. Is it reasonable to say that the scooter is the least popular choice? Explain.

EXAMPLE 2 Using a Graph

Writing down key facts as you read a problem can help you solve it. In Example 2, you know: 100 students were surveyed, 48 of them like skiing, and 200 people are in the group you're predicting for.

Winter Sports The circle graph shows the favorite winter sport of 100 students. Predict how many students out of 200 you would expect to respond "Skiing."

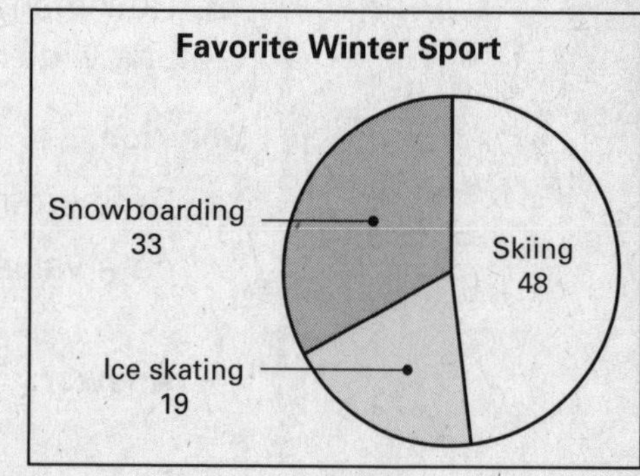

Solution

Find the relationship between the number of students surveyed and the number of students in the group you're making a prediction for:

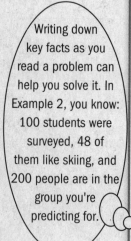

Multiply the number of students who prefer skiing by ____ to predict the number of students out of the group of 200 that will respond "Skiing":

____ × ____ = ____.

Answer: About ____ students in a group of 200 should respond "Skiing."

Your turn now **Use the circle graph in Example 2.**

4. Predict the number of students out of 500 you would expect to respond "Snowboarding."

Mean, Median, and Mode

Goal: Describe data using mean, median, mode, and range.

Vocabulary

Mean:

Median:

Mode:

Range:

EXAMPLE 1 **Finding a Mean**

CD Collections The numbers of CDs in students' collections are listed below. Find the mean of the data.

35 30 34 30 33 34 28

Solution

To find the mean of the numbers of CDs, ______ the number of CDs in the students' collections. Then divide by ______, the number of collections.

Mean = $\frac{\quad}{\quad}$ = $\frac{\quad}{\quad}$ = ______

Answer: The mean of the numbers of CDs is ______ CDs.

EXAMPLE 2 Finding Median, Mode, and Range

CD Collections Find the median, mode(s), and range of the CD collections in Example 1.

Solution

Put the numbers of CDs in order from ______ to ______.

______ ______ ______ ______ ______ ______ ______

Median: The middle number is ______, so the median is ______.

Mode: ______ and ______ occur ______. There are ______ mode(s), ______.

Range: Range = Largest number of CDs − Smallest number of CDs

= ______ − ______

= ______

EXAMPLE 3 Choosing the Best Average

Baseball The total numbers of runs in a series of baseball games are listed below. Choose the best average(s) for the data.

10 3 0 8 15 3 11 6

Solution

Mean: ______ ÷ ______ = ______. The mean is ______ the data values.

Median: ______ ÷ ______ = ______. The median is ______ the data values.

Mode: The mode is ______. The mode is ______ the data values.

Answer: The ______ is not typical of the data. The ______ best represent the data.

Be sure your notes include an example with an even number of data values, such as Example 3. Make note of the fact that the median is the mean of the two middle numbers.

Your turn now **Find the mean, median, mode(s), and range.**

1. 15, 24, 17, 14, 21, 26, 30	**2.** 42, 35, 40, 28, 35
3. 4, 13, 9, 5, 5, 14, 6, 8	**4.** 89, 104, 98, 90, 89, 96, 110, 10
5. Choose the best average(s) to represent the data in Exercise 4.	

Words to Review

Give an example of the vocabulary word.

Inch

Foot

Yard

Mile

Millimeter

Centimeter

Meter

Kilometer

Perimeter

Area

Scale drawing

Scale

Data

Frequency table

Line plot

Bar graph

Double bar graph

Ordered pair

Coordinates

Line graph

Circle graph

Mean

Median

Mode

Range

Review your notes and Chapter 2 by using the Chapter Review on pages 100–101 of your textbook.

LESSON
3.1

Decimals and Place Value

Goal: Read and write decimals.

For Your Notebook

Vocabulary

Decimal:

EXAMPLE 1 Expressing a Number in Different Ways

a. Write 50 hundredths using only tenths.

50 hundredths

☐ × ☐ hundredths

☐ × ☐ tenth

☐ tenths

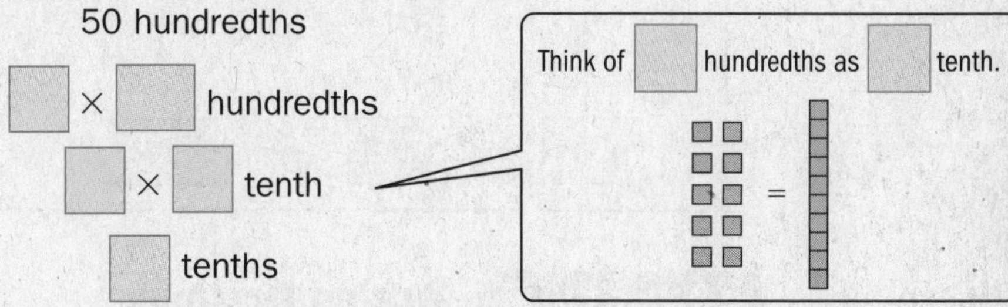
Think of ☐ hundredths as ☐ tenth.
=

b. Write 1 one and 7 tenths using only tenths.

1 one and 7 tenths

☐ tenths and ☐ tenths

☐ tenths

Use the fact that 1 one equals ☐ tenths.

You might want to record relationships between base-ten pieces in your notebook, such as 1 one = 10 tenths.

Your turn now **Copy and complete the statement.**

1. 800 hundredths = ___?___ tenths	**2.** 3 ones and 5 tenths = ___?___ tenths

Decimals and Place Value

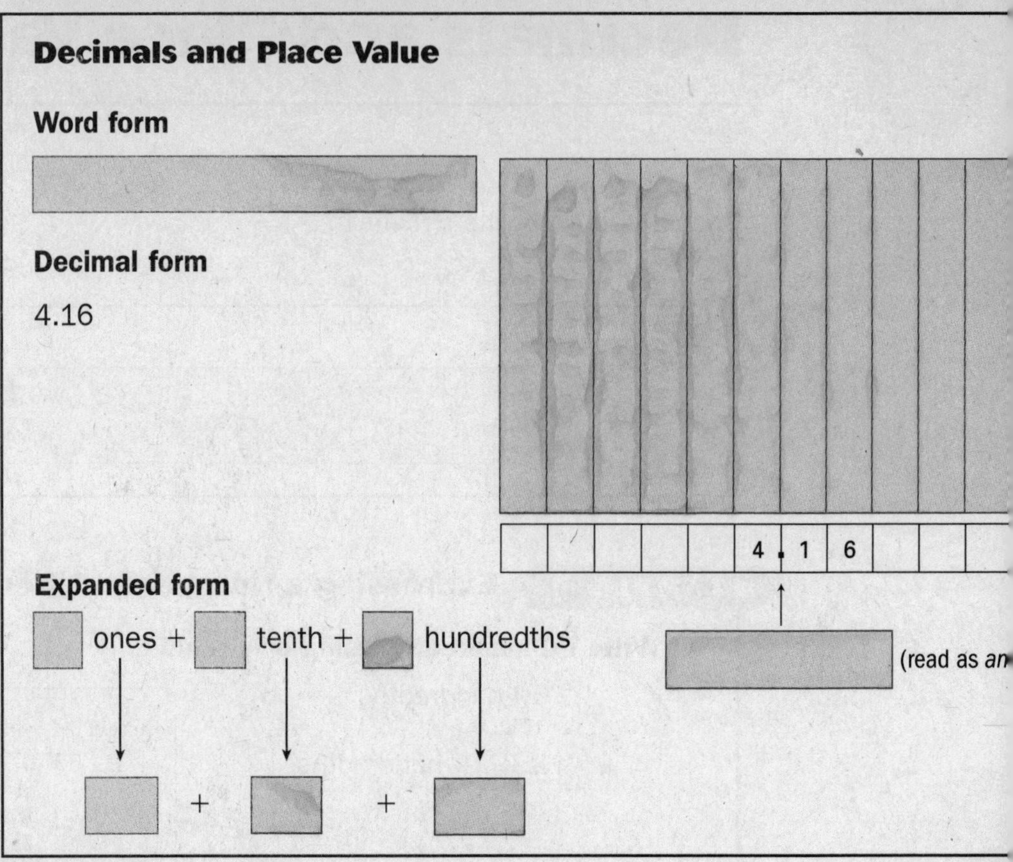

EXAMPLE 2 Writing Decimals

Distance A friend tells you that the distance between her house and your house is thirty-two and seven tenths miles. Write this distance as a decimal.

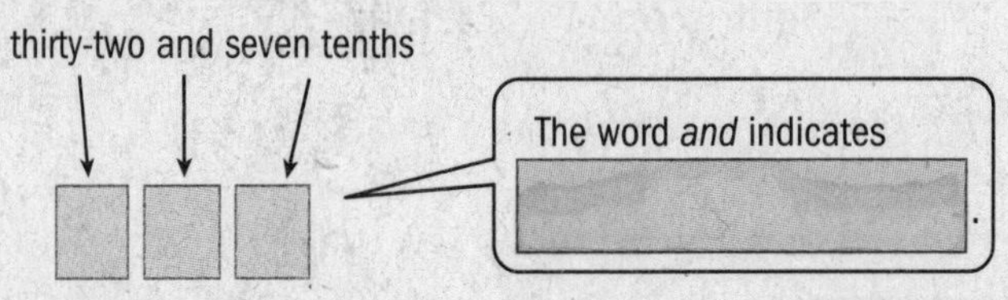

EXAMPLE 3 Reading Decimals

Orbit Earth makes one complete trip around the Sun in 356.256 days. Wri
the number of days in one complete trip in words.

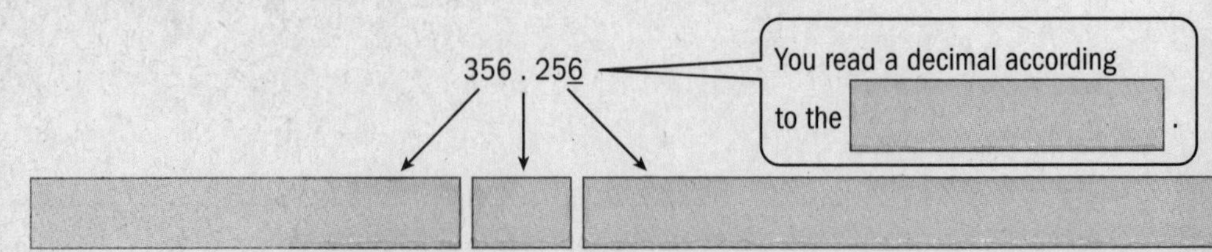

Your turn now

3. Write *forty-one and nine hundred-thousandths* as a decimal.	
4. Write 8.032 in words.	**5.** Write 505.83 in words.

Measuring Metric Lengths

Goal: Use decimals to express metric measurements.

EXAMPLE 1 Writing Measurements as Decimals

Lizards A zoo keeper is recording information about the zoo's lizards. One o the lizards has a tail that is about 10 centimeters long. What is a more pre cise measurement for the lizard's tail?

Solution

To answer the question about the lizard's tail, use a metric ruler and write your answer as a decimal number of centimeters.

Remember that when measuring an object, line up one end of the object with the zero mark on the ruler.

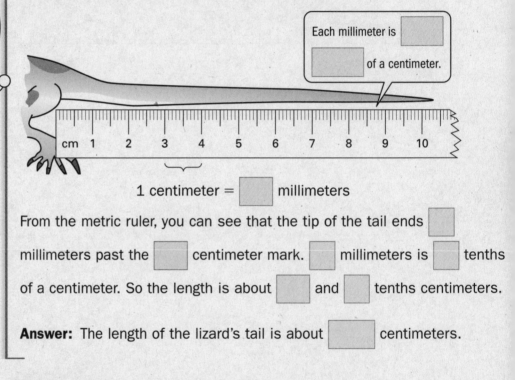

Each millimeter is ______ ______ of a centimeter.

cm 1 2 3 4 5 6 7 8 9 10

1 centimeter = ______ millimeters

From the metric ruler, you can see that the tip of the tail ends ______ millimeters past the ______ centimeter mark. ______ millimeters is ______ tenths of a centimeter. So the length is about ______ and ______ tenths centimeters.

Answer: The length of the lizard's tail is about ______ centimeters.

Your turn now **Write the length of the line segment as a decimal numbe of centimeters.**

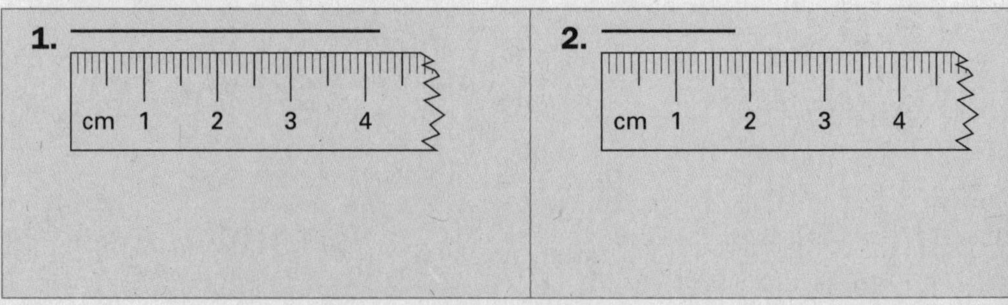

Metric Units of Length

millimeter (mm)	centimeter (cm)	meter (m)
1 mm = ____ cm	1 cm = ____ mm	1 m = ____ mm
1 mm = ____ m	1 cm = ____ m	1 m = ____ cm
		1 m = ____ km

EXAMPLE 2 **Measuring in Centimeters**

Need help with metric units of length? See page 56 of your textbook.

Find the length of the line segment to the nearest tenth of a centimeter.

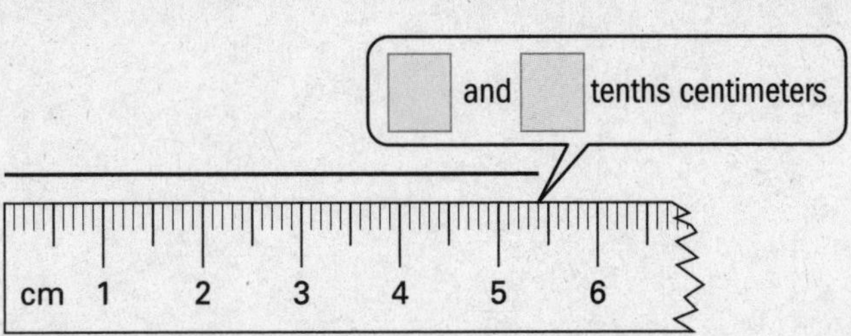

Answer: The length of the line segment is about ____.

EXAMPLE 3 **Measuring in Meters**

Lizards Find the length of the lizard to the nearest hundredth of a meter.

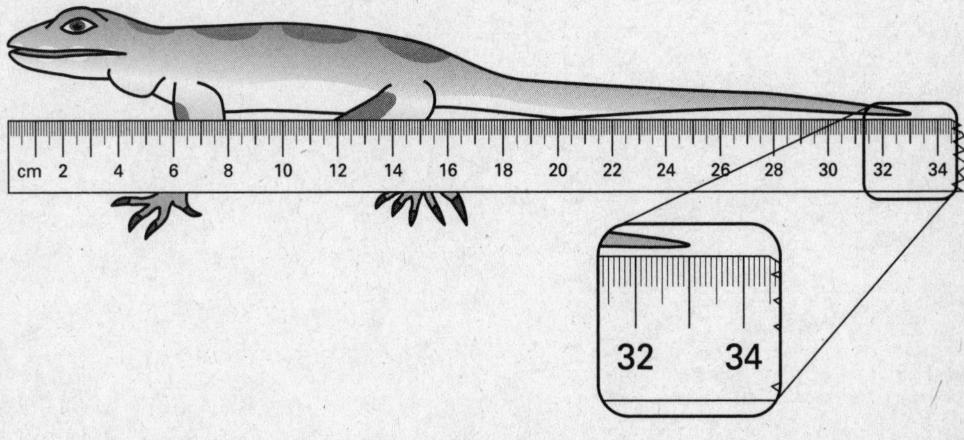

It takes more of a smaller unit of length to equal a measurement written in a larger unit of length. For example, it takes 300 cm to equal 3 m.

The length of the lizard is about ____ centimeters. Because 1 centimeter is ____ hundredth of a meter, ____ centimeters is ____ hundredths of a meter.

Answer: The length of the lizard is about ____ meter.

Your turn now **Find the length of the line segment to the given unit.**

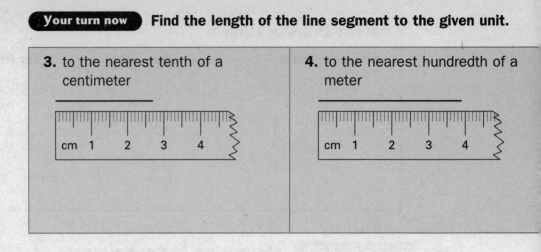

3. to the nearest tenth of a centimeter	**4.** to the nearest hundredth of a meter
	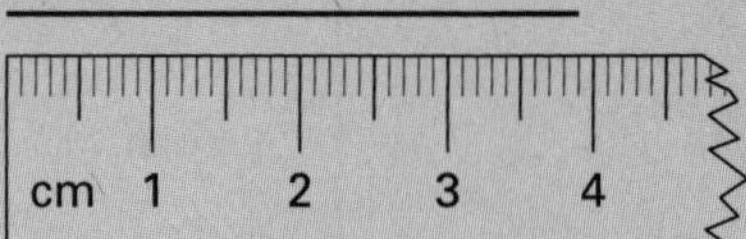

Ordering Decimals

Goal: Compare and order decimals.

EXAMPLE 1 Comparing Metric Lengths

Writing Utensils Carolyn has a pen and a mechanical pencil in her book bag. The pen measures 15.7 centimeters and the mechanical pencil measures 15.3 centimeters. Which writing utensil is longer, the pen or the mechanical pencil?

Solution

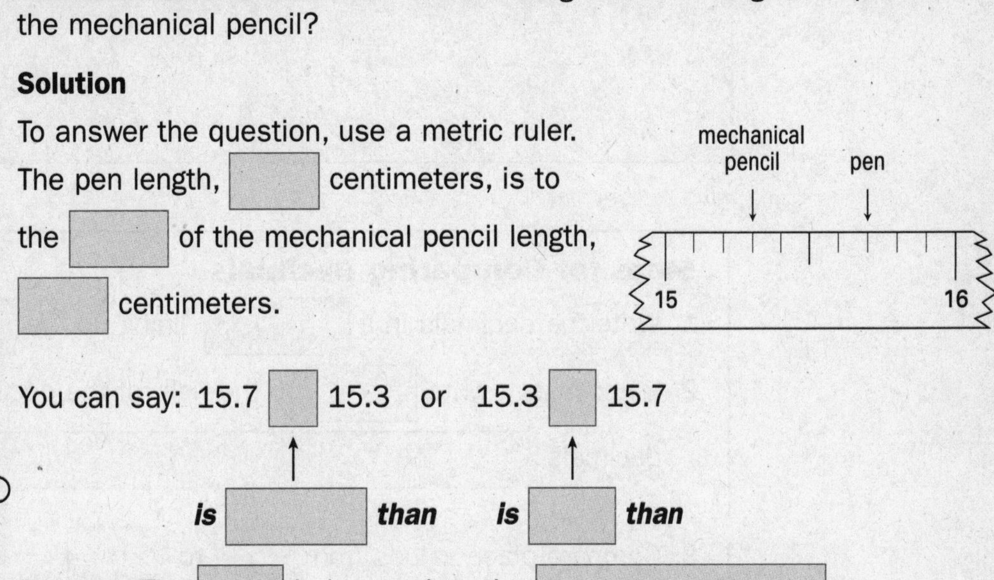

To answer the question, use a metric ruler. The pen length, ____ centimeters, is to the ____ of the mechanical pencil length, ____ centimeters.

You can say: 15.7 ____ 15.3 or 15.3 ____ 15.7

is ____ *than* *is* ____ *than*

Less than and *greater than* symbols always point to the lesser number.

Answer: The ____ is longer than the ____.

EXAMPLE 2 Ordering Decimals on a Number Line

Order the numbers from least to greatest: 2.3, 2.18, 2.06, 2, and 2.25.

Graph each number on a number line. Begin by marking tenths from ____ to ____. Then mark hundredths by dividing each tenth into ____ sections.

By writing the numbers above their plotted points on the number line, you can easily order the numbers.

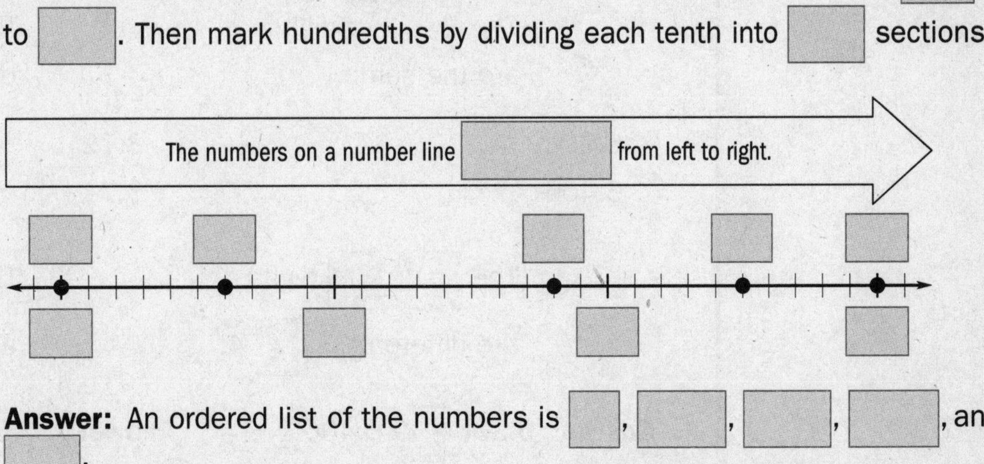

The numbers on a number line ____ from left to right.

Answer: An ordered list of the numbers is ____, ____, ____, ____, and ____.

Your turn now **Use the number line from Example 2.**

1. Order the numbers from least to greatest: 2.2, 2.09, 2.1, 2.01, and 2.29.

2. Write three numbers that are greater than 5.7 and less than 5.8.

Steps for Comparing Decimals

1. Write the decimals in a ______, lining up the ______.

2. If necessary, write ______ to the right of the decimals so that all decimals ______.

3. Compare place values from ______ to ______.

EXAMPLE 3 Comparing Decimals

Copy and complete the statement with <, >, or =.

a. 6.398 __?__ 6.406

The ______ digits are the same.

6.398
6.406

The ______ digits are different: 3 ______ 4.

Answer: 6.398  6.406

b. 3.72 __?__ 3.7

The ______ digits are the same.

3.72
3.7 ______ ← ______

The ______ digits are different: 2 ______ 0.

Answer: 3.72 ______ 3.7

EXAMPLE 4 Ordering Decimals

Order the countries by the price for one gallon of gasoline from greatest to least.

The digits are the same through the ______ place. Compare ______: 1.**8**0, 1.**7**2, 1.**5**1, and 1.**1**7.

Country	Price (in dollars)
Australia	1.72
Canada	1.51
Mexico	1.80
United States	1.17

Answer: The countries, from the greatest price for a gallon of gasoline to the least price for a gallon of gasoline, are ______, ______, ______, and ______.

Your turn now **Copy and complete the statement with <, >, or =.**

3. 8.21 __?__ 8.12	**4.** 9.3 __?__ 9.30	**5.** 0.207 __?__ 0.213

Rounding Decimals

Goal: Round decimals.

EXAMPLE 1 Using a Number Line to Round

Use a number line to round 5.26 to the nearest tenth.

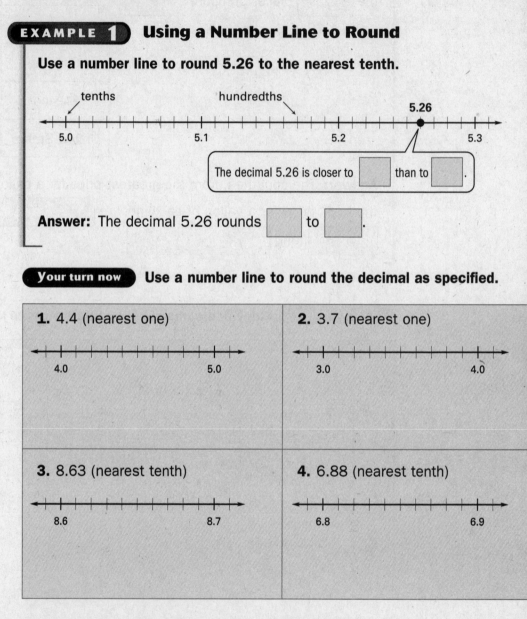

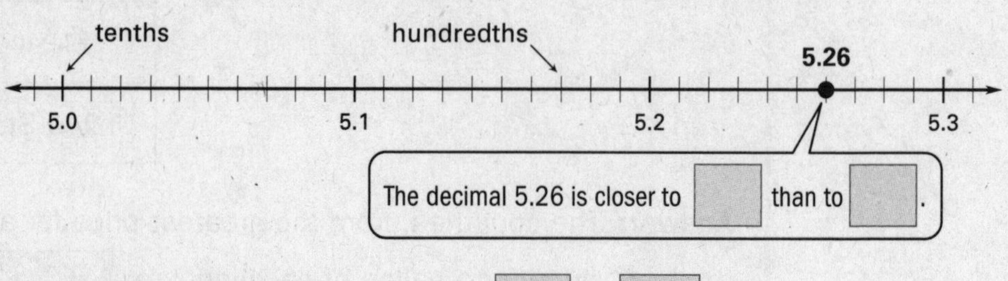

The decimal 5.26 is closer to than to .

Answer: The decimal 5.26 rounds to .

Your turn now **Use a number line to round the decimal as specified.**

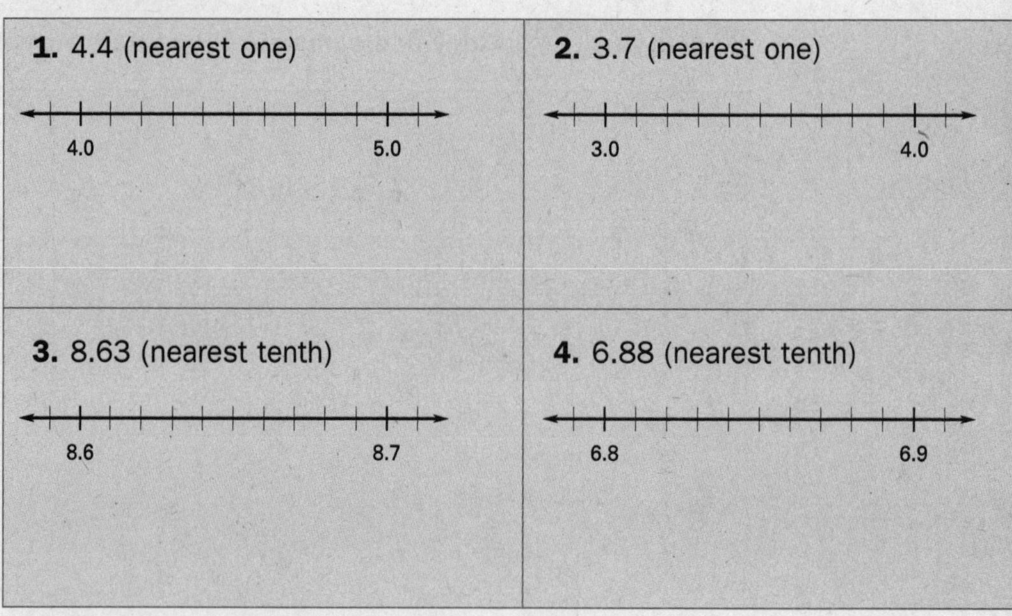

1. 4.4 (nearest one) 4.0 5.0	**2.** 3.7 (nearest one) 3.0 4.0
3. 8.63 (nearest tenth) 8.6 8.7	**4.** 6.88 (nearest tenth) 6.8 6.9

Rule for Rounding Decimals

To round a decimal to a given place value, look at the digit in the place to the .

- If the digit is 4 or less, round .
- If the digit is 5 or greater, round .

EXAMPLE 2 Rounding Decimals

Round the decimal to the place value of the underlined digit.

a. $1.\underline{4}1$ → ____ The digit to the ____ of 4 is ____, so round ____.

b. $9.3\underline{7}6$ → ____ The digit to the ____ of 7 is ____, so round ____.

c. $3.92\underline{8}17$ → ____ The digit to the ____ of 8 is ____, so round ____.

d. $7.\underline{9}53$ → ____ The digit to the ____ of 9 is ____, so round ____.

WATCH OUT!
n rounding problems ike part (d) of Example 2, do not drop the final ero. Keep it to mark he place value you ounded to.

Your turn now **Round the decimal as specified.**

5. 7.39 (nearest tenth)	**6.** 3.097 (nearest hundredth)
7. 5.47 (nearest one)	**8.** 2.9885 (nearest thousandth)

EXAMPLE 3 Rounding to the Leading Digit

Sand A grain of sand has a diameter of 0.0008512 inch. Round the diameter of the grain of sand to the leading digit.

Solution

The first ____ digit at the left of 0.0008512 is ____, and it is in the ____ place. You should round the diameter to the nearest ____.

0.0008512 ____ is in the ____ place.

Because ____ is to the right of the ____ place, round ____ ____ to ____.

Answer: The diameter of the grain of sand rounded to the leading digit is ____ inch.

Your turn now **Round the decimal to the leading digit.**

9. 0.069	**10.** 0.0082	**11.** 0.0971	**12.** 0.008419

EXAMPLE 4 Using Decimals for Large Numbers

Big Cities The populations of the four largest cities in the United States in a recent year are shown below. Round each population to the nearest hundred thousand. Then write each rounded population as a decimal number of millions. Display your results in a bar graph.

Solution

City	Population	Round	Write in millions
New York	8,008,278		million
Los Angeles	3,694,820		million
Chicago	2,896,016		million
Houston	1,953,631		million

As you work on the exercises, remember to write down any questions you want to ask your teacher.

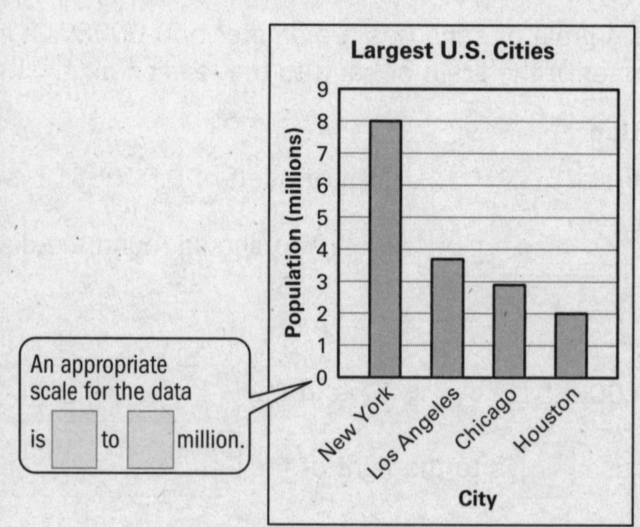

Decimal Estimation

Goal: Estimate sums and difference of decimals.

Vocabulary

Front-end estimation:

EXAMPLE 1 Estimating Sums and Differences

Vehicle Production The table shows the number of passenger cars and commercial vehicles made by different countries in a recent year. About how many vehicles were made in the United States altogether? About how many more passenger cars did Japan produce than Germany?

Country	Passenger cars (millions)	Commercial vehicles (millions)
Germany	4.8	0.4
Japan	8.4	1.8
United States	5.5	7.2

When answering a question, make sure that you include the correct number of units. In Example 1, the numbers of vehicles are given in *millions* of vehicles.

Solution

a. To estimate the answer to the first question, round each decimal to the nearest whole number. Then add.

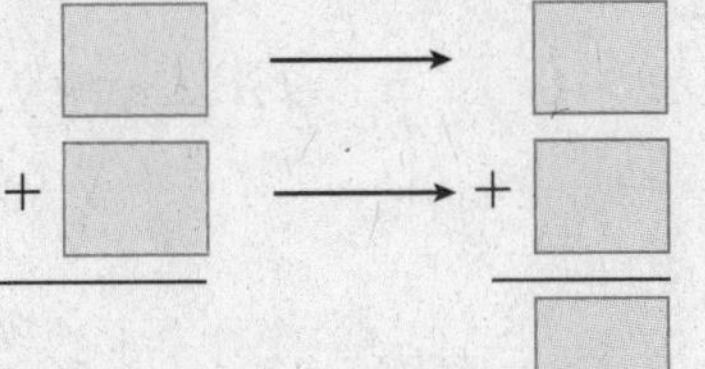

Round ______ to ______.

Round ______ to ______.

Answer: About ______ million total vehicles were made in the United States.

b. To estimate the answer to the second question, round each decimal to the nearest whole number. Then subtract.

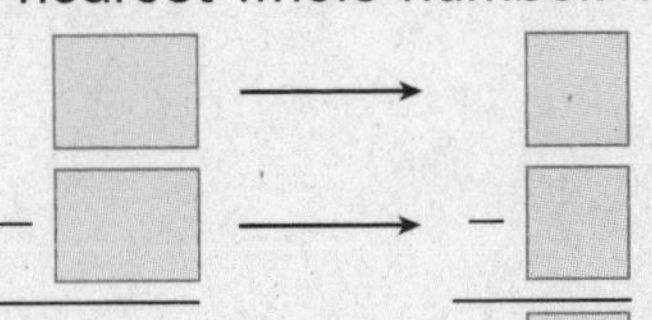

Round ______ to ______.

Round ______ to ______.

Answer: Japan made about ______ million more passenger cars than Germany.

Your turn now **Use the information provided in Example 1.**

1. Estimate the total number of vehicles made in Japan.

2. Estimate how many more commercial vehicles than passenger cars were made in the United States.

EXAMPLE 2 Predicting Results

Writing You spent 12 hours researching for a report for one of your classes. You spent a total of 8.3 hours writing the report. Estimate how much more time you spent on researching than on writing. Is this estimate *high* or *low*?

Before rounding, it can be helpful to use zeros to write each decimal with the same number of decimal places.

$$\begin{array}{r} \square \\ - \square \\ \hline \end{array} \longrightarrow \begin{array}{r} \square \\ - \square \\ \hline \square \end{array}$$

Round ____ ____ to ____.

Answer: You spent about ____ more hours on researching than on writing.

This estimate is ____ because ____ ____.

EXAMPLE 3 Using Front-End Estimation

Mail You are mailing a package of books to your brother in college. You have enough money to mail a 6-pound package. The books weigh 1.25 pounds, 1.72 pounds, 1.54 pounds, and 0.45 pound. Can you mail the package?

Solution

Find the sum of all the weights.

1. Add the front-end digits.

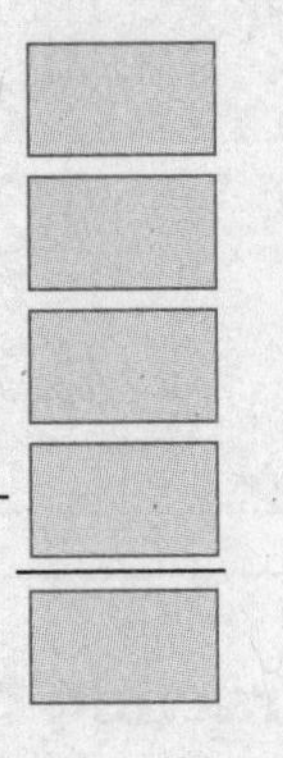

2. Estimate the sum of the remaining digits.

3. Add your results.

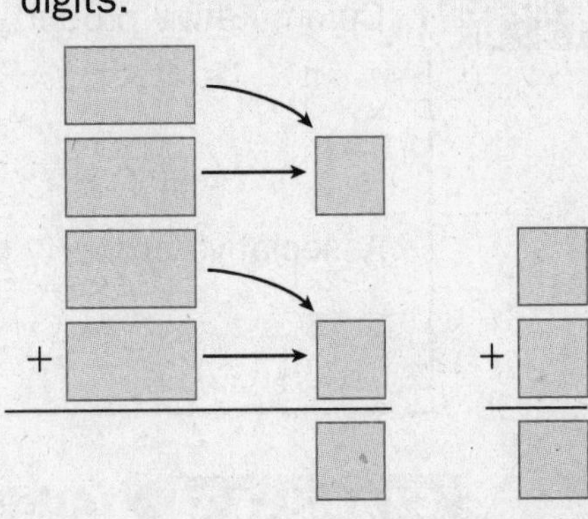

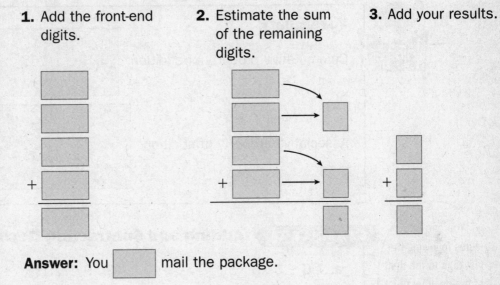

Answer: You ______ mail the package.

Your turn now **Use front-end estimation to estimate the sum.**

3. 5.74 + 8.32 + 2.54 + 1.51

4. 4.48 + 2.46 + 5 + 3.13

5. How can you estimate the difference in Example 2 so that your answer is a low estimate?

LESSON 3.6

Adding and Subtracting Decimals

Goal: Add and subtract decimals.

Vocabulary

Commutative property of addition:

Associative property of addition:

You can add zeros following the last digit to the right of the decimal point to help you line up the decimal points.

EXAMPLE 1 **Adding and Subtracting Decimals**

a. 7.6 + 3.28

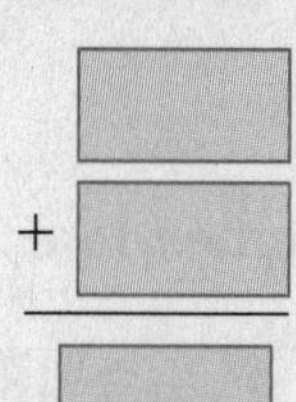

b. 9 − 2.15

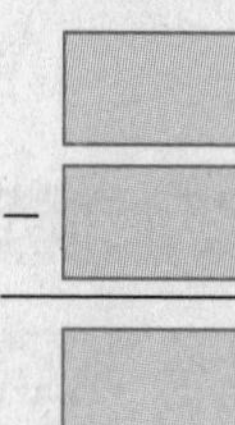

EXAMPLE 2 **Evaluating Algebraic Expressions**

Evaluate 30 − *x* when *x* = 6.14.

$30 - x =$ ______ Substitute ______ for ______.

$=$ ______

Your turn now **Evaluate the expression when *x* = 8.25 and *y* = 4.2.**

1. $2.9 + x$	**2.** $14.38 - y$	**3.** $x - y$

EXAMPLE 3 Using Mental Math to Add Decimals

Building Materials Find the total cost for a bag of nails that is $1.75, two pieces of wood that are $10.15 each, and a can of paint that is $8.25.

List the prices:

$ ____

$ ____

$ ____

$ ____

Rearrange the prices and group pairs of prices.

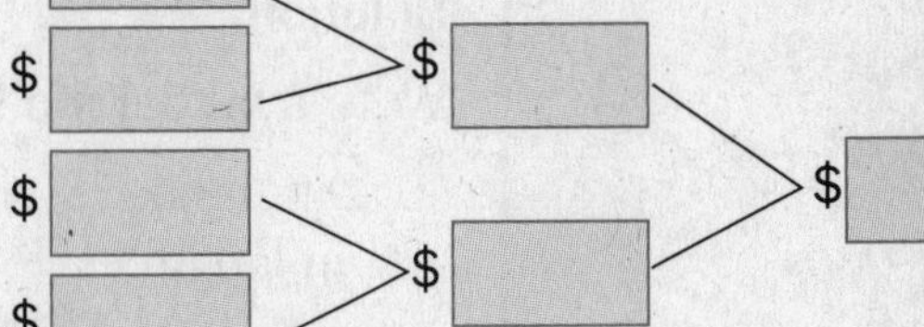

$ ____

$ ____

$ ____

$ ____

$ ____

$ ____

$ ____

Answer: The building materials will cost $ ____.

Properties of Addition

Commutative Property You can add numbers ____.

Numbers ____ = 8 + 3 **Algebra** $x + y =$ ____

Associative Property The value of a sum does not depend on ____.

Numbers ____ = 5 + (1 + 7) **Algebra** $(x + y) + z =$ ____

Your turn now Tell which property is illustrated. Then find the sum.

4. 6.2 + 3.7 = 3.7 + 6.2

5. (1.9 + 4.4) + 8.6 = 1.9 + (4.4 + 8.6)

EXAMPLE 4 Writing a Model

Rivers The Mississippi River is about 3765.86 kilometers long. The Potomac River is about 616.38 kilometers long. The St. Lawrence River is about 1287.48 kilometers long. How much longer is the Mississippi River than the Potomac River and St. Lawrence River combined?

Solution

Write a verbal model to help you find the difference in the lengths.

Difference in length	=	Length of Mississippi	− (	Length of Potomac	+	Length of St. Lawrence)	
	=	____	− (	____	+	____)	Substitute
	=	____	−	____			Add.
	=	____					Subtract.

Need help with the order of operations? See page 21 of your textbook.

Answer: The Mississippi River is ____ kilometers longer than the Potomac River and the St. Lawrence River combined.

✓ **Check** Use estimation to check that your answer is reasonable. Round 3765.86 to ____, 616.38 to ____, and 1287.48 to ____. Because ____ − (____ + ____) = ____, the answer ____ reasonable.

Words to Review

Give an example of the vocabulary word.

Decimal

Front-end estimation

Commutative property of addition

Associative property of addition

Review your notes and Chapter 3 by using the Chapter Review on pages 144–145 of your textbook.

Multiplying Decimals and Whole Numbers

Goal: Multiply decimals and whole numbers.

For Your Notebook

Vocabulary

Commutative property of multiplication:

Associative property of multiplication:

EXAMPLE 1 **Multiplying Decimals by Whole Numbers**

Find the product 8 × 0.009.

Because 0.009 has ☐ decimal places, the answer will have ☐ decimal places.

You may want to think of Example 1 in words. *8 times 9 thousandths is ? thousandths.* Then you can see why a zero is needed as a placeholder in the product.

☐
× ☐
☐

Write a ☐ as a placeholder so that the answer has ☐ decimal places.

Your turn now **Find the product. Then write the product in words.**

1. 2 × 0.007	**2.** 6 × 0.018	**3.** 3.4 × 9	**4.** 7.14 × 5

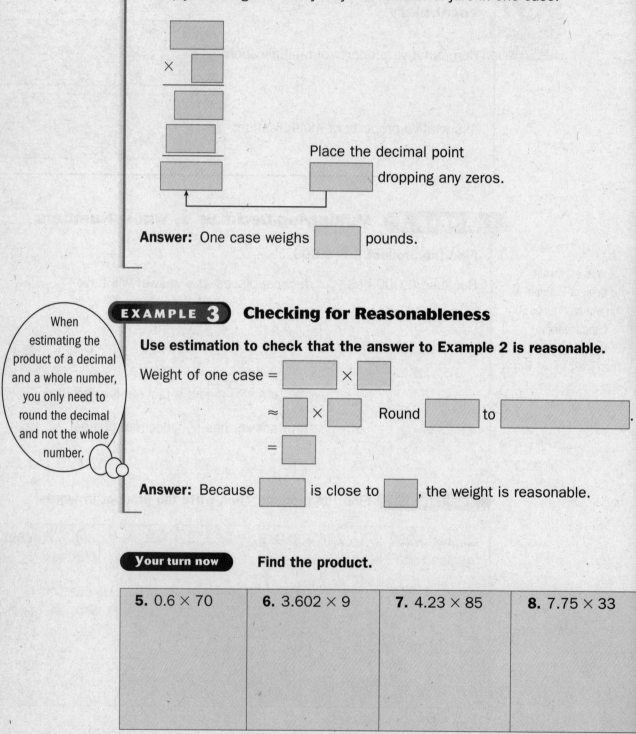

EXAMPLE 2 Solving a Problem

Spaghetti Sauce A food company packages its spaghetti sauce in jars that weigh 1.625 pounds. The jars are then shipped in cases that contain 12 jars of sauce each. How much does one case of spaghetti sauce weigh?

Solution

Multiply the weight of one jar by the number of jars in one case.

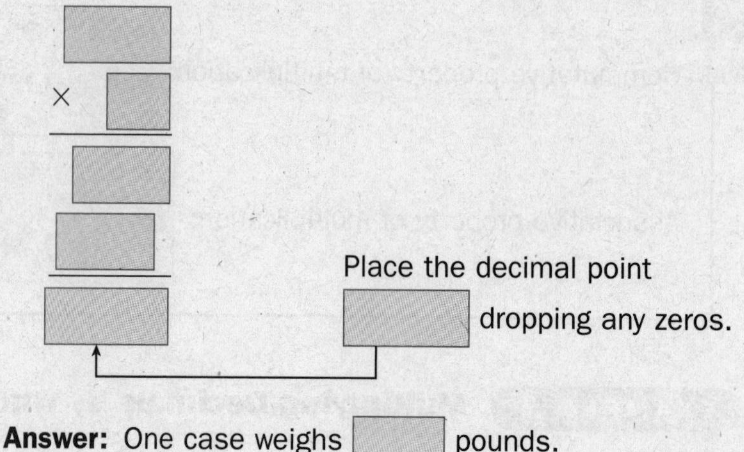
×
Place the decimal point
dropping any zeros.

Answer: One case weighs ______ pounds.

When estimating the product of a decimal and a whole number, you only need to round the decimal and not the whole number.

EXAMPLE 3 Checking for Reasonableness

Use estimation to check that the answer to Example 2 is reasonable.

Weight of one case = ______ × ______

≈ ______ × ______ Round ______ to ______.

= ______

Answer: Because ______ is close to ______, the weight is reasonable.

Your turn now **Find the product.**

5. 0.6 × 70	6. 3.602 × 9	7. 4.23 × 85	8. 7.75 × 33

Your turn now **Use estimation to check that the answer is reasonable.**

9. 4.135×17; 70.295	**10.** 19.309×6; 1158.54
11. Explain why the answer 312 is *not* reasonable for the product 8×3.9.	
12. Explain why the answer 2.34 *is* reasonable for the product .	

Properties of Multiplication

Commutative Property In a product, you can multiply numbers ____.

Numbers $7 \times 5.4 =$ ____ **Algebra** ____ $= b \cdot a$

Associative Property The value of a product does not depend on ____.

Numbers $(7 \times 5.4) \times 3 =$ ____

Algebra ____ $= a \cdot (b \cdot c)$

EXAMPLE 4 Using Properties of Multiplication

Tell whether the *commutative* or *associative* property of multiplication allows you to rewrite the problem as shown. Explain your choice.

a. $8 \times 6.34 \times 5 = 6.34 \times 8 \times 5$

____ has changed, so this is an example of the ____ property of multiplication.

b. $(6.34 \times 8) \times 5 = 6.34 \times (8 \times 5)$

____ have changed, so this is an example of the ____ property of multiplication.

The Distributive Property

Goal: Use the distributive property to evaluate expressions.

Vocabulary

Distributive property: ______

Numbers $7(3 + 4) = \square(\square) + \square(\square)$; $\square(\square) = 4(9) - 4(5)$

Algebra $\square(\square + \square) = ab + ac$ $\quad a(b - c) = \square - \square$

EXAMPLE 1 Evaluating Expressions

Amusement Park Tickets A family of six is going to an amusement park. The admission is \$42 per person, but the family has a coupon for \$5 off of each ticket. How much will the family pay altogether for admission to the park?

Solution

Method 1 To answer the question, first find the cost of one ticket using the coupon. Then multiply to find the total amount the family has to pay.

Number of family members × Cost of one ticket using coupon

$= \square \times (\square)$

$= \square(\square)$

$= \square$

Remember that $a(b)$ is another way to write $a \times b$.

Method 2 To answer the question, first find the amount the family will have to pay without using the coupon and find the total worth of the coupon for all family members. Then subtract to find the total amount the family has to pay.

Cost without using coupon − Total worth of coupon

$= (\square \times \square) - (\square \times \square)$

$= \square - \square$

$= \square$

Answer: The family will pay \$______ altogether for admission to the park.

EXAMPLE 2 Using the Distributive Property

a. 3(40 + 9) = ☐(☐) + ☐(☐)

= ☐ + ☐

= ☐

b. 20(7.2 − 3.9) = ☐(☐) − ☐(☐)

= ☐ − ☐

= ☐

Your turn now **Use the distributive property to evaluate.**

1. 3(15 + 8)	**2.** 9(30 − 4)	**3.** 100(7.6 − 5)	**4.** 0.4(25 + 17)

EXAMPLE 3 Evaluating Using Mental Math

a. To find 8(59), rewrite ☐.

8(59) = ☐(☐ − ☐)

= ☐(☐) − ☐(☐)

= ☐ − ☐

= ☐

Another way to solve Example 3(a) would be to rewrite 59 as the sum 50 + 9.

b. To find 6(7.2), rewrite ☐.

☐(☐) = ☐(☐ + ☐)

= ☐(☐) + ☐(☐)

= ☐ + ☐

= ☐

EXAMPLE 4 Using a Formula

Serving Platter A rectangular serving platter is 14 inches long and 10.5 inches wide. What is the area of the serving platter?

Solution

Use the formula *Area* = *length* × *width*.

Area = ____(____) — Use ____ for the length and ____ for the width.

= ____(____ + ____) — Rewrite 10.5 as ____ + ____.

= ____(____) + ____(____) — Use the distributive property.

= ____ + ____ — Multiply.

= ____ — Add.

Answer: The area of the serving platter is ____ square inches.

Your turn now **Use mental math to find the product.**

5. 7(43)	**6.** 3(98)	**7.** 4(14.5)	**8.** 9(2.3)

Multiplying Decimals

Goal: Multiply decimals by decimals.

EXAMPLE 1 Using a Model to Multiply Decimals

Rainfall Shawna has been recording the amount of rainfall in her town for a science project. The first week she recorded 0.7 inch of rain. The amount of rainfall for the second week was 0.5 times the amount of rain that fell during the first week. How much rain fell during the second week?

Solution

To find the amount of rain that fell during the second week, use a model to find the product 0.7×0.5.

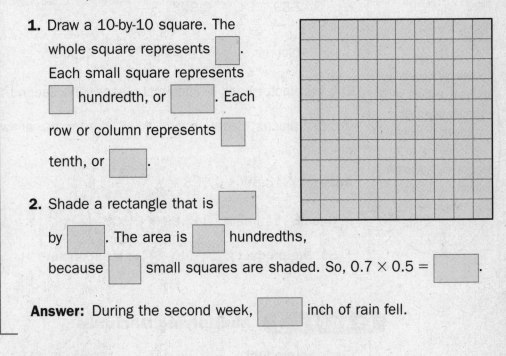

1. Draw a 10-by-10 square. The whole square represents ____. Each small square represents ____ hundredth, or ____. Each row or column represents ____ tenth, or ____.

2. Shade a rectangle that is ____ by ____. The area is ____ hundredths, because ____ small squares are shaded. So, $0.7 \times 0.5 =$ ____.

Answer: During the second week, ____ inch of rain fell.

Your turn now **Draw a model to find the product.**

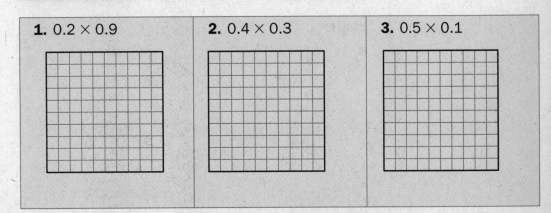

1. 0.2×0.9	**2.** 0.4×0.3	**3.** 0.5×0.1
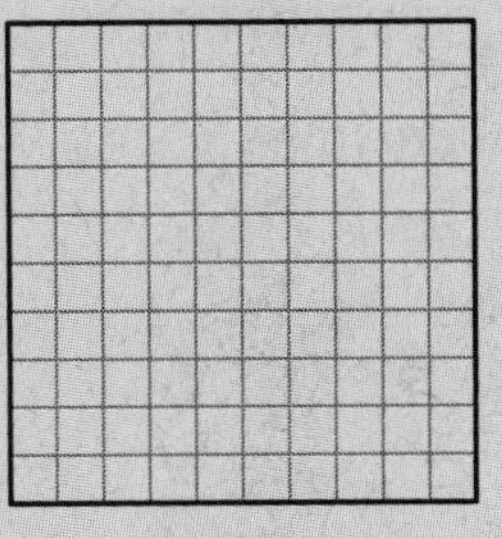	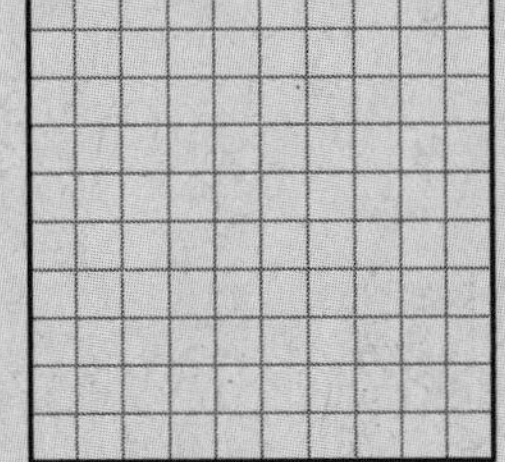	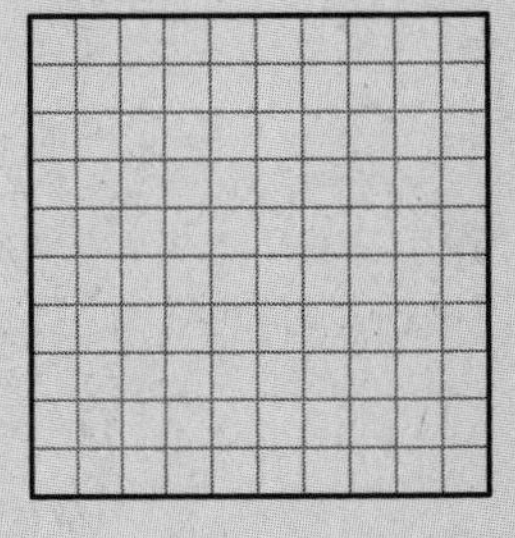

Multiplying Decimals

Words Multiply decimals as you do whole numbers. Then place the decimal point. The number of decimal places is ______ ______.

Numbers 6.92 × 12.3 = ______

___ places ___ place ___ places

EXAMPLE 2 Placing a Decimal Point in a Product

Place the decimal point in the correct location.

342.89 × 0.908 = ______

___ places ___ places ___ places

When you estimate to check a decimal product, you can use compatible numbers or round each decimal to its leading digit. Another estimate in Example 2 would be 300 × 1 = 300.

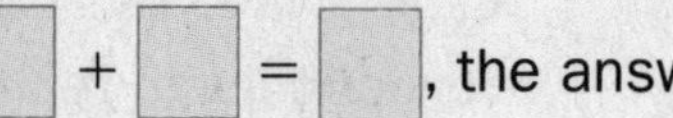

The first factor has ___ decimal places. The second factor has ___ decimal places. Because ___ + ___ = ___, the answer has ___ decimal places.

Answer: 342.89 × 0.908 = ______.

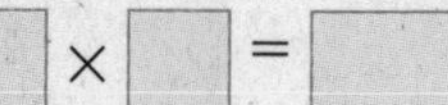

✓ **Check** Estimate: 342.89 × 0.908 ≈ ___ × ___ = ___.

So, the product ______ is reasonable.

EXAMPLE 3 Multiplying Decimals

Find the product.

a. 6.05 × 3.7 **b.** 1.732 × 0.04 **c.** 6.345 × 4.4

Solution

a. 6.05 ___ decimal places

× 3.7 + ___ decimal place

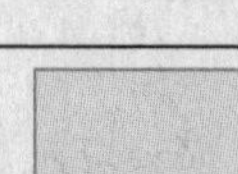

___ decimal places

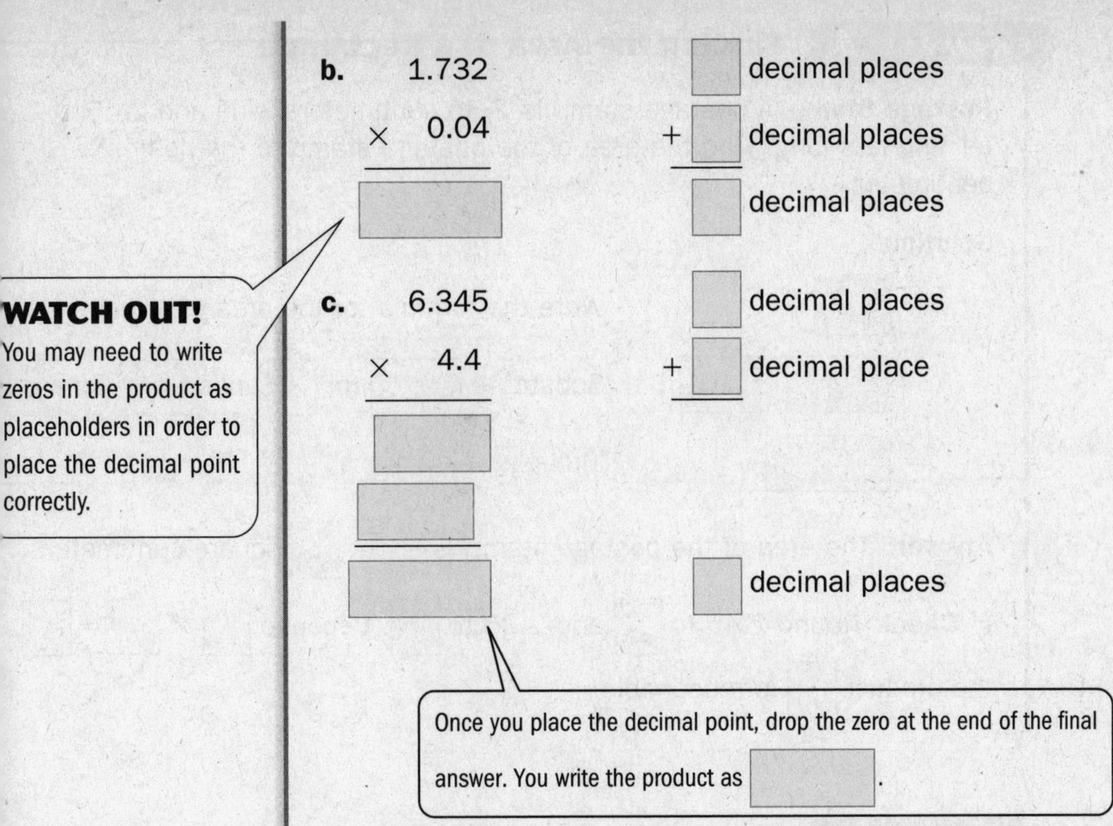

b. 1.732
× 0.04
decimal places
+ decimal places
decimal places
WATCH OUT!
You may need to write zeros in the product as placeholders in order to place the decimal point correctly.
c. 6.345
× 4.4
decimal places
+ decimal place
decimal places

Once you place the decimal point, drop the zero at the end of the final answer. You write the product as ______.

Your turn now **Multiply. Use estimation to check your answer.**

4. 4.75 × 5.6	**5.** 16.8 × 3.7	**6.** 7.178 × 0.3	**7.** 0.84 × 0.06

EXAMPLE 4 Finding the Area of a Rectangle

Postage Stamp A postage stamp is 2.35 centimeters wide and 2.45 centimeters long. Find the area of the postage stamp to the nearest centimeter.

Solution

$A =$ ______ Write the formula for the area of a rectangle.

$= ($ ______ $)($ ______ $)$ Substitute ______ for ______ and ______ for ______.

$=$ ______ Multiply.

Answer: The area of the postage stamp is about ______ square centimeters.

✓ **Check** Round 2.45 to ______ and 2.35 to ______. Because ______ × ______ = ______, the product ______ is reasonable.

Your turn now **Find the area of the rectangle or square.**

8. A square with side length 4.5 feet

9. A rectangle with length 7.6 centimeters and width 2.32 centimeters

Dividing by Whole Numbers

Goal: Divide decimals by whole numbers.

Dividing a Decimal by a Whole Number

Words When dividing a decimal by a whole number, place the decimal point in the quotient ______.

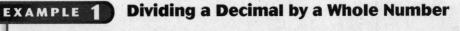

Numbers

$$4\overline{)27.2} = 6.8$$

Place the decimal point in the quotient ______.

EXAMPLE 1 Dividing a Decimal by a Whole Number

CDs A computer store charges $9.95 for a 5-pack of rewritable CDs. How much does one CD cost at this price?

Solution

To answer the question, find 9.95 ÷ 5.

1. Place the decimal point.

$5\overline{)9.95}$

2. Then divide.

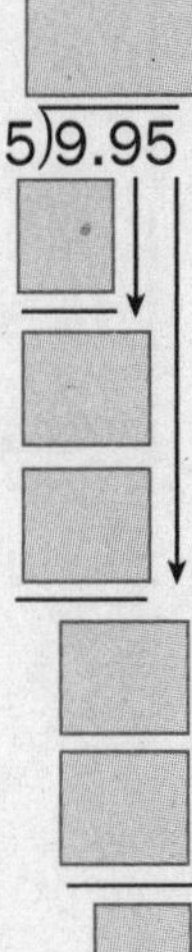

Answer: One CD costs $ ______.

Your turn now **Find the quotient.**

1. $4\overline{)30.4}$	2. $3\overline{)27.9}$	3. $9\overline{)4.77}$

EXAMPLE 2 Writing Additional Zeros

Find the quotient 13 ÷ 4.

1. Place the decimal point and begin dividing.

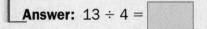

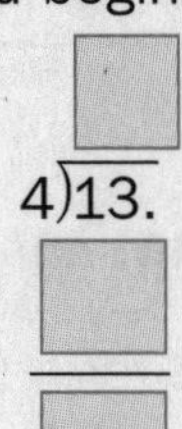

2. Write additional zeros in the dividend as needed.

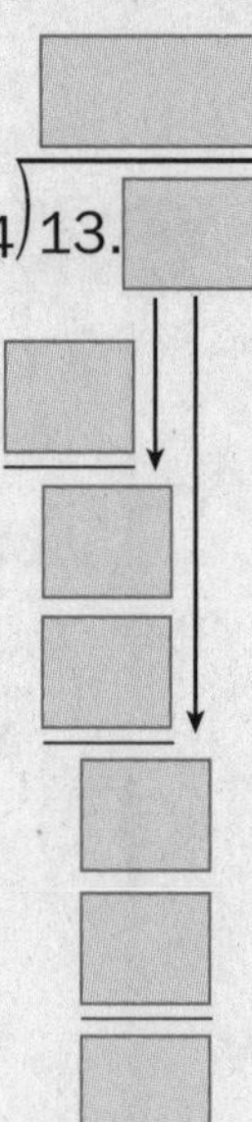

Answer: 13 ÷ 4 = ______

EXAMPLE 3 **Using Zeros as Placeholders**

Road Trip Three people are going on a 425-mile trip. They want to divide the driving up evenly among the three people. How far does each person have to drive? Round your answer to the nearest tenth of a mile.

Solution

3)425. ___ Write zeros in the dividend as needed.

Stop when the quotient reaches the ___ place.

To round to a given decimal place, divide until the quotient has one more decimal place than needed. Then round back.

Answer: Each person has to drive about ___ miles.

Your turn now **Divide. Round to the nearest tenth if necessary.**

4. 6)45	**5.** 8)26	**6.** 7)30.52	**7.** 13)38.56

Multiplying and Dividing by Powers of Ten

Goal: Use mental math to help multiply and divide.

Multiplying by Powers of Ten

Multiplying by Whole Number Powers of 10 Move the decimal point one place *to the* ______ for each ______ in the whole number power of 10.

Numbers 4.278 × 100 = ______

Multiplying by Decimal Powers of 10 Move the decimal point one place *to the* ______ for each ______ in the decimal power of 10.

Numbers 427.8 × 0.001 = ______

EXAMPLE 1 Multiply Decimals Using Mental Math

When you move a decimal point to the right or left, you may need to write zeros as placeholders.

a. 0.008 × 1000 = ______ Move ______ places to the ______.

b. 85.96 × 0.0001 = ______ Move ______ places to the ______.

Your turn now **Find the product using mental math.**

1. 17.34 × 10	**2.** 4.03 × 1000	**3.** 218.8 × 0.01	**4.** 18 × 0.001

EXAMPLE 2 Multiply Decimals by Powers of Ten

Airports The graph shows the number of people that traveled through airports during 2000. How many people traveled through Chicago's O'Hare airport?

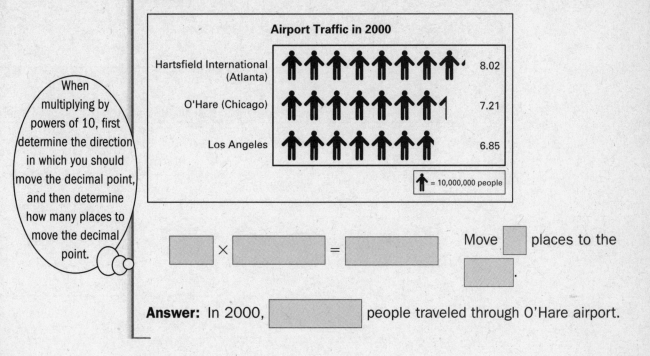

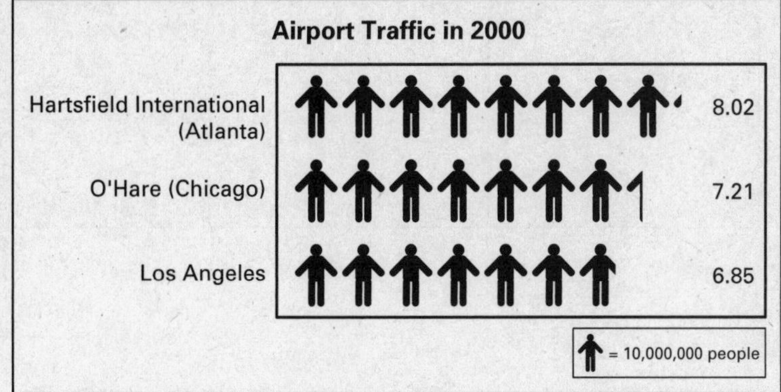

When multiplying by powers of 10, first determine the direction in which you should move the decimal point, and then determine how many places to move the decimal point.

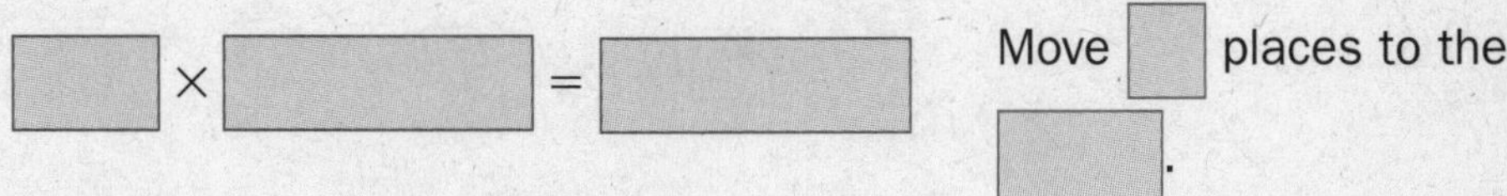

Answer: In 2000, people traveled through O'Hare airport.

Dividing by Powers of Ten

Dividing by Whole Number Powers of 10 Move the decimal point one place *to the* for each in the whole number power of 10.

Numbers $78 \div 100 =$

Dividing by Decimal Powers of 10 Move the decimal point one place *to the* for each in the decimal power of 10.

Numbers $78 \div 0.001 =$

EXAMPLE 3 Divide Decimals Using Mental Math

a. $907.4 \div 10 =$ Move place to the .

b. $907.4 \div 0.01 =$ Move places to the .

Your turn now **Find the quotient using mental math.**

5. 38.7 ÷ 100	**6.** 704 ÷ 1000	**7.** 2 ÷ 0.1	**8.** 1.9 ÷ 0.001

Dividing by Decimals

Goal: Divide by decimals.

Dividing by a Decimal

Words When you divide by a decimal, multiply both the divisor and the dividend by ______ that will make the ______ a whole number.

Numbers 4.5)6.75 Multiply 4.5 and 6.75 by ______. ⟶ 45)______ (quotient 1.5)

EXAMPLE 1 Writing Divisors as Whole Numbers

Rewrite the division problem so that the divisor is a whole number.

When you divide by a decimal with one decimal place, multiply the divisor and the dividend by 10. For a divisor with two decimal places, multiply by 100, and so on.

a. 4.27 ÷ 3.6

3.6)4.27 ⟵ Multiply the divisor and dividend by ______.

Answer: ______ ÷ ______

b. 8 ÷ 0.42

0.42)8.______ ⟵ Write ______ as placeholders.

Multiply the divisor and dividend by ______.

Answer: ______ ÷ ______

Your turn now **Rewrite the division problem so that the divisor is a whole number.**

1. 0.5)7.8	**2.** 4.1)8.97	**3.** 0.33)0.59	**4.** 0.024)679

EXAMPLE 2 Using Zeros While Dividing

WATCH OUT!
Sometimes you need to place zeros as placeholders in the quotient.

Find the quotient.

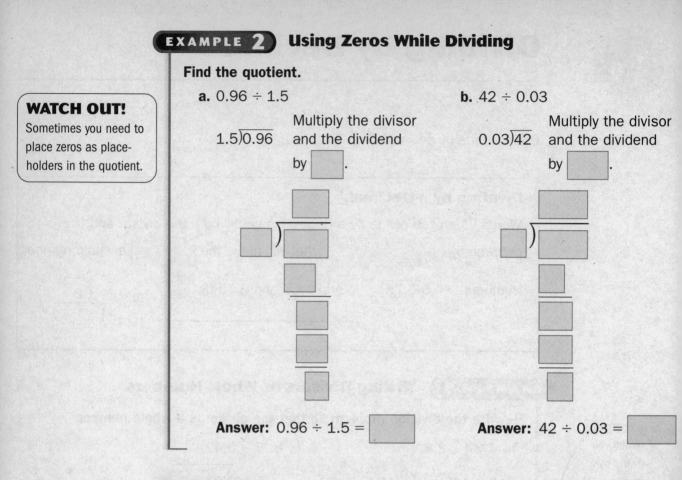

a. 0.96 ÷ 1.5

$1.5\overline{)0.96}$ Multiply the divisor and the dividend by ____.

Answer: 0.96 ÷ 1.5 = ____

b. 42 ÷ 0.03

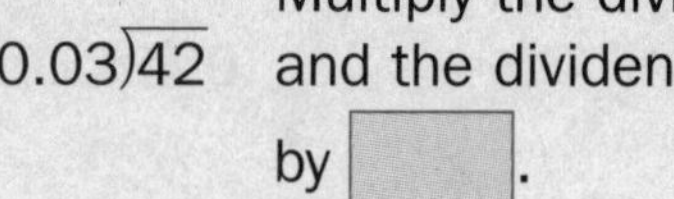

$0.03\overline{)42}$ Multiply the divisor and the dividend by ____.

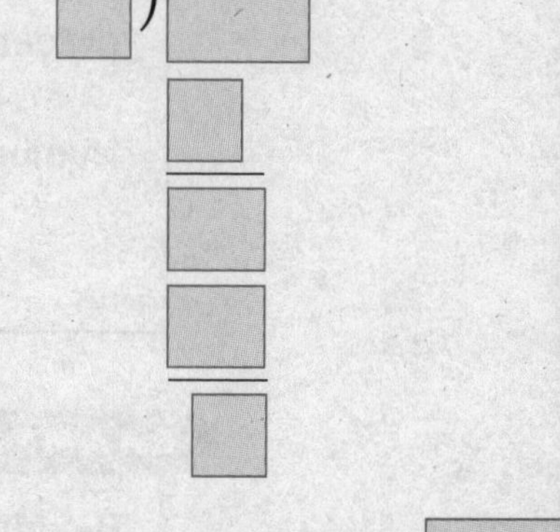

Answer: 42 ÷ 0.03 = ____

EXAMPLE 3 Solving Problems Involving Decimals

Potatoes While at the grocery store, you buy $6.25 worth of potatoes. If on pound of potatoes costs $1.25, how many pounds of potatoes did you buy?

Solution

To find the number of pounds of potatoes you bought, divide the total cost o the potatoes by the cost of one pound of potatoes.

Divide $____ by $____.

$1.25\overline{)6.25}$ Multiply the divisor and dividend by ____.

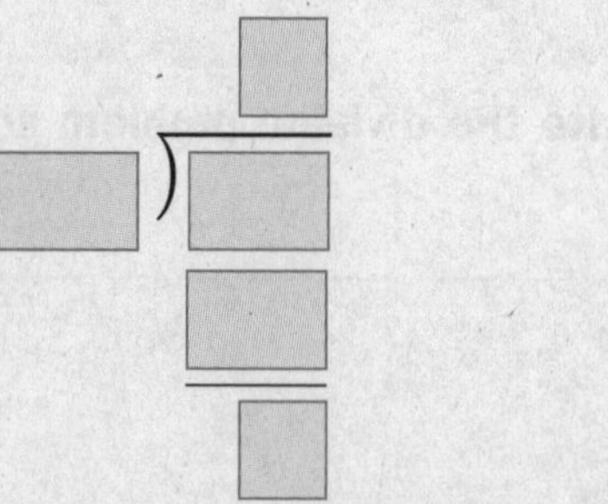

Answer: You bought ____ pounds of potatoes.

✓ **Check** Estimate: 6.25 ÷ 1.25 ≈ ____ ÷ ____ = ____. So, the answer of ____ pounds is reasonable.

Your turn now **Divide. Round to the nearest tenth if necessary.**

1. $0.4\overline{)0.94}$	**2.** $1.7\overline{)4.35}$	**3.** $0.36\overline{)31.8}$	**4.** $3.2\overline{)28}$
9. You buy $5.20 worth of apples. If apples cost $1.60 a pound, how many pounds of apples did you buy?			

Mass and Capacity

Goal: Use metric units of mass and capacity.

For Your Notebook

Vocabulary

mass:

gram:

milligram:

kilogram:

capacity:

liter:

milliliter:

kiloliter:

EXAMPLE 1 **Choosing Units of Mass**

An item has a mass of 6.4 kilograms. Is it a *videotape* or a *guitar*? Explain.

The mass of a ______ is about 1 kilogram, so 6.4 kilograms is the mass of about 6 ______. The mass of a ______ is closest to the mass of 6 ______, so the item is a ______.

As you preview this lesson, you may want to review what you learned about benchmarks for metric units of length in Lesson 2.1.

EXAMPLE 2 Choosing Units of Capacity

Tell whether the most appropriate unit to measure the capacity of the item is *milliliters*, *liters*, or *kiloliters*.

a. mixing bowl **b.** swimming pool

Solution

a. The capacity of a mixing bowl is closest to the capacity of _____ _____. You should use _____.

b. The capacity of a swimming pool is closest to the capacity of _____. You should use _____.

EXAMPLE 3 Choosing Metric Units

Choose an appropriate metric unit to measure the item.

a. mass of a refrigerator magnet **b.** capacity of a measuring spoon

When choosing an appropriate metric unit, use your benchmarks as a guide.

Solution

a. The mass of a refrigerator magnet is much greater than _____ and less than _____. So, you should use a _____.

b. The capacity of a measuring spoon is much less than _____ _____. So, you should use a _____.

Your turn now **Choose an appropriate metric unit to measure the item.**

1. mass of a stone statue	**2.** capacity of a food storage bag

LESSON 4.8

Changing Metric Units

Goal: Change from one metric unit of measure to another.

EXAMPLE 1 Changing Units Using Multiplication

Change 0.52 L to milliliters.

1. Decide whether to multiply or divide.
2. Select the power of 10.

Change to a smaller unit by ______.

mL ⟷ L

0.52 ____ ____ = ____

Answer: 0.52 L = ______ mL

EXAMPLE 2 Changing Units Using Division

Change 42.7 g to kilograms.

1. Decide whether to multiply or divide.
2. Select the power of 10.

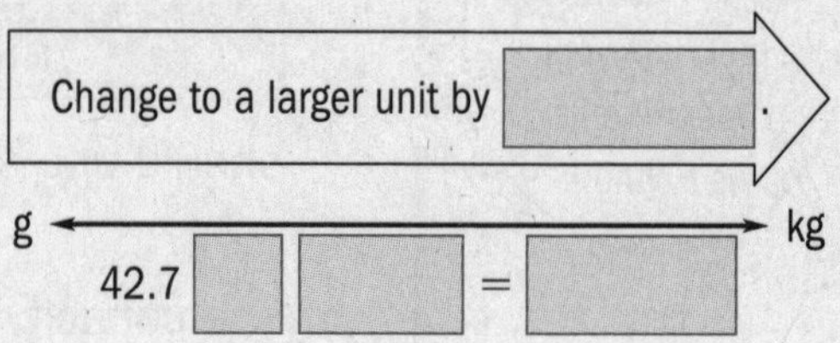

Answer: 42.7 g = ______ kg

Your turn now **Copy and complete the statement.**

1. 540 g = _?_ kg	**2.** 1.8 mL = _?_ L	**3.** 0.37 m = _?_ cm

EXAMPLE 3 Comparing Measures

Which is longer, 340 m or 0.35 km?

Change 340 m to kilometers so the units are the same for both measures.

340 m = (340 ☐ ☐) km ☐ m = ☐ km

= ☐ km

Then compare measures.

Because ☐ km ☐ 0.35 km, you know that 340 m ☐ 0.35 km.

Answer: ☐ is longer than ☐.

You can change either unit to the other. In Example 3, you could have changed 0.35 kilometers to meters instead.

Your turn now **Copy and complete the statement with <, >, or =.**

4. 80 mm __?__ 6.7 cm	**5.** 620 mL __?__ 7 L	**6.** 0.03 kg = __?__ 30 g

EXAMPLE 4 Using a Verbal Model

Shelving A storage shelf can hold up to 39.8 kg of materials. A paint can has a mass of about 995 g. How many paint cans can four storage shelves hold?

Solution

1. Write a verbal model to find the number of cans that one shelf can hold.

   Number of cans on one shelf = _____ ÷ _____

2. Before substituting into the verbal model, the units must be the same. So change 39.8 kg to grams.

   39.8 kg = (39.8 ___ ___) g = _____ g

Whenever you are solving problems involving units of measure, check to see if you need to convert any of the units.

3. Substitute the given values into the verbal model.

   Number of cans on one shelf = _____ ÷ _____

   = _____

4. Find the number of paint cans that four shelves can hold by multiplying the number of shelves by the number of paint cans that one shelf can hold.

   ___ × ___ = _____

Answer: Four storage shelves can hold _____ paint cans.

Words to Review

Give an example of the vocabulary word.

Commutative property of multiplication

Associative property of multiplication

Distributive property

Mass

Gram

Milligram

Kilogram

Capacity

Liter

Milliliter

Kiloliter

Review your notes and Chapter 4 by using the Chapter Review on pages 198–199 of your textbook.

Prime Factorization

Goal: Write whole numbers as the product of prime factors.

For Your Notebook

Vocabulary

Divisible:

Prime number:

Composite number:

Prime factorization:

Factor tree:

EXAMPLE 1 **Finding Factors**

Gardening You are planting tulip bulbs in rows in your garden. The bulbs will be arranged so that each row contains the same number of bulbs. Can 15 tulip bulbs or 18 tulip bulbs be arranged in more ways?

Solution

To answer the question, list all the factors of 15 and 18 by writing each number as a product of two numbers in as many ways as possible.

15: ☐ × ☐
☐ × ☐
☐ × ☐

18: ☐ × ☐
☐ × ☐
☐ × ☐
☐ × ☐

Stop when a pair of factors repeats.

The factors of 15 are ☐.

The factors of 18 are ☐.

Answer: ☐ bulbs can be arranged in more ways than ☐ bulbs, because ☐ has more ☐ than ☐.

Divisibility Rules for 2, 3, 5, 6, 9, and 10

A whole number is divisible by:

- 2 if the number is ____.
- 3 if the sum of ____ is divisible by ____.
- 5 if it ends with ____.
- 6 if it is ____.
- 9 if the sum of ____ is divisible by ____.
- 10 if it ends with ____.

EXAMPLE 2 Using Divisibility Rules

Test 120 for divisibility by 2, 3, 5, 6, 9, and 10.

120 ____ divisible by 2 because it ____.

120 ____ divisible by 3 because ____ + ____ + ____ = ____, which ____ divisible by ____.

120 ____ divisible by 5 because it ends with ____.

120 ____ divisible by 6 because it is ____ and divisible by ____.

120 ____ divisible by 9 because ____ + ____ + ____ = ____, which ____ divisible by ____.

120 ____ divisible by 10 because it ends with ____.

Answer: 120 is divisible by ____.

Your turn now **List all the factors of the number.**

1. 10	**2.** 16	**3.** 20	**4.** 22

Test the number for divisibility by 2, 3, 5, 6, 9, and 10.

5. 80	**6.** 126	**7.** 585	**8.** 1296

Another way to tell if a number is composite is to use divisibility rules. For example, 21 is divisible by 3. So, 3 is a factor of 21 and 21 is composite.

EXAMPLE 3 Classifying as Prime or Composite

Tell whether the number is *prime* or *composite*.

a. 63

b. 71

Solution

a. List the factors of 63: ______.

Answer: The number 63 is ______. It has factors ______ 1 and itself.

b. List the factors of 71: ______.

Answer: The number 71 is ______. Its factors ______ 1 and itself.

Your turn now **Tell whether the number is *prime* or *composite*.**

9. 17	**10.** 16	**11.** 23	**12.** 28

EXAMPLE 4 Writing a Prime Factorization

Write the prime factorization of 80.

Only prime and composite numbers are used in a factor tree. So, the number 1 is not used in a factor tree.

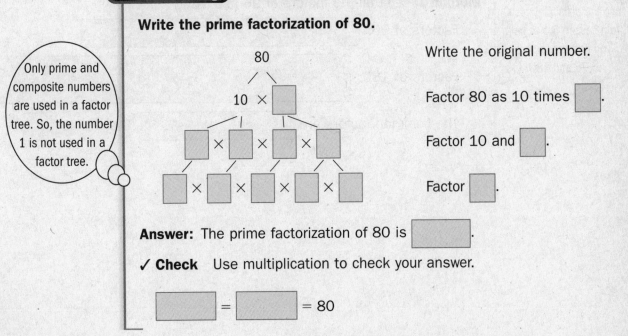

80

10 × ______

______ × ______ × ______ × ______

______ × ______ × ______ × ______ × ______

Write the original number.

Factor 80 as 10 times ______.

Factor 10 and ______.

Factor ______.

Answer: The prime factorization of 80 is ______.

✓ **Check** Use multiplication to check your answer.

______ = ______ = 80

Greatest Common Factor

Goal: Find the greatest common factor of two or more numbers.

For Your Notebook

Vocabulary

Common factor:

Greatest Common Factor (GCF):

EXAMPLE 1 **Finding the GCF of Two Numbers**

Drawing Class You are preparing kits for a drawing class. The kits will contain sheets of blank paper and sheets of grid paper. You have 180 sheets of blank paper and 96 sheets of grid paper. You want each kit to have the same number of each kind of paper, and you want to use all of the paper. What is the greatest number of kits you can make?

Solution

The greatest number of kits that you can make is the GCF of 96 and 180. Two methods for finding the GCF are shown.

Keep in mind that you can use the divisibility tests from Lesson 5.1 to help you find the factors of 96 and 180.

Method 1 List all the factors of 96 and 180.

Factors of 96: ______

Factors of 180: ______

The common factors are ______. The GCF is ___.

Method 2 Write the prime factorizations of 96 and 180. Then find the ______ of the common prime factors.

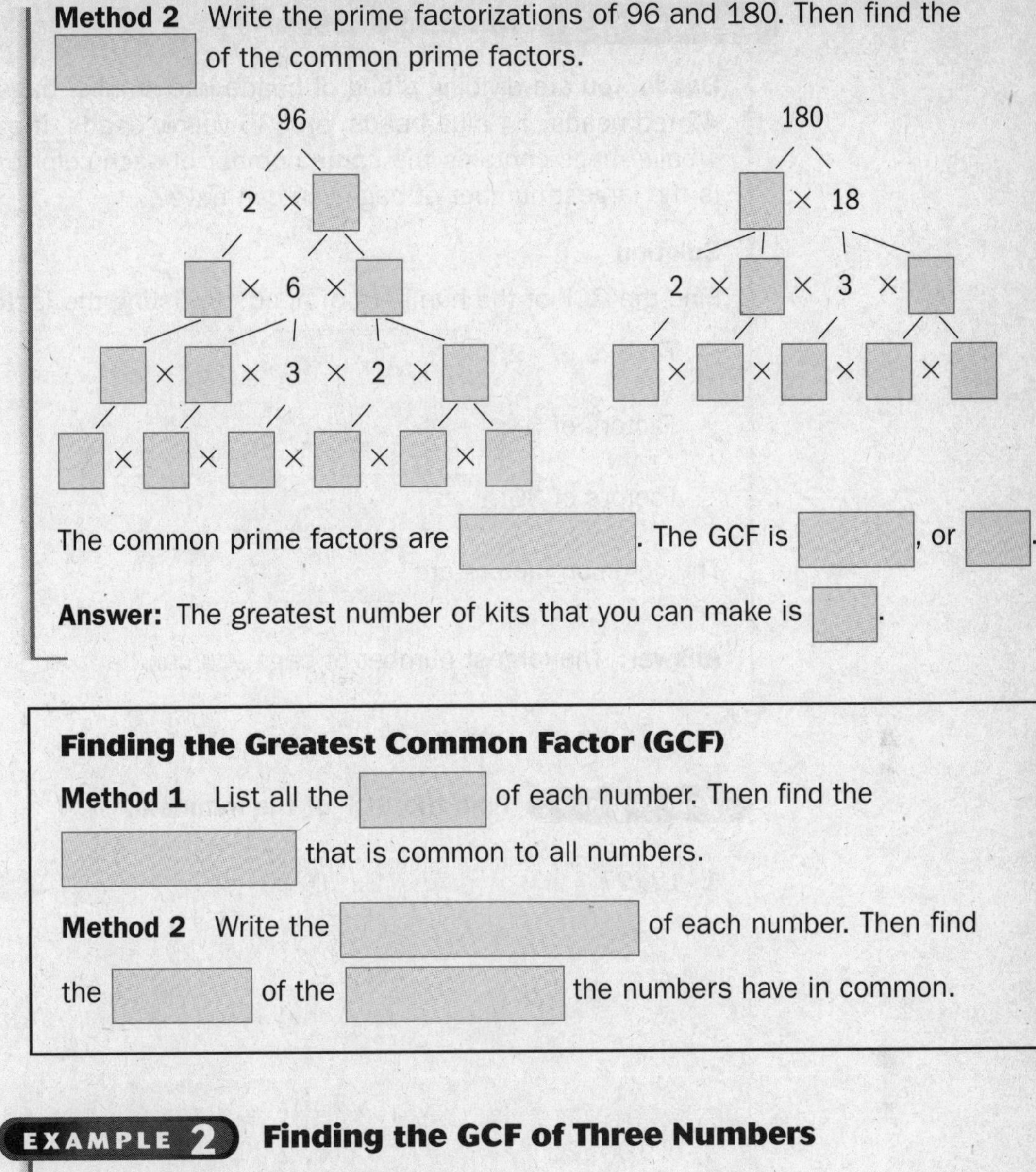

The common prime factors are ______. The GCF is ______, or ______.

Answer: The greatest number of kits that you can make is ______.

Finding the Greatest Common Factor (GCF)

Method 1 List all the ______ of each number. Then find the ______ that is common to all numbers.

Method 2 Write the ______ of each number. Then find the ______ of the ______ the numbers have in common.

EXAMPLE 2 Finding the GCF of Three Numbers

Find the GCF of 16, 24, and 28.

Factors of 16: ______

Factors of 24: ______

Factors of 28: ______

Answer: The GCF of 16, 24, and 28 is ______.

Remember that when listing the factors of a number, you need to list the number itself and the number 1.

EXAMPLE 3 Making a List

Beads You are dividing a bag of beads into smaller bags. You have 42 red beads, 54 blue beads, and 36 yellow beads. If each of the smaller bags contains the same number of each color of bead, what is the largest number of bags you can have?

Solution

Find the GCF of the numbers of beads by listing the factors.

Factors of 42: ________

Factors of 54: ________

Factors of 36: ________

The common factors are ________.

Answer: The largest number of bags you can have is ____ bags.

Your turn now **Find the GCF of the numbers.**

1. 12, 27	**2.** 20, 36	**3.** 24, 90
4. 6, 10, 12	**5.** 16, 24, 36	**6.** 15, 45, 75

Equivalent Fractions

Goal: Write equivalent fractions.

For Your Notebook

Vocabulary

Fraction:

Equivalent fractions:

Simplest form:

EXAMPLE 1 **Writing Equivalent Fractions**

Write two fractions that are equivalent to $\frac{1}{6}$.

$\frac{1}{6} = \frac{\square \times \square}{\square \times \square} = \frac{\square}{\square}$ Multiply the numerator and denominator by 2.

$\frac{1}{6} = \frac{\square \times \square}{\square \times \square} = \frac{\square}{\square}$ Multiply the numerator and denominator by 3.

In your notebook, you might want to record models of the equivalent fractions shown in Example 1.

Answer: The fractions $\frac{\square}{\square}$ and $\frac{\square}{\square}$ are equivalent to $\frac{1}{6}$.

Your turn now **Write two fractions that are equivalent to the given fraction.**

1. $\frac{1}{7}$	**2.** $\frac{2}{5}$	**3.** $\frac{6}{7}$	**4.** $\frac{3}{8}$

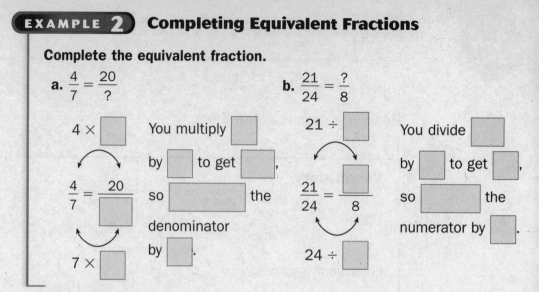

EXAMPLE 2 Completing Equivalent Fractions

Complete the equivalent fraction.

a. $\frac{4}{7} = \frac{20}{?}$

$4 \times$ ☐

$\frac{4}{7} = \frac{20}{☐}$

$7 \times$ ☐

You multiply ☐ by ☐ to get ☐, so ☐ the denominator by ☐.

b. $\frac{21}{24} = \frac{?}{8}$

$21 \div$ ☐

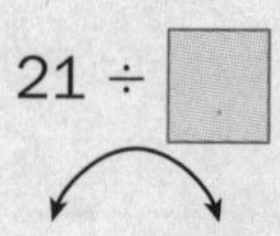

$\frac{21}{24} = \frac{☐}{8}$

$24 \div$ ☐

You divide ☐ by ☐ to get ☐, so ☐ the numerator by ☐.

Your turn now **Copy and complete the statement.**

5. $\frac{2}{9} = \frac{8}{?}$	**6.** $\frac{7}{10} = \frac{?}{40}$	**7.** $\frac{18}{24} = \frac{?}{4}$	**8.** $\frac{10}{45} = \frac{2}{?}$

EXAMPLE 3 Simplifying Fractions

Stamps In a grab bag of 100 stamps, 26 of the stamps are from the United States. Write this as a fraction in simplest form.

Solution

Write "26 out of 100" as a fraction. Then simplify.

If the numerator and denominator are large numbers, you could start by dividing the numerator and denominator by any common factor until you get a numerator and denominator whose GCF is easier to find.

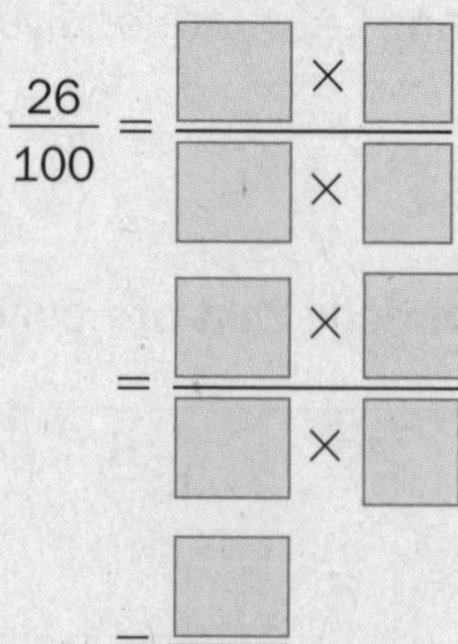

$\frac{26}{100} = \frac{☐ \times ☐}{☐ \times ☐}$ Use the GCF to write the numerator and denominator as products.

$= \frac{☐ \times ☐}{☐ \times ☐}$ Divide the numerator and denominator by the GCF.

$= \frac{☐}{☐}$ Simplest form

Answer: The fraction, in simplest form, of the stamps that are from the United States is ☐.

Your turn now **Write the fraction in simplest form.**

9. $\frac{6}{24}$	**10.** $\frac{4}{32}$	**11.** $\frac{12}{18}$	**12.** $\frac{27}{54}$

EXAMPLE 4 Applying Fractions

Stickers You bought a pack of 100 stickers. Write a fraction in simplest form to describe the portion of each kind of sticker in the pack.

a. There are 12 frog stickers in the pack.

$$\frac{12}{\square} = \frac{\square \times \square}{\square \times \square} = \frac{\square}{\square}$$

$\square$ of the stickers are frogs.

b. There are 18 turtle stickers in the pack.

$$\frac{\square}{100} = \frac{\square \times \square}{\square \times \square} = \frac{\square}{\square}$$

$\square$ of the stickers are turtles.

c. There are 70 fish stickers in the pack.

$$\frac{70}{\square} = \frac{\square \times \square}{\square \times \square} = \frac{\square}{\square}$$

$\square$ of the stickers are fish.

Least Common Multiple

Goal: Find least common multiples.

Vocabulary

Multiple:

Common multiple:

Least Common Multiple (LCM):

EXAMPLE 1 **Finding a Common Multiple**

Haircuts You get your hair cut every 6 weeks and your brother gets his hair cut every 4 weeks. If you both get your hair cut today, when will you get your hair cut on the same day in the next 48 weeks?

Solution

You can use common multiples to answer the question about haircuts. Begin by writing the multiples of 6 and 4. Then identify the common multiples through 48.

Multiples of 6:

Multiples of 4:

The common multiples of 6 and 4 are ______.

Answer: You and your brother will get your hair cut on the same day in ______ weeks.

Your turn now **Find two common multiples of the numbers.**

1. 2, 5	**2.** 3, 4	**3.** 8, 12	**4.** 4, 16

5. A garbage company picks up nonrecyclable items every 7 days and recyclable items every 12 days. If the company picks up both kinds of items today, in how many days will the company pick up both kinds of items next?

Finding the Least Common Multiple (LCM)

The least common multiple of two or more numbers is the ______ of the common ______. Below are two methods to find the LCM.

Method 1 Start listing the ______ of each number. Then find the ______ of the common ______.

Method 2 Write the ______ of the numbers. Multiply together the ______, using each ______ the ______ number of times it is a factor of any of the numbers.

If the only common factor of two numbers is 1, then their least common multiple is the product of the two numbers.

EXAMPLE 2 **Finding the LCM**

Find the LCM of 6 and 16.

Multiples of 6: ___, ___, ___, ___, ___, ___, ___, ___, . . .

Multiples of 16: ___, ___, ___, ___, ___, ___, . . .

Answer: The LCM of 6 and 16 is ___.

EXAMPLE 3 Using Prime Factorization

Find the LCM of 30 and 36 using prime factorization.

1. Write the prime factorizations. Circle any common factors.

30 = ______

36 = ______

2. Multiply together the ______, using each circled factor the ______ number of times it occurs in either factorization.

______ = ______

Answer: The LCM of 30 and 36 is ______.

Your turn now **Find the LCM of the numbers.**

6. 6, 15	**7.** 5, 8, 10	**8.** 40, 70

Ordering Fractions

Goal: Compare and order fractions.

Vocabulary

Least Common Denominator (LCD):

EXAMPLE 1 Comparing Fractions Using the LCD

Compare $\frac{3}{4}$ and $\frac{5}{6}$.

You can use any common denominator to compare two fractions, but it is usually easiest to use the LCD.

1. Find the LCD: Because the LCM of ___ and ___ is ___, the LCD is ___.

2. Use the LCD to write equivalent fractions.

$\frac{3}{4} = \frac{\square \times \square}{\square \times \square} = \frac{\square}{\square}$ $\qquad$ $\frac{5}{6} = \frac{\square \times \square}{\square \times \square} = \frac{\square}{\square}$

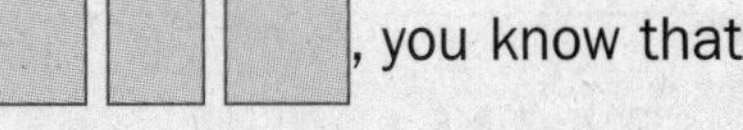

3. Compare: Because ___ ___ ___, you know that ___ ___ ___.

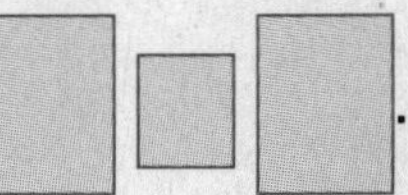

So, ___ ___ ___.

EXAMPLE 2 Ordering Fractions

Order the fractions $\frac{5}{6}$, $\frac{3}{8}$, and $\frac{7}{12}$ from least to greatest.

1. Find the LCD: Because the LCM of ___, ___, and  is ___, the LCD is ___.

2. Use the LCD to write equivalent fractions.

$\frac{5}{6} = \frac{\_\_ \times \_\_}{\_\_ \times \_\_} = \frac{\_\_}{\_\_}$ $\frac{3}{8} = \frac{\_\_ \times \_\_}{\_\_ \times \_\_} = \frac{\_\_}{\_\_}$

$\frac{7}{12} = \frac{\_\_ \times \_\_}{\_\_ \times \_\_} = \frac{\_\_}{\_\_}$

WATCH OUT!
Don't forget to multiply the numerator by the same number you multiply the denominator by when writing an equivalent fraction.

3. Compare: Because ___ < ___, you know that  ___ < ___.

Because 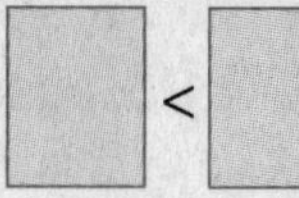 ___ < ___, you know that 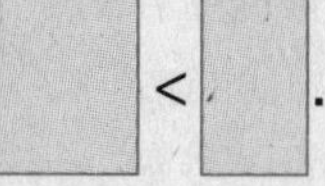 ___ < ___.

Answer: The fractions, from least to greatest, are ___,  ___, and ___.

Your turn now **Order the fractions from least to greatest.**

1. $\frac{8}{15}, \frac{5}{6}, \frac{2}{3}$	**2.** $\frac{3}{5}, \frac{7}{15}, \frac{13}{20}$	**3.** $\frac{2}{5}, \frac{1}{4}, \frac{3}{8}$

EXAMPLE 3 Ordering Fractions to Solve a Problem

Chair Repair You are replacing the screws in a chair. You tried a screw that was $\frac{3}{4}$ inch long, but it was too long. Should you try a screw that is $\frac{9}{16}$ inch long or a screw that is $\frac{7}{8}$ inch long?

Solution

Order the fractions from least to greatest:

1. Find the LCD: Because the LCM of ____, ____, and ____ is ____, the LCD is ____.

2. Use the LCD to write equivalent fractions.

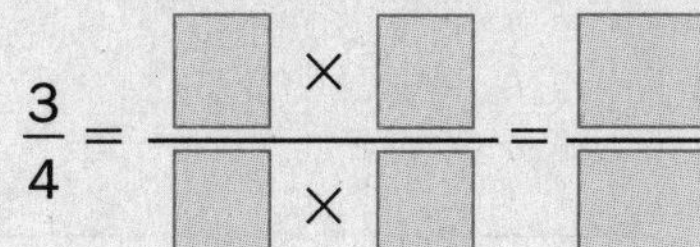

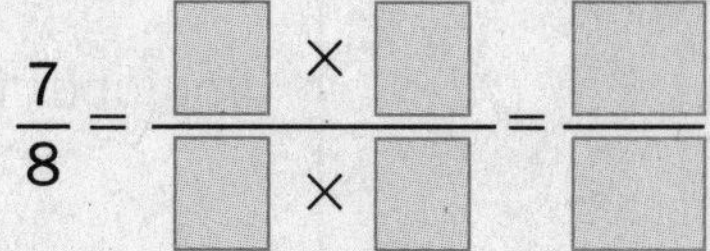

3. Order the fractions: The fractions, from least to greatest, are

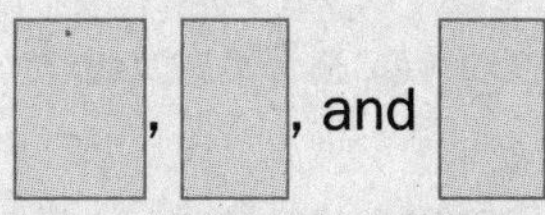

Answer: You should try the screw that is ____ inch long.

Mixed Numbers and Improper Fractions

Goal: Rewrite mixed numbers and improper fractions.

For Your Notebook

Vocabulary

Mixed number:

Improper fraction:

EXAMPLE 1 Measuring to a Fraction of an Inch

Picture Frame You need to measure the length of a photo so that you can buy the correct size of frame for the photo. Write the length as a mixed number and as an improper fraction.

Solution

First write the length as a mixed number: ______ inches.

Then count eighths to write the length as an improper fraction: ______ inches

There are ______ eighths in ______.

in. 1 2 3 4 5 6

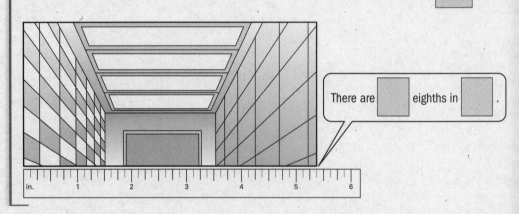

Your turn now **Draw a line segment that has the given length.**

1. $\frac{5}{2}$ in.

2. $3\frac{3}{8}$ in.

EXAMPLE 2 Rewriting Mixed Numbers

Write $6\frac{3}{7}$ as an improper fraction.

$6\frac{3}{7} = \frac{\square + \square}{\square}$ 1 whole $= \frac{\square}{\square}$, so 6 wholes =

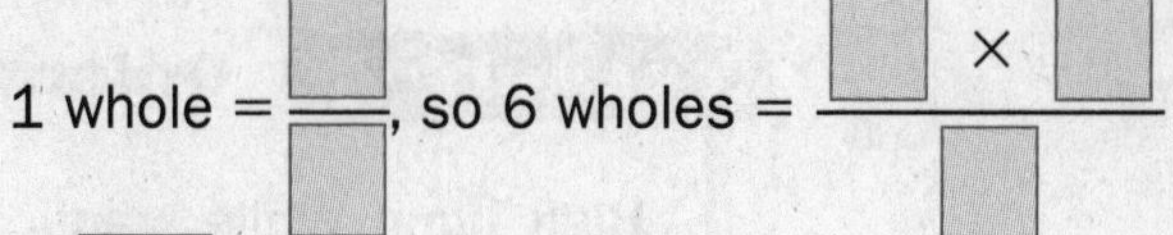

or

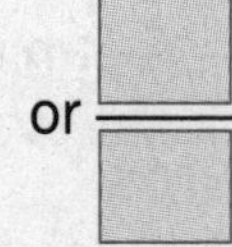

=

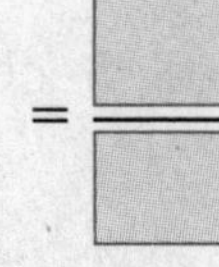

Simplify the numerator.

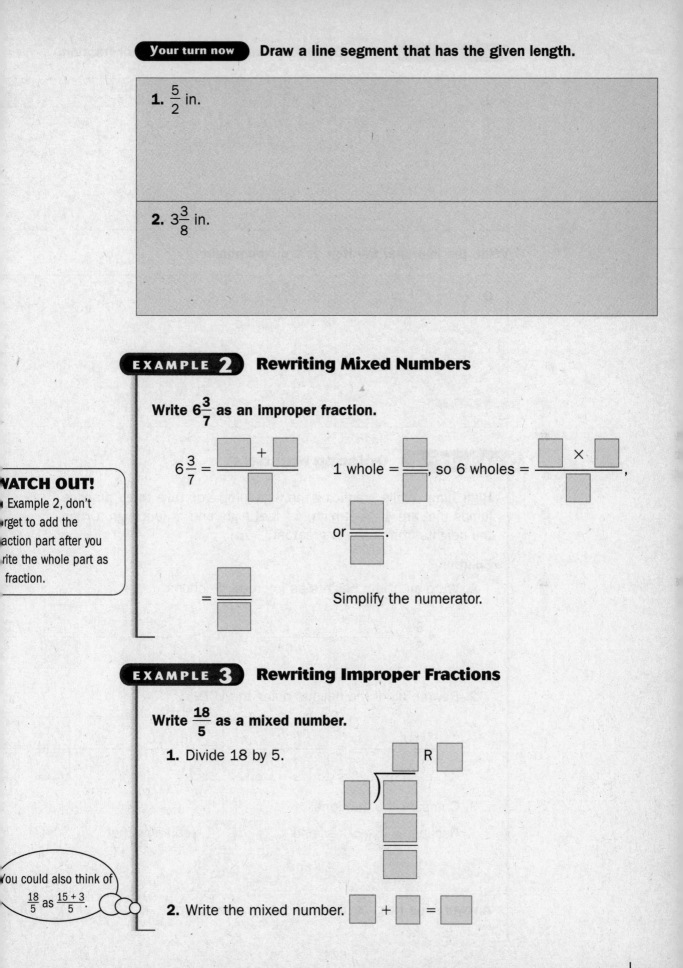

WATCH OUT!
In Example 2, don't forget to add the fraction part after you write the whole part as a fraction.

EXAMPLE 3 Rewriting Improper Fractions

Write $\frac{18}{5}$ as a mixed number.

1. Divide 18 by 5.

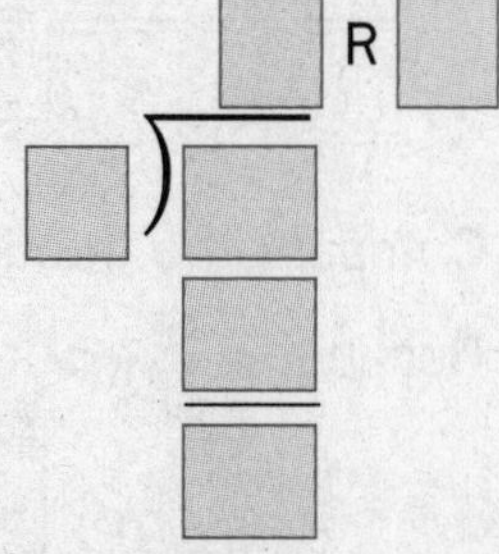

2. Write the mixed number. $\square + \square = \square$

You could also think of $\frac{18}{5}$ as $\frac{15+3}{5}$.

Your turn now **Write the mixed number as an improper fraction.**

3. $2\frac{3}{5}$	4. $3\frac{1}{8}$	5. $5\frac{4}{9}$

Write the improper fraction as a mixed number.

6. $\frac{24}{7}$	7. $\frac{48}{15}$	8. $\frac{52}{11}$

EXAMPLE 4 Ordering Numbers

High Jump While practicing the high jump, you take three practice jumps that are $4\frac{3}{8}$ feet high, $4\frac{1}{4}$ feet high, and $\frac{18}{4}$ feet high. Order the heights from least to greatest.

Solution

1. Write all of the heights as improper fractions.

$$4\frac{3}{8} = \frac{\square + \square}{\square} = \frac{\square}{\square} \qquad 4\frac{1}{4} = \frac{\square + \square}{\square} = \frac{\square}{\square} \qquad \frac{18}{4}$$

2. Rewrite all of the heights using the LCD, $\square$.

$$\frac{\square}{\square} \qquad \frac{\square}{\square} = \frac{\square \times \square}{\square \times \square} = \frac{\square}{\square} \qquad \frac{18}{4} = \frac{\square \times \square}{\square \times \square} = \frac{\square}{\square}$$

3. Compare the fractions.

Because $\square < \square$ and $\square < \square$, you know that

$\square < \square$ and $\square < \square$.

Answer: The heights, from least to greatest, are $\square$, $\square$, and $\square$ feet

LESSON 5.7

Changing Decimals to Fractions

Goal: Write a decimal as a fraction.

EXAMPLE 1 Writing Decimals as Fractions

Write the decimal as a fraction in simplest form.

a. $0.6 = \frac{\square}{\square}$ Write six ______ as a fraction.

$= \frac{\square}{\square}$ Simplify.

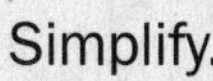

b. $0.28 = \frac{\square}{\square}$ Write twenty-eight ______ as a fraction.

$= \frac{\square}{\square}$ Simplify.

With practice, you will learn to recognize the fraction forms of several common decimals. Here are some examples.

$0.5 = \frac{1}{2}$

$0.2 = \frac{1}{5}$

$0.25 = \frac{1}{4}$

$0.125 = \frac{1}{8}$

$0.75 = \frac{3}{4}$

$0.4 = \frac{2}{5}$

EXAMPLE 2 Writing Decimals as Mixed Numbers

Precipitation The total amounts of precipitation in Portland, Oregon, and Albuquerque, New Mexico, in 2000 are given below. Write each amount as a mixed number in simplest form.

a. Amount of precipitation in Portland, Oregon: 30.2 inches

b. Amount of precipitation in Albuquerque, New Mexico: 8.24 inches

Solution

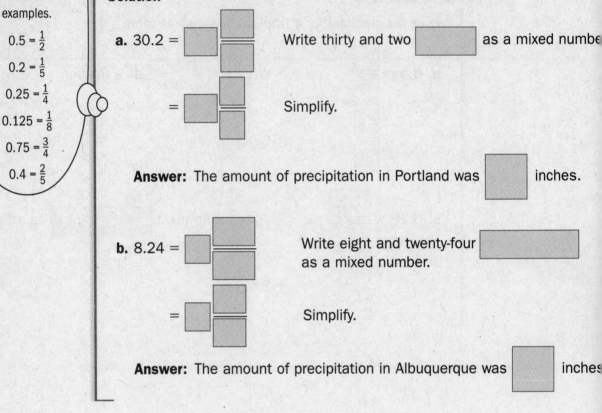

a. 30.2 = Write thirty and two as a mixed number.

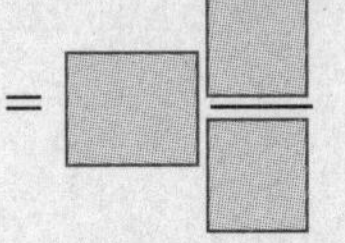

= Simplify.

Answer: The amount of precipitation in Portland was 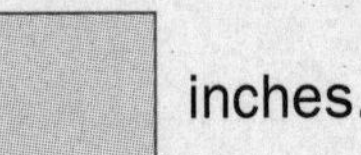 inches.

b. 8.24 = Write eight and twenty-four as a mixed number.

= Simplify.

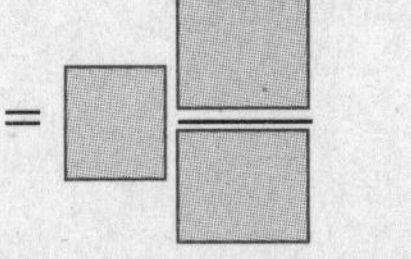

Answer: The amount of precipitation in Albuquerque was 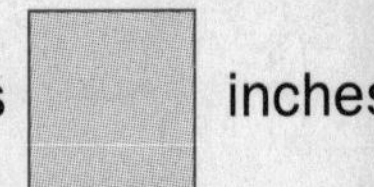 inches.

EXAMPLE 3 **Decimals with Zeros**

Recall that you read a decimal according to its last place value. For example, 2.007 is read "two and seven thousandths."

Write the decimal as a fraction or mixed number in simplest form.

a. 4.08 = ☐ $\frac{☐}{☐}$ Write four and eight ☐ as a mixed number.

= ☐ $\frac{☐}{☐}$ Simplify.

b. 0.312 = $\frac{☐}{☐}$ Write three hundred twelve ☐ as a fraction.

= $\frac{☐}{☐}$ Simplify.

Your turn now **Write the decimal as a fraction or mixed number in simplest form.**

1. 0.2	**2.** 1.48	**3.** 3.004	**4.** 0.806

Changing Fractions to Decimals

Goal: Write fractions as decimals.

For Your Notebook

Vocabulary

Terminating decimal:

Repeating decimal:

EXAMPLE 1 Writing a Fraction as a Decimal

U.S. Government In the 107th Congress, fourteen out of the fifty states had 10 or more representatives in the House of Representatives. This can be written as the fraction $\frac{14}{50}$. Write this fraction as a decimal.

Solution

To answer the question, write the fraction $\frac{14}{50}$ as a decimal by dividing 14 by 50.

50)14.00

← The remainder is ___.

Need help with division? See page 170 of your textbook.

Answer: The quotient is ___, so ___ of the states had 10 or more representatives.

Writing a Fraction as a Decimal

Words To write a fraction as a decimal, divide the ___ by the ___.

Numbers $\frac{2}{5}$ means ___ ÷ ___ **Algebra** $\frac{\square}{\square}$ means $a \div b$ $(b \neq 0)$

Your turn now **Write the fraction as a decimal.**

1. $\frac{1}{5}$	2. $\frac{7}{10}$	3. $\frac{3}{4}$	4. $\frac{5}{8}$

EXAMPLE 2 Writing a Mixed Number as a Decimal

Write $4\frac{7}{8}$ as a decimal.

1. Divide 7 by 8.

$8\overline{)7.000}$

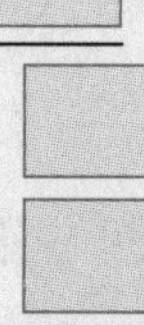

The remainder is ☐.

2. Add the whole number and the decimal.

☐ + ☐ = ☐

Answer: The mixed number $4\frac{7}{8}$, written as a decimal, is ☐.

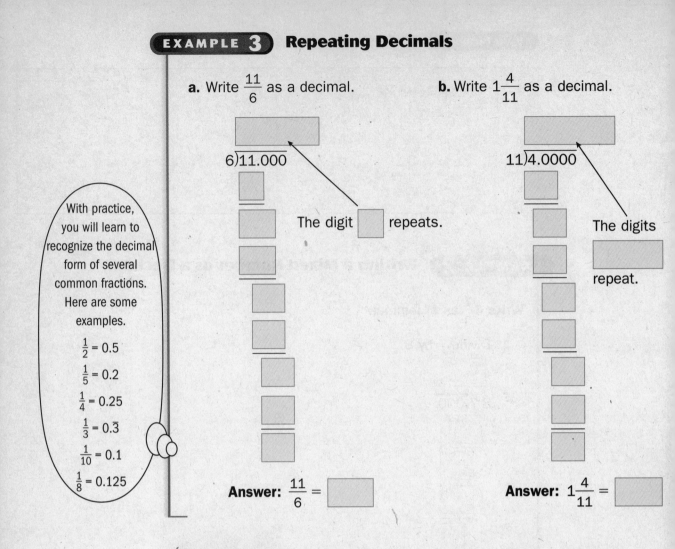

EXAMPLE 3 Repeating Decimals

a. Write $\frac{11}{6}$ as a decimal.

$6\overline{)11.000}$

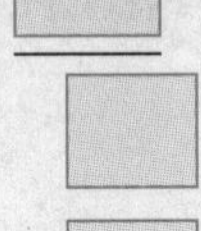

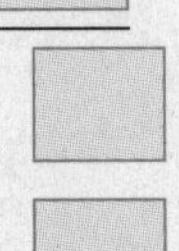

The digit ___ repeats.

Answer: $\frac{11}{6} =$ ___

b. Write $1\frac{4}{11}$ as a decimal.

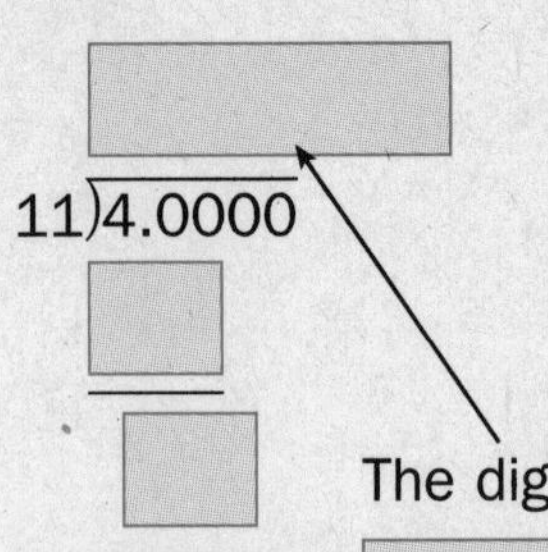

$11\overline{)4.0000}$

The digits

repeat.

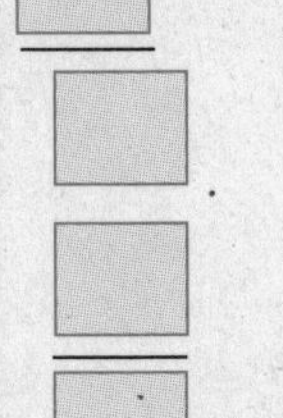

Answer: $1\frac{4}{11} =$ ___

With practice, you will learn to recognize the decimal form of several common fractions. Here are some examples.

$\frac{1}{2} = 0.5$

$\frac{1}{5} = 0.2$

$\frac{1}{4} = 0.25$

$\frac{1}{3} = 0.\overline{3}$

$\frac{1}{10} = 0.1$

$\frac{1}{8} = 0.125$

Your turn now **Write the fraction or mixed number as a decimal.**

1. $2\frac{4}{5}$	**2.** $3\frac{7}{8}$	**3.** $\frac{5}{9}$	**4.** $4\frac{5}{11}$

Words to Review

Give an example of the vocabulary word.

Divisible

Prime number

Composite number

Prime factorization

Factor tree

Common factor

Greatest Common Factor (GCF)

Fraction

Equivalent fractions

Simplest form

Multiple

Common multiple

Least Common Multiple (LCM)

Least Common Denominator (LCD)

Mixed number

Improper fraction

Proper fraction

Terminating or repeating decimal

Review your notes and Chapter 5 by using the Chapter Review on pages 260–261 of your textbook.

LESSON 6.1

Fraction Estimation

Goal: Estimate with fractions and mixed numbers.

EXAMPLE 1 Rounding Fractions

Round the fraction.

a. $\frac{1}{9} \approx$ ☐ Because 1 is ☐ 9, round $\frac{1}{9}$ to ☐.

b. $\frac{6}{11} \approx$ ☐ Because 6 is ☐ 11, round $\frac{6}{11}$ to ☐.

c. $\frac{7}{8} \approx$ ☐ Because 7 is ☐ 8, round $\frac{7}{8}$ to ☐.

EXAMPLE 2 Rounding Mixed Numbers

If the fraction or mixed number that you are rounding is halfway between two numbers, you usually round to the greater number.

Round the mixed number.

a. $5\frac{1}{4} \approx$ ☐ Because $\frac{1}{4}$ is ☐ $\frac{1}{2}$, round $5\frac{1}{4}$ ☐ to ☐.

b. $6\frac{2}{3} \approx$ ☐ Because $\frac{2}{3}$ is ☐ $\frac{1}{2}$, round $6\frac{2}{3}$ ☐ to ☐.

Your turn now **Round the fraction or mixed number.**

1. $\frac{1}{5}$	**2.** $\frac{9}{10}$	**3.** $1\frac{7}{12}$	**4.** $3\frac{2}{5}$

EXAMPLE 3 Estimating a Difference

Estimate the difference $7\frac{1}{3} - 2\frac{5}{6}$.

$7\frac{1}{3} - 2\frac{5}{6} \approx$ ☐ − ☐ Round each mixed number.

= ☐ Find the difference.

EXAMPLE 4 Estimating a Sum

Home Repair You are replacing the wood frame around a door. You need 13 feet of wood for the sides and $3\frac{7}{8}$ feet of wood for the top of the frame. You want to know how much wood you need.

a. Should your estimate of the amount of wood be *high* or *low*?

b. Estimate the amount of wood needed.

Usually when you are estimating a sum involving fractions or mixed numbers, you want to round to the nearest half or nearest whole number. In real-life situations, however, you may want to round all fractions or mixed numbers up (or down) to get a high (or low) estimate.

Solution

a. Your estimate of the amount of wood you need should be ☐ so that you will ☐.

b. Estimate the sum $13\frac{1}{4} + 3\frac{7}{8}$.

$13\frac{1}{4} + 3\frac{7}{8} \approx$ ☐ + ☐ Round each fraction ☐ to get a ☐ estimate.

= ☐ Find the sum.

Answer: You will need about ☐ feet of wood.

Your turn now Estimate the sum or difference.

5. $\frac{2}{3} + \frac{6}{7}$	**6.** $\frac{7}{13} - \frac{1}{6}$	**7.** $5\frac{1}{8} - 3\frac{9}{14}$	**8.** $2\frac{8}{9} + 4\frac{1}{2}$

9. A recipe for omelets calls for $1\frac{2}{3}$ cups cheddar cheese to go inside the omelets and $\frac{1}{4}$ cup cheddar cheese to go on top as a garnish. Estimate how much cheddar cheese you will need altogether.

LESSON 6.2

Fractions with Common Denominators

Goal: Find actual sums and differences of fractions.

Adding Fractions with Common Denominators

Words To add two fractions with a common denominator, write the ______ of the ______ over the ______.

Numbers $\frac{2}{9} + \frac{5}{9} = \frac{\square}{\square}$ **Algebra** $\frac{\square}{\square} + \frac{\square}{\square} = \frac{a + b}{c}$ $(c \neq 0)$

EXAMPLE 1 Adding Fractions

$\frac{2}{7} + \frac{6}{7} = \frac{\square + \square}{\square}$ Add the numerators.

$= \frac{\square}{\square}$ Simplify the numerator.

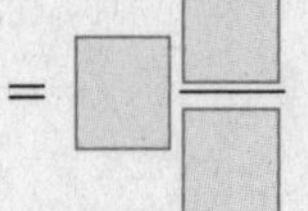

$= \square\frac{\square}{\square}$ Rewrite the improper fraction as a mixed number.

Need help with rewriting improper fractions as mixed numbers? See page 244 of your textbook.

Your turn now **Find the sum. Simplify if possible.**

1. $\frac{1}{5} + \frac{2}{5}$	2. $\frac{4}{9} + \frac{2}{9}$	3. $\frac{3}{8} + \frac{7}{8}$	4. $\frac{11}{12} + \frac{5}{12}$

Subtracting Fractions with Common Denominators

Words To subtract two fractions with a common denominator, write the ______ of the ______ over the ______.

Numbers $\frac{6}{7} - \frac{3}{7} = \frac{\square}{\square}$ **Algebra** $\frac{\square}{\square} - \frac{\square}{\square} = \frac{a-b}{c}\ (c \neq 0)$

EXAMPLE 2 **Subtracting Fractions**

Need help with writing fractions in simplest form? See page 228 of your textbook.

$\frac{9}{16} - \frac{3}{16} = \frac{\square - \square}{\square}$ Subtract the numerators.

$= \frac{\square}{\square}$ Simplify the numerator.

$= \frac{\square}{\square}$ Simplify the fraction.

EXAMPLE 3 Using a Verbal Model

Soil Particles The U.S. Bureau of Soils classifies soil particles according to their diameters. For example, a particle with a diameter of $\frac{6}{25}$ millimeter is called fine sand and a particle with a diameter of $\frac{1}{25}$ millimeter is called silt. What is the difference in the diameters of the particles?

Solution

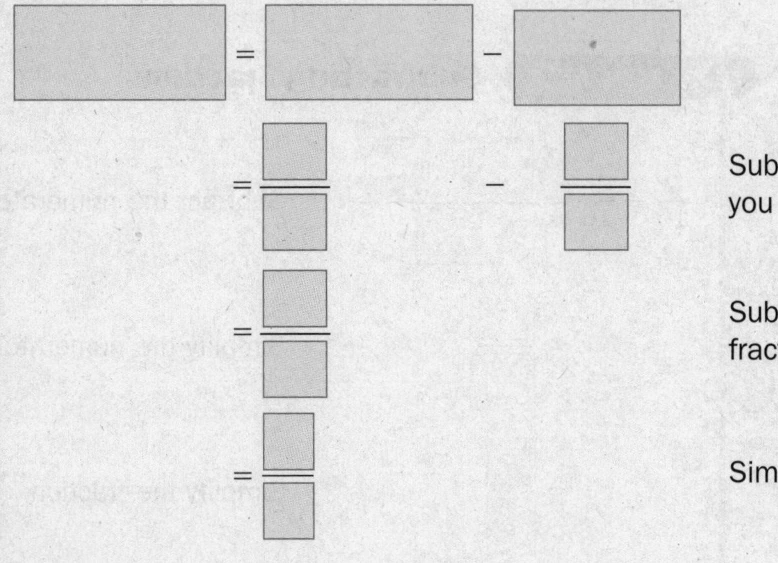

Substitute amounts you know.

Subtract the fractions.

Simplify.

Answer: The diameters differ by ______ millimeter.

Your turn now **Find the difference. Simplify if possible.**

5. $\frac{6}{7} - \frac{5}{7}$	6. $\frac{3}{4} - \frac{1}{4}$	7. $\frac{9}{10} - \frac{7}{10}$	8. $\frac{11}{12} - \frac{5}{12}$

LESSON 6.3

Fractions with Different Denominators

Goal: Add and subtract fractions with different denominators.

Adding and Subtracting Fractions

1. Find the ______ of the fractions.

2. Rewrite the fractions using the ______.

3. ______ the fractions. ______ if possible.

EXAMPLE 1 **Adding Fractions**

Art Class You are buying art supplies for an art class. Of the total amount of money you will spend on supplies, $\frac{1}{4}$ of the total amount will be spent on paper and $\frac{3}{5}$ of the total amount will be spent on paints and charcoal pencils. How much of the total amount of money will you spend on paper, paints, and charcoal pencils?

Solution

To answer the question, find the sum $\frac{\square}{\square} + \frac{\square}{\square}$.

$$\frac{\square \times \square}{\square \times \square} = \frac{\square}{\square}$$ Rewrite both fractions using the LCD, ______.

$$+\frac{\square \times \square}{\square \times \square} = +\frac{\square}{\square}$$

$$\frac{\square}{\square}$$ Add the fractions.

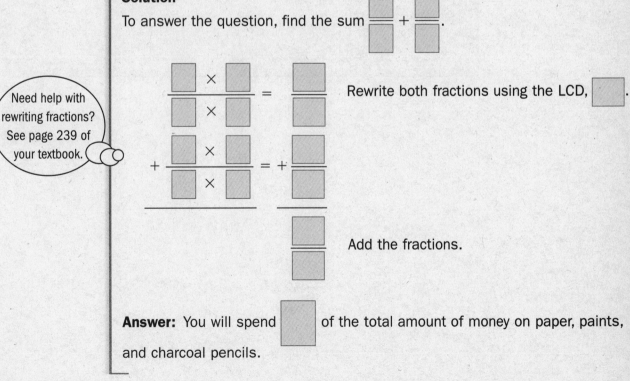

Need help with rewriting fractions? See page 239 of your textbook.

Answer: You will spend ______ of the total amount of money on paper, paints, and charcoal pencils.

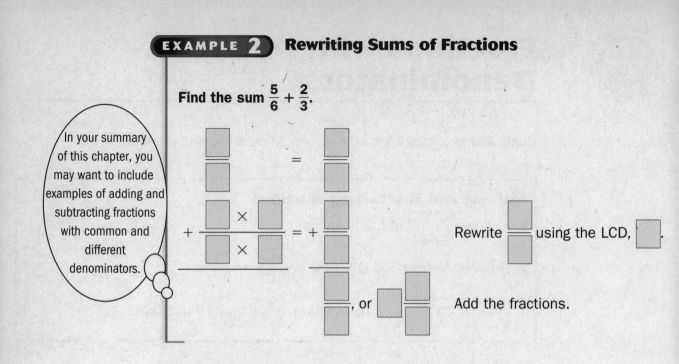

EXAMPLE 2 Rewriting Sums of Fractions

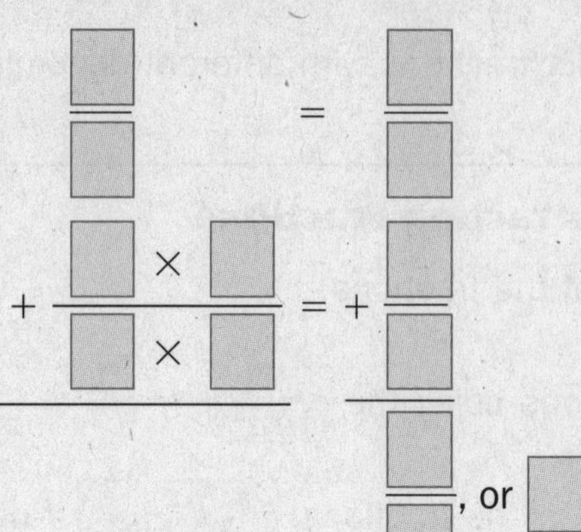

In your summary of this chapter, you may want to include examples of adding and subtracting fractions with common and different denominators.

Find the sum $\frac{5}{6} + \frac{2}{3}$.

Rewrite using the LCD, .

Add the fractions.

Your turn now Find the sum. Simplify if possible.

1. $\frac{3}{8} + \frac{1}{4}$	2. $\frac{1}{2} + \frac{3}{5}$	3. $\frac{2}{3} + \frac{3}{4}$	4. $\frac{5}{6} + \frac{4}{9}$

EXAMPLE 3 Subtracting Fractions

Science Project For a semester-long science project, you are recording the growth of your hair. During the month of September, your hair grew $\frac{5}{6}$ inch. In October, your hair grew $\frac{3}{4}$ inch. How much more did you hair grow in September than in October?

Solution

You need to find the difference $\frac{\square}{\square} - \frac{\square}{\square}$.

$$\frac{\square \times \square}{\square \times \square} = \frac{\square}{\square}$$ Rewrite both fractions using the LCD, $\square$.

$$-\frac{\square \times \square}{\square \times \square} = -\frac{\square}{\square}$$

$$\frac{\square}{\square}$$ Subtract the fractions.

Answer: Your hair grew $\square$ inch longer in September.

Your turn now **Find the difference. Simplify if possible.**

5. $\frac{7}{8} - \frac{5}{6}$	**6.** $\frac{4}{9} - \frac{1}{3}$	**7.** $\frac{2}{3} - \frac{1}{5}$	**8.** $\frac{5}{9} - \frac{2}{15}$

9. You estimate that $\frac{3}{4}$ of a driving trip will be spent on the highway, $\frac{1}{5}$ on city streets, and the rest on country roads. How much greater of a portion of your trip will be spent on the highway than on city streets?

Adding and Subtracting Mixed Numbers

Goal: Add and subtract mixed numbers.

Adding and Subtracting Mixed Numbers

1. Rewrite the fractions using the ______.
2. Add or subtract the ______, then the ______.
3. ______ if possible.

EXAMPLE 1 **Adding Mixed Numbers**

Guitar Practice Last week, you practiced playing the guitar for $6\frac{1}{5}$ hours. This week, you practiced for $8\frac{2}{5}$ hours. How much time did you spend practicing the guitar during the last two weeks?

Solution

To solve the problem, find the sum ______ + ______.

Remember that when adding fractions, you write the sum of the numerators over the common denominator.

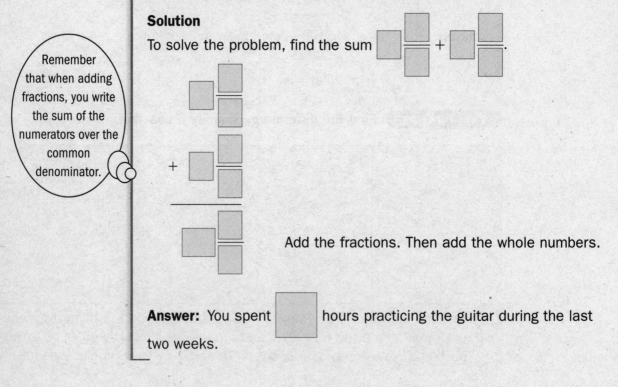

Add the fractions. Then add the whole numbers.

Answer: You spent ______ hours practicing the guitar during the last two weeks.

Your turn now **Find the sum.**

1. $3\frac{3}{5} + 2\frac{1}{5}$	2. $4\frac{2}{9} + 1\frac{5}{9}$	3. $6\frac{4}{7} + 5\frac{1}{7}$	4. $2\frac{4}{11} + 1\frac{6}{11}$

EXAMPLE 2 Simplifying Mixed Number Sums

Find the sum $2\frac{1}{6} + 1\frac{1}{3}$.

$$\square\frac{\square}{\square} = \square\frac{\square}{\square}$$

$$+\,\square\frac{\square \times \square}{\square \times \square} = +\,\square\frac{\square}{\square}$$

Rewrite $\frac{\square}{\square}$ using the LCD, $\square$.

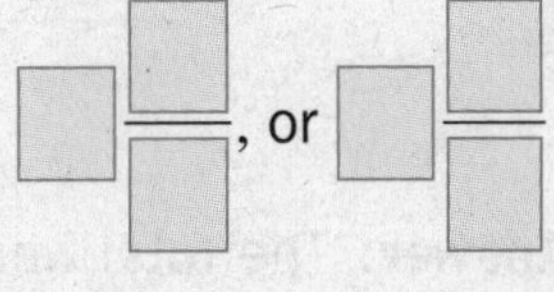

Add the fractions, then the whole numbers. Simplify.

EXAMPLE 3 Solving Addition Problems

Books Your science book weighs $2\frac{3}{5}$ pounds and your history book weighs $3\frac{1}{2}$ pounds. What is the total weight of the books?

Solution

You need to find the sum 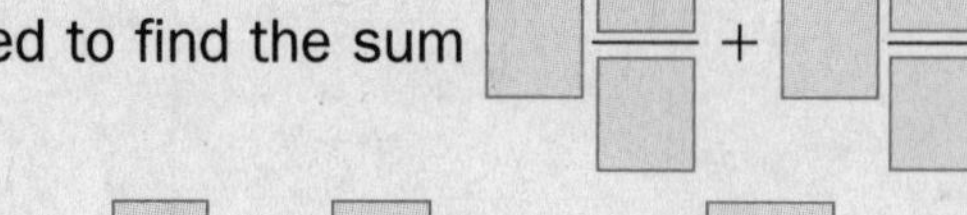.

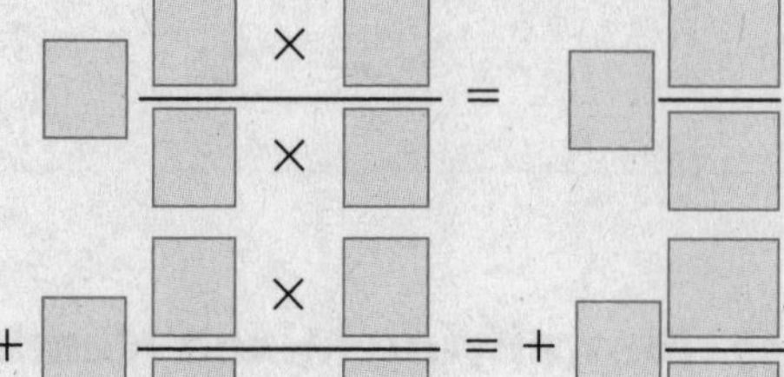

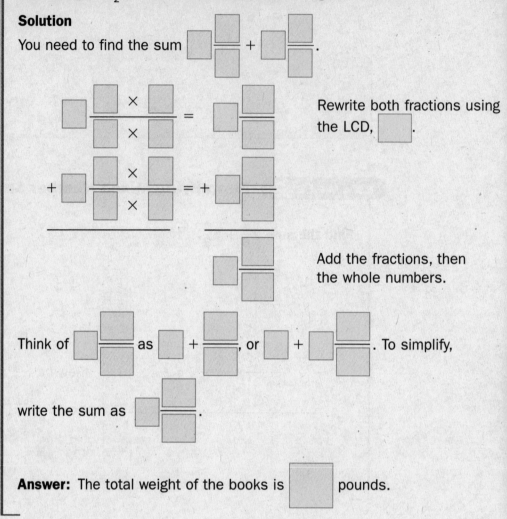

Rewrite both fractions using the LCD, ____.

Add the fractions, then the whole numbers.

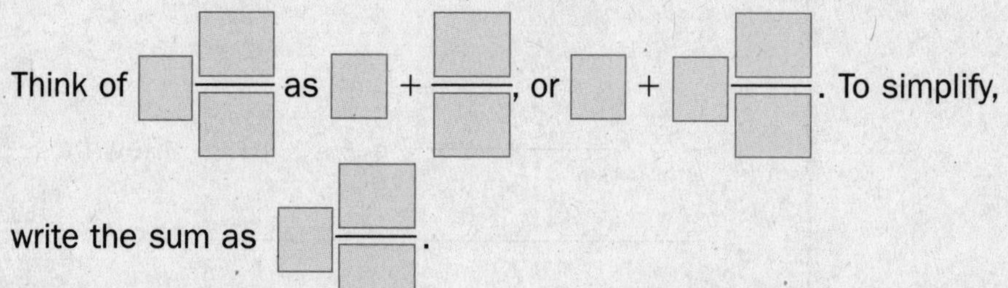

Think of ____ as ____ + ____, or ____ + ____. To simplify,

write the sum as ____.

Answer: The total weight of the books is ____ pounds.

Your turn now **Find the sum. Simplify if possible.**

5. $1\frac{1}{2} + 2\frac{3}{8}$	**6.** $4\frac{2}{5} + 6\frac{1}{3}$	**7.** $5\frac{4}{9} + 8\frac{2}{3}$	**8.** $3\frac{5}{12} + 2\frac{5}{6}$

9. A plant stand is $16\frac{3}{5}$ inches tall. There is a plant on the top of the stand that is $5\frac{2}{3}$ inches tall. What is the total height of the plant and the stand?

10. It takes $3\frac{1}{2}$ hours to drive from your house to your cousin's house and the same time to return home. How long are you in the car for a round trip?

EXAMPLE 4 Subtracting Mixed Numbers

Racing The track at Pimlico Race Course in Baltimore, Maryland is $1\frac{3}{16}$ miles long. The track at Belmont Park in Elmont, New York is $1\frac{1}{2}$ miles long. How much longer is the track at Belmont Park?

Solution

You need to find the difference

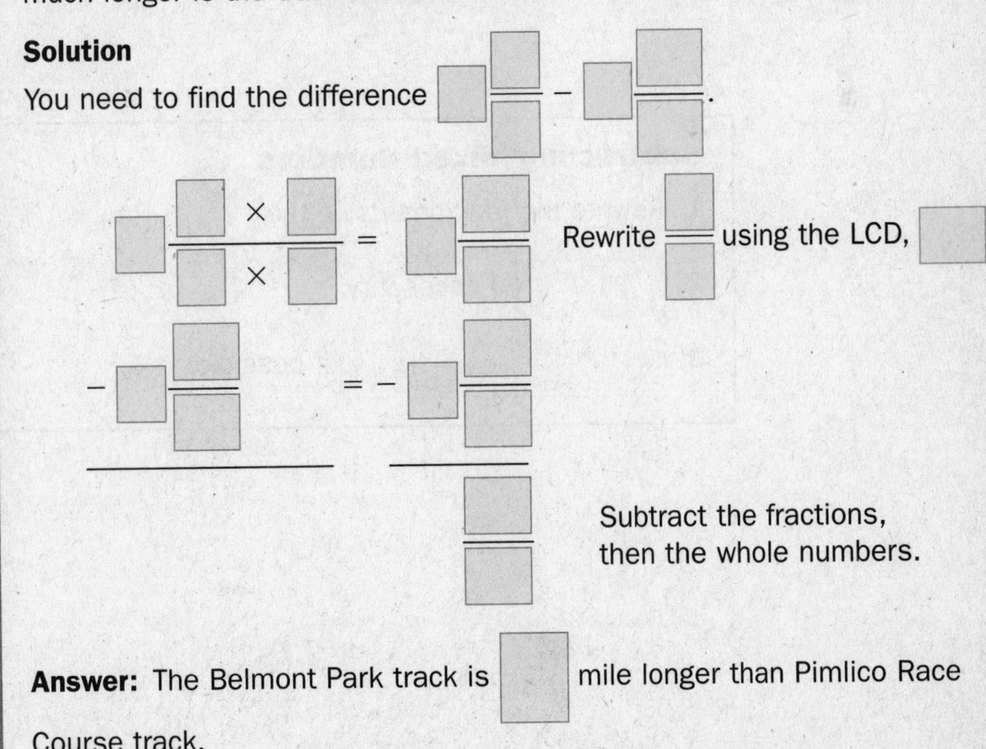

Rewrite using the LCD, .

Subtract the fractions, then the whole numbers.

Answer: The Belmont Park track is mile longer than Pimlico Race Course track.

LESSON 6.5

Subtracting Mixed Numbers by Renaming

Goal: Subtract mixed numbers by renaming.

EXAMPLE 1 Subtracting Mixed Numbers

Find the difference $4\frac{1}{5} - 2\frac{3}{5}$.

Solution

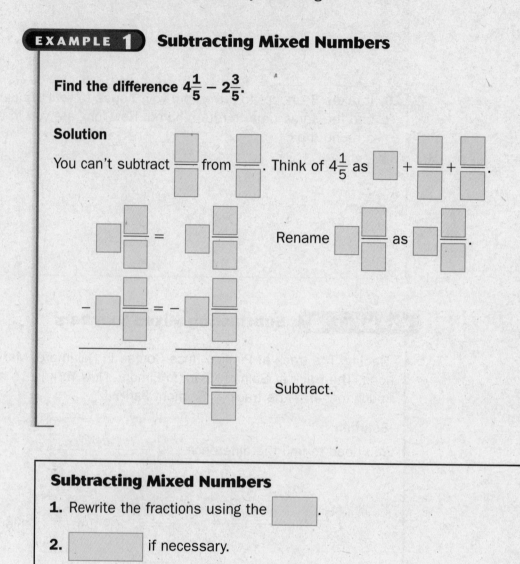

You can't subtract 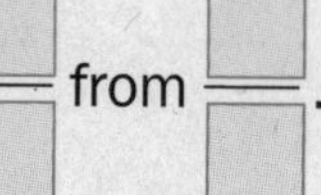 from . Think of $4\frac{1}{5}$ as 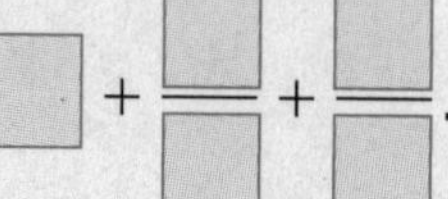.

= Rename 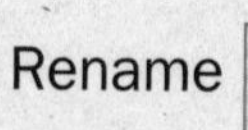 as 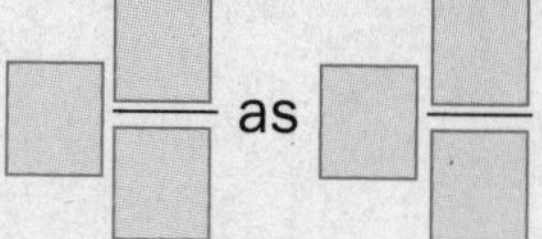.

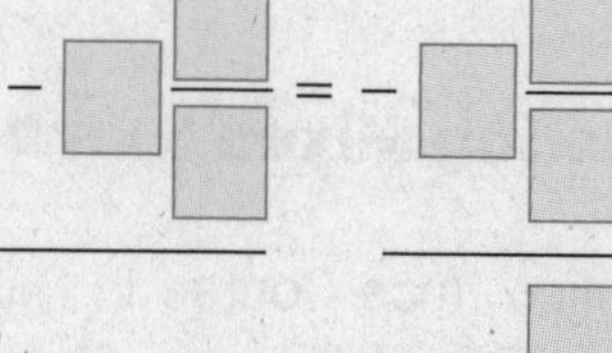

Subtract. 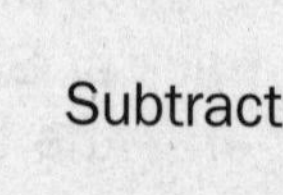

Subtracting Mixed Numbers

1. Rewrite the fractions using the .
2. if necessary.
3. . if possible.

Your turn now Find the difference. Simplify if possible.

1. $6\frac{1}{6} - 4\frac{5}{6}$	2. $3\frac{1}{3} - 1\frac{2}{3}$	3. $5\frac{3}{8} - 2\frac{5}{8}$	4. $7\frac{2}{9} - 4\frac{7}{9}$

When subtracting a mixed number from a whole number, rename one whole part as a fraction whose denominator is the same as the other denominator in the problem.

EXAMPLE 2 Subtracting from a Whole Number

Find the difference $7 - 2\frac{1}{8}$.

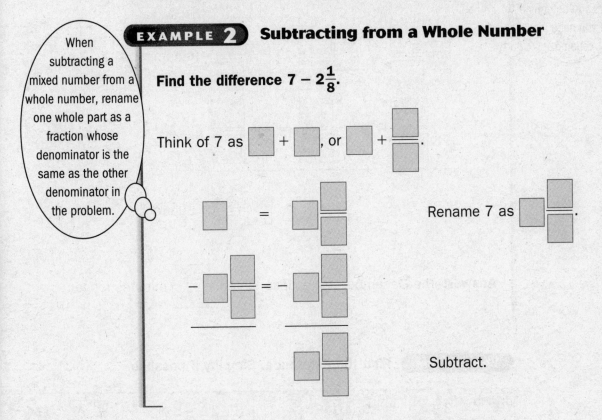

Think of 7 as ☐ + ☐, or ☐ + $\frac{☐}{☐}$.

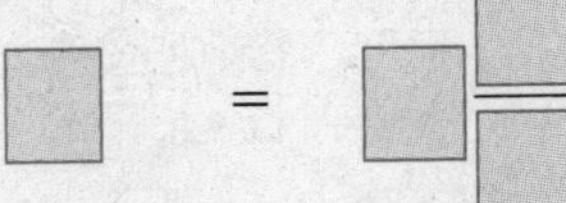

Rename 7 as ☐$\frac{☐}{☐}$.

$- ☐\frac{☐}{☐} = - ☐\frac{☐}{☐}$

Subtract.

EXAMPLE 3 Solving Subtraction Problems

Solar Eclipse On April 8, 2005, a solar eclipse will occur which will last $\frac{7}{10}$ minute. A solar eclipse on December 4, 2002 lasted $2\frac{1}{15}$ minutes. How much longer was the December 4th eclipse?

When subtracting mixed numbers, rewrite the mixed numbers with a common denominator before you determine if you need to rename.

Solution

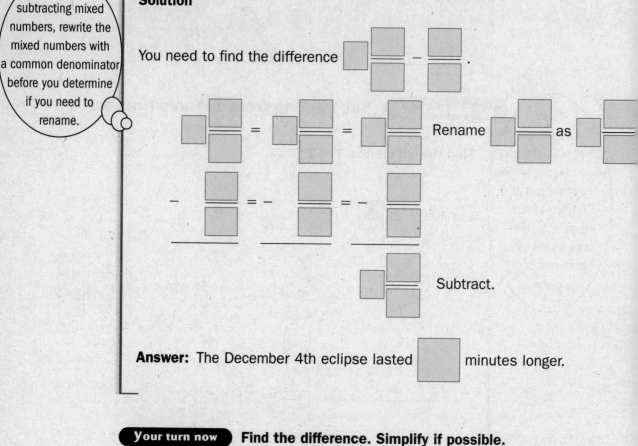

You need to find the difference ___ − ___.

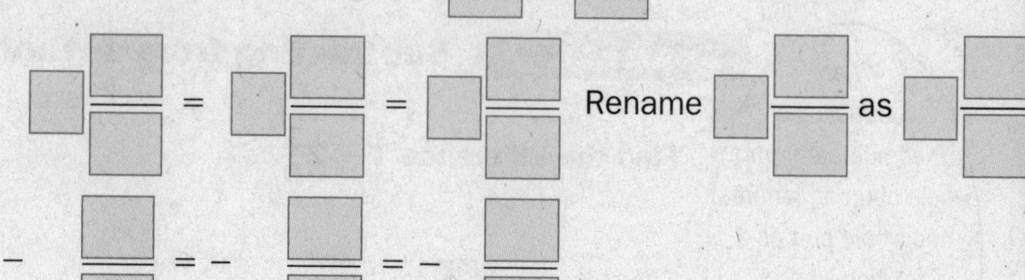

Rename ___ as ___.

Subtract.

Answer: The December 4th eclipse lasted ___ minutes longer.

Your turn now **Find the difference. Simplify if possible.**

5. $4 - 3\frac{1}{3}$	**6.** $10 - 8\frac{5}{6}$	**7.** $2\frac{1}{3} - 1\frac{1}{2}$	**8.** $5\frac{3}{8} - 3\frac{3}{4}$

LESSON 6.6

Measures of Time

Goal: Add and subtract measures of time.

For Your Notebook

Vocabulary

Elapsed time: ______

EXAMPLE 1 **Adding Measures of Time**

Marathon Your best running time in a marathon was 5 hours, 26 minutes, and 38 seconds. Your second best running time took 3 minutes and 25 seconds longer than your best time. What was your second best running time?

Solution

To answer the question, add 3 minutes and 25 seconds to 5 hours, 26 minutes, and 38 seconds.

When adding times vertically, make sure that you line up hours with hours, minutes with minutes, and seconds with seconds.

	___ h	___ min	___ sec	
+		___ min	___ sec	
	___ h	___ min	___ sec	Add the hours, the minutes, and the seconds.

Think of ___ sec as ___ min ___ sec. Then add ___ min to ___ min.

Answer: Your second best running time was ___ hours, ___ minutes, and ___ seconds.

EXAMPLE 2 **Subtracting Measures of Time**

	14 h	15 min
−	6 h	45 min

Think of 14 h 15 min as ___ h ___ min.

	___ h	___ min	Rename.
−	___ h	___ min	
	___ h	___ min	Subtract.

Your turn now **Add or subtract the measures of time.**

1.	2.
3 h 42 min 12 sec + 1 h 33 min 19 sec	6 min 24 sec − 3 min 50 sec

EXAMPLE 3 **Finding Elapsed Time**

School You get up to go to school at 6:45 A.M. and arrive home from school at 3:55 P.M. How much time has passed since you got up for school and arrived home from school?

WATCH OUT!
You can't always subtract two times to find elapsed time. For example, to find the elapsed time from 8:00 A.M. to 4:25 P.M., you can't compute 4 h 25 min − 8 h. You need to break the problem into parts.

Solution

Break the problem into parts.

1. Find the elapsed time from 6:45 A.M. to 12:00 P.M.

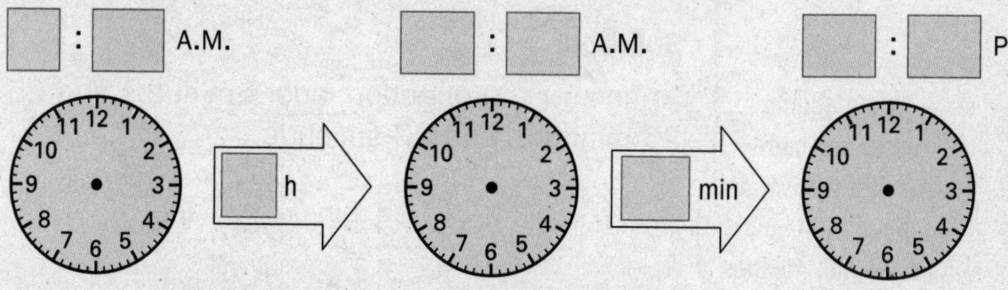

2. Find the elapsed time from 12:00 P.M. to 3:55 P.M.

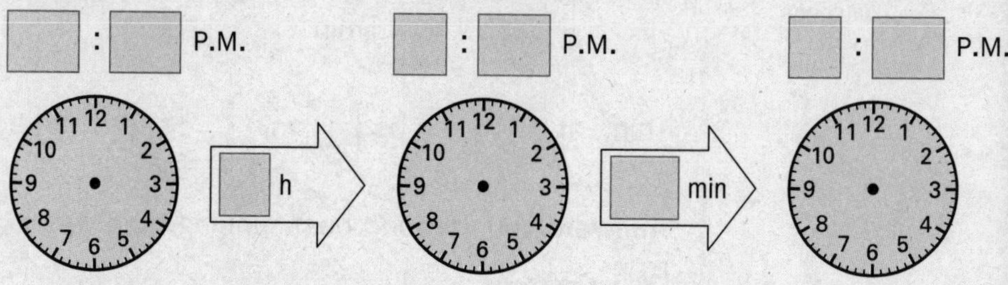

3. Add the two elapsed times.

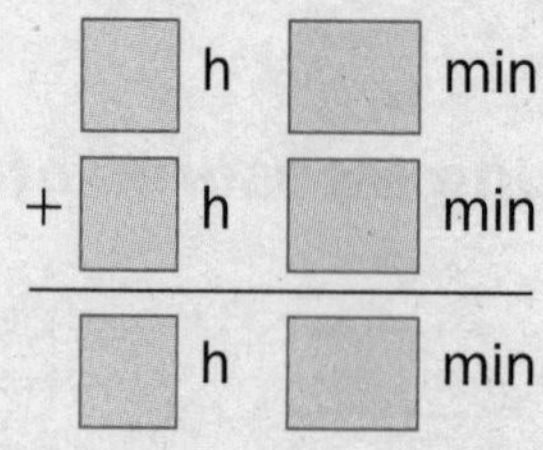

Think of ___ min as ___ h ___ min. Then add ___ h to ___ h.

Answer: Since you got up for school and arrived home from school, ___ hours and ___ minutes have passed.

Your turn now **Find the elapsed time.**

3. 4:00 A.M. to 10:00 A.M.	**4.** 6:30 A.M. to 10:45 A.M.
5. 11:35 A.M. to 4:10 P.M.	**6.** 9:40 P.M. to 2:10 P.M.

7. You make a long-distance phone call to your friend. The call begins at 7:43 P.M. and ends at 8:22 P.M. How long were you on the phone?

Words to Review

Give an example of the vocabulary word.

Fraction

Simplest form

Least common denominator

Mixed number

Improper fraction

Elapsed time

Round

Review your notes and Chapter 6 by using the Chapter Review on pages 304–305 of your textbook.

Multiplying Fractions and Whole Numbers

Goal: Multiply fractions and whole numbers.

Multiplying Fractions by Whole Numbers

Words To multiply a fraction by a whole number, multiply the ______ of the fraction by the ______ and write the ______ over the ______. ______ if possible.

Numbers $4 \times \frac{2}{9} = \frac{\square}{\square}$ **Algebra** $a \cdot \frac{\square}{\square} = \frac{a \cdot b}{c}$ $(c \neq 0)$

EXAMPLE 1 Multiply Fractions by Whole Numbers

When you write the rule for multiplying fractions by whole numbers in your notebook, you may want to include a model like the one in the activity on page 313 of your textbook.

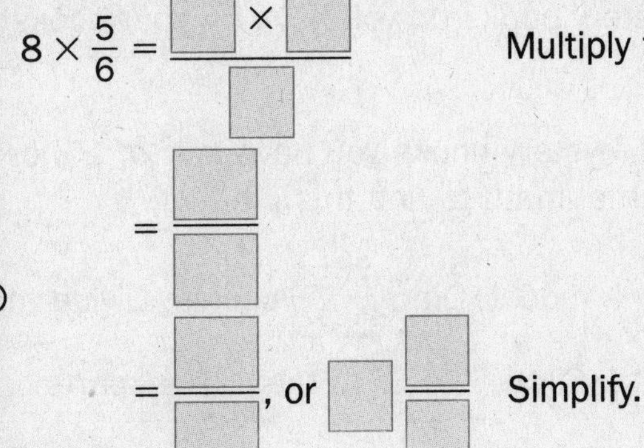

$8 \times \frac{5}{6} = \frac{\square \times \square}{\square}$ Multiply the numerator by the whole number.

$= \frac{\square}{\square}$

$= \frac{\square}{\square}$, or $\square\frac{\square}{\square}$ Simplify.

EXAMPLE 2 Multiply Whole Numbers by Fractions

You can find the product the same way whether the whole number is written on the left or right. In part (a) of Example 2, $\frac{2}{9} \times 3 = 3 \times \frac{2}{9}$.

a. $\frac{2}{9} \times 3 = \frac{\square}{\square}$ Multiply the ______ by the ______.

$= \frac{\square}{\square}$ Simplify.

b. $\frac{5}{4} \times 3 = \frac{\square}{\square}$ Multiply the ______ by the ______.

$= \square\frac{\square}{\square}$ Simplify.

Your turn now **Find the product. Simplify if possible.**

1. $3 \times \frac{2}{7}$	**2.** $8 \times \frac{2}{5}$	**3.** $\frac{4}{3} \times 4$	**4.** $\frac{7}{9} \times 3$
5. Look at the results in Example 2. Then predict whether the product will be *greater than 3* or *less than 3* when 3 is multiplied by $\frac{7}{8}$.			

EXAMPLE 3 Using Mental Math or a Model

Books You have 15 books on your bookshelf, $\frac{2}{5}$ of which are mystery books. How many mystery books do you have on your bookshelf?

Solution

The number of mystery books you have is $\frac{2}{5}$ *of* 15, or $\frac{2}{5} \times 15$. You can use a model or mental math to find this product.

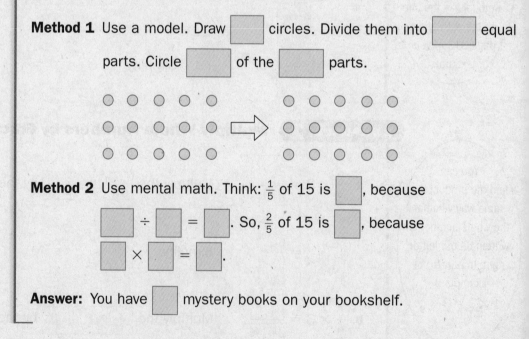

Method 1 Use a model. Draw ______ circles. Divide them into ______ equal parts. Circle ______ of the ______ parts.

Method 2 Use mental math. Think: $\frac{1}{5}$ of 15 is ______, because ______ ÷ ______ = ______. So, $\frac{2}{5}$ of 15 is ______, because ______ × ______ = ______.

Answer: You have ______ mystery books on your bookshelf.

EXAMPLE 4 Estimating a Product

Saving Money Alicia has a summer job that pays $157 a week. Each week, she will put $\frac{3}{4}$ of her earnings in a savings account. Estimate how much money Alicia will put in the account each week.

Solution

Amount put into account = ____ × ____ Multiply fraction of earnings put into account by the weekly amount earned.

≈ ____ × ____ Replace ____ with a number compatible with ____.

= ____ Think: $\frac{1}{4}$ of ____ is ____, so $\frac{3}{4}$ of ____ is ____.

Answer: Alicia will put about $ ____ in the account each week.

Your turn now **Use mental math.**

6. Find $\frac{4}{5}$ of 20.	**7.** Find $48 \times \frac{3}{8}$.	**8.** Estimate $\frac{2}{3} \times 19$.

CHAPTER 7.2

Multiplying Fractions

Goal: Multiply fractions.

EXAMPLE 1 Using a Model to Multiply Fractions

Sleep The average person sleeps for about $\frac{1}{3}$ of a 24-hour day. About $\frac{1}{5}$ of the time spent sleeping is spent in REM (rapid eye movement) sleep. What fraction of a 24-hour day is spent in REM sleep?

Solution

Use a model to find $\frac{1}{5}$ of $\frac{1}{3}$, or $\frac{1}{5} \times \frac{1}{3}$.

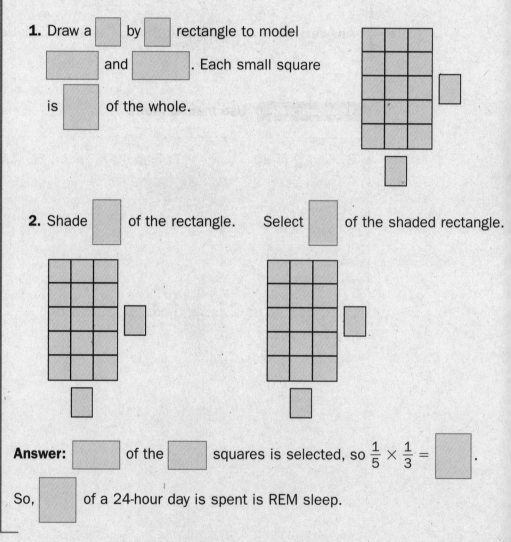

1. Draw a ______ by ______ rectangle to model ______ and ______. Each small square is ______ of the whole.

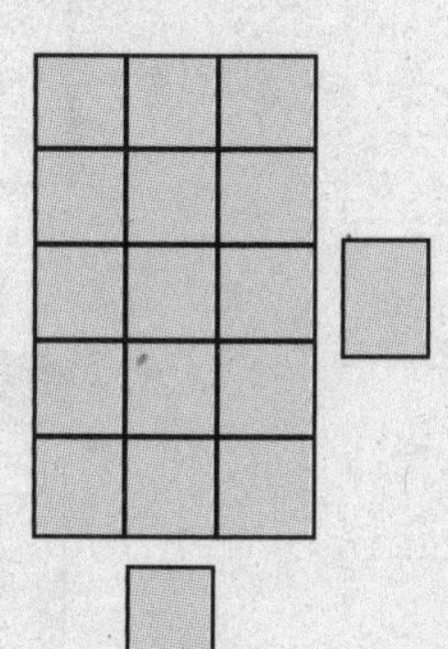

2. Shade ______ of the rectangle. Select ______ of the shaded rectangle.

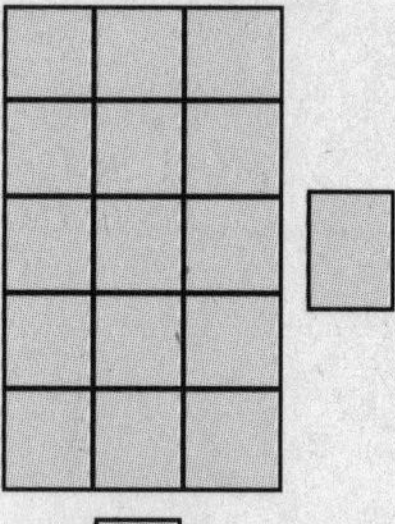

Answer: ______ of the ______ squares is selected, so $\frac{1}{5} \times \frac{1}{3} =$ ______.

So, ______ of a 24-hour day is spent is REM sleep.

Your turn now **Draw a model to find the product.**

1. $\frac{1}{2} \times \frac{1}{3}$	2. $\frac{2}{3} \times \frac{1}{5}$	3. $\frac{3}{4} \times \frac{3}{5}$

Multiplying Fractions

Words product of fractions = $\frac{\text{product of the } \square}{\text{product of the } \square}$

Numbers $\frac{1}{3} \times \frac{4}{5} = \frac{\square}{\square}$

Algebra $\frac{a}{b} \cdot \frac{c}{d} = \frac{\square \cdot \square}{\square \cdot \square}$ $(b, d \neq 0)$

EXAMPLE 2 Multiplying Two Fractions

$\frac{5}{8} \times \frac{3}{2} = \frac{\square \times \square}{\square \times \square}$ Use the rule for multiplying fractions.

$= \frac{\square}{\square}$ Multiply. The product is in simplest form.

EXAMPLE 3 Evaluating an Algebraic Expression

Algebra **Evaluate the expression $\frac{1}{4}n$ when $n = \frac{3}{5}$.**

$\frac{1}{4}n = \square \times \square$ Substitute $\square$ for n.

$= \frac{\square \times \square}{\square \times \square}$ Use the rule for multiplying fractions.

$= \frac{\square}{\square}$ Multiply. The product is in simplest form.

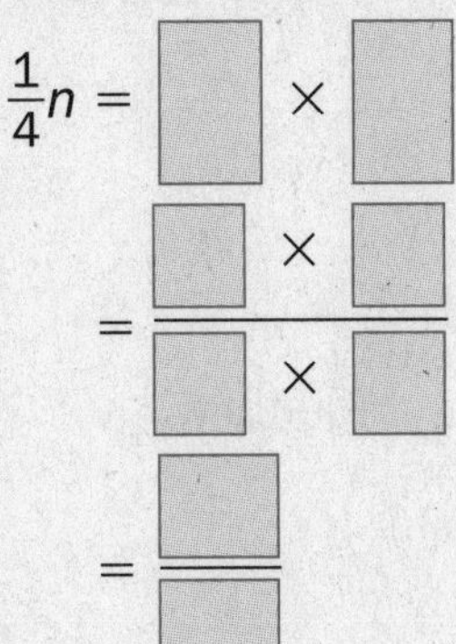

Notice in
Example 3 that
the product is
less than either
fraction.

Your turn now **In Exercises 4–7, find the value.**

4. Find the product $\frac{1}{2} \times \frac{3}{8}$.	**5.** Find the product $\frac{1}{5} \times \frac{4}{7}$.
6. Evaluate $\frac{2}{9}n$ when $n = \frac{4}{3}$.	**7.** Evaluate $\frac{4}{5}x$ when $x = \frac{6}{7}$.

8. Is the product in Example 2 less than both fractions?

EXAMPLE 4 Simplifying Before Multiplying

$\frac{1}{18} \times \frac{4}{15} = \frac{\square \times \square}{\square \times \square}$ Use the rule for multiplying fractions.

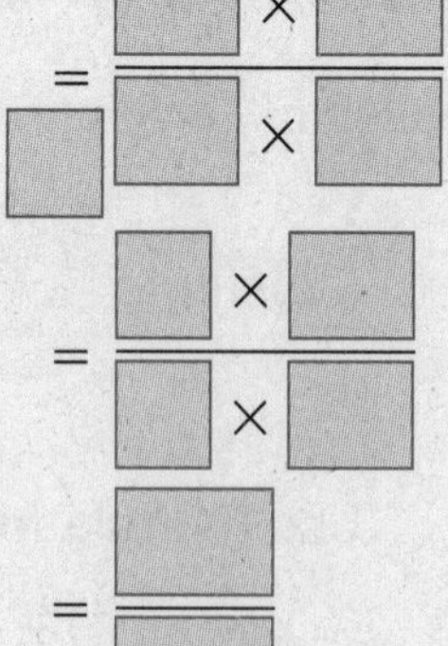

$= \frac{\square \times \square}{\square \times \square}$ $\square$ is a factor of 4 and $\square$.

Divide 4 and $\square$ by $\square$.

$= \frac{\square \times \square}{\square \times \square}$ Rewrite.

$= \frac{\square}{\square}$ Multiply.

To simplify in Example 4, find the greatest factor of 4 that is also a factor of 18 or 15.

EXAMPLE 5 Multiplying Three Fractions

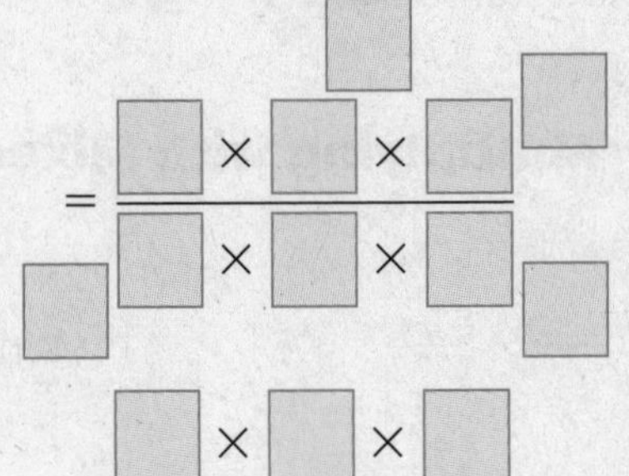

$\frac{1}{4} \times \frac{3}{5} \times \frac{2}{9} = \frac{\square \times \square \times \square}{\square \times \square \times \square}$ Use the rule for multiplying fractions.

$= \frac{\square \times \square \times \square}{\square \times \square \times \square}$ $\square$ is a factor of 3 and $\square$. $\square$ is a factor of 2 and $\square$.

$= \frac{\square \times \square \times \square}{\square \times \square \times \square}$ Rewrite.

$= \frac{\square}{\square}$ Multiply.

WATCH OUT!
Rewrite the fraction after dividing out common factors. You will be less likely to make an error when you multiply.

Your turn now **Multiply. Write the answer in simplest form.**

9. $\frac{2}{7} \times \frac{5}{8}$	**10.** $\frac{4}{9} \times \frac{3}{16}$	**11.** $\frac{5}{24} \times \frac{6}{35}$
12. $\frac{5}{8} \times \frac{2}{3} \times \frac{1}{15}$	**13.** $\frac{4}{11} \times \frac{3}{8} \times \frac{11}{15}$	**14.** $\frac{5}{6} \times \frac{1}{10} \times \frac{12}{13}$

15. What do all of the products in Exercises 9–14 have in common?

LESSON
7.3

Multiplying Mixed Numbers

Goal: Multiply mixed numbers.

EXAMPLE 1 **Multiplying with Mixed Numbers**

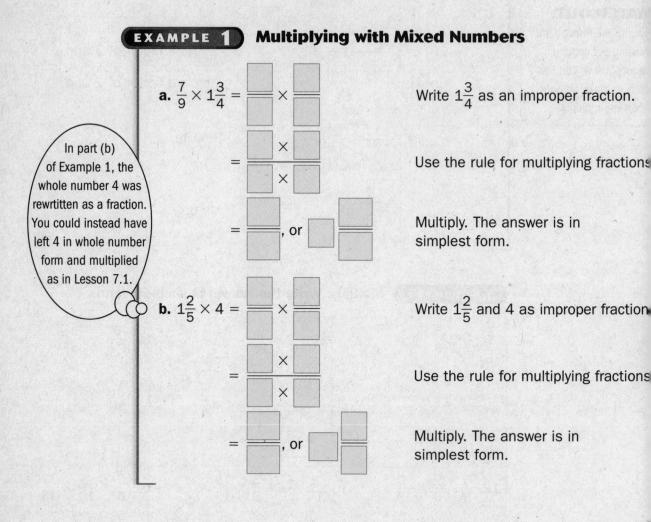

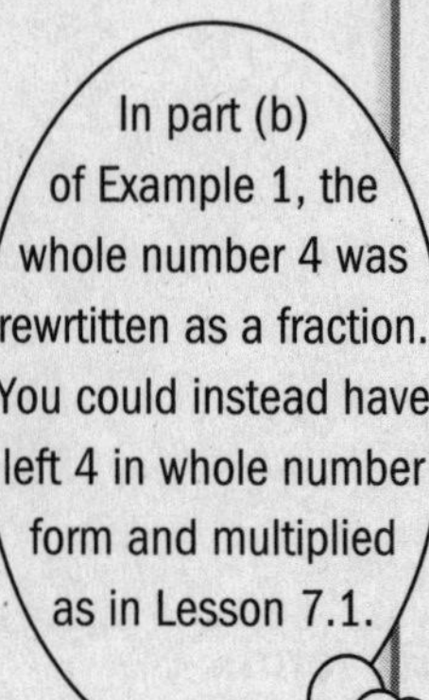
In part (b)
of Example 1, the
whole number 4 was
rewrtitten as a fraction.
You could instead have
left 4 in whole number
form and multiplied
as in Lesson 7.1.

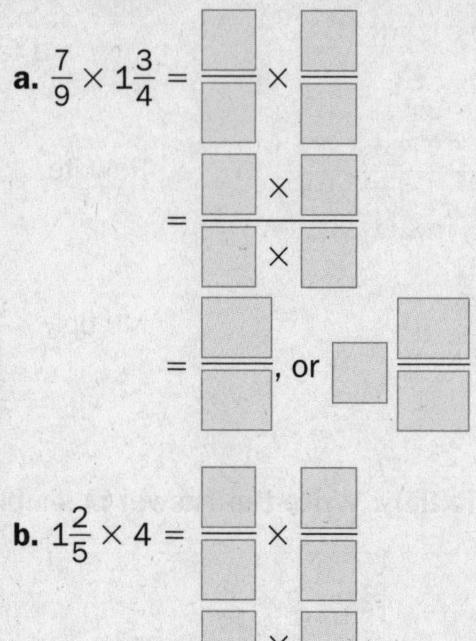

a. $\frac{7}{9} \times 1\frac{3}{4} = \frac{\square}{\square} \times \frac{\square}{\square}$ Write $1\frac{3}{4}$ as an improper fraction.

$= \frac{\square \times \square}{\square \times \square}$ Use the rule for multiplying fractions.

$= \frac{\square}{\square}$, or $\square\frac{\square}{\square}$ Multiply. The answer is in simplest form.

b. $1\frac{2}{5} \times 4 = \frac{\square}{\square} \times \frac{\square}{\square}$ Write $1\frac{2}{5}$ and 4 as improper fractions.

$= \frac{\square \times \square}{\square \times \square}$ Use the rule for multiplying fractions.

$= \frac{\square}{\square}$, or $\square\frac{\square}{\square}$ Multiply. The answer is in simplest form.

EXAMPLE 2 Simplifying Before Multiplying

$3\frac{3}{8} \times 4\frac{2}{3} = \frac{\square}{\square} \times \frac{\square}{\square}$ Write $3\frac{3}{8}$ and $4\frac{2}{3}$ as improper fractions.

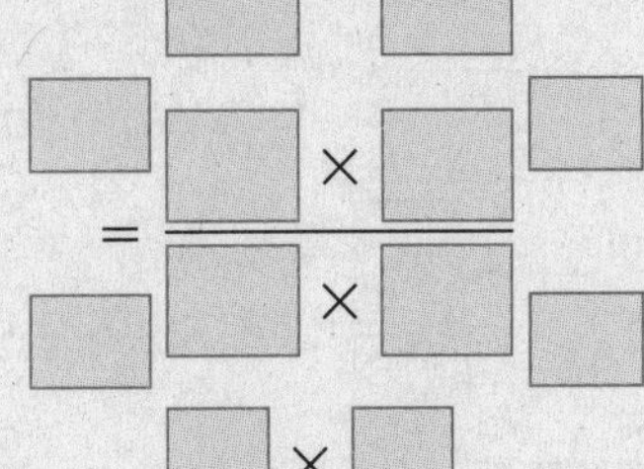

Use the rule for multiplying fractions. Divide out common factors.

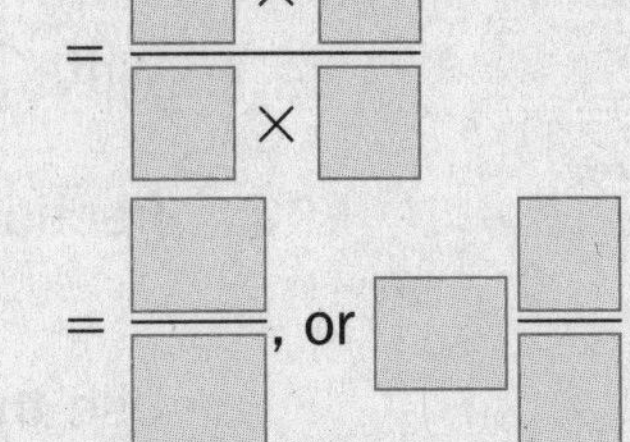

Rewrite.

Multiply. The answer is in simplest form.

Remember that when rounding mixed numbers, you should round to the nearest whole number.

✓ **Check** Round $3\frac{3}{8}$ to $\square$ and $4\frac{2}{3}$ to $\square$. Because $\square \times \square = \square$, the product $\square\frac{\square}{\square}$ is reasonable.

Your turn now **Multiply. Write the answer in simplest form.**

1. $4\frac{1}{4} \times \frac{3}{5}$	**2.** $6 \times 2\frac{5}{6}$	**3.** $3\frac{3}{4} \times 2\frac{2}{3}$	**4.** $3\frac{2}{5} \times 2\frac{5}{6}$

EXAMPLE 3 Multiplying to Solve Problems

Fields A rectangular field is $42\frac{1}{2}$ feet long and $33\frac{1}{3}$ feet wide. What is the area of the field?

Solution

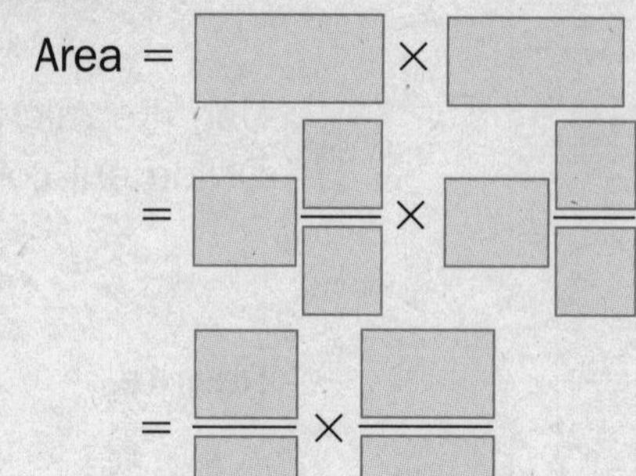

Write formula for area of a rectangle.

Substitute for 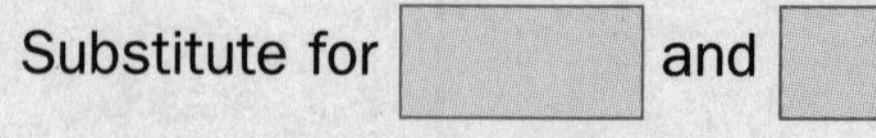 and

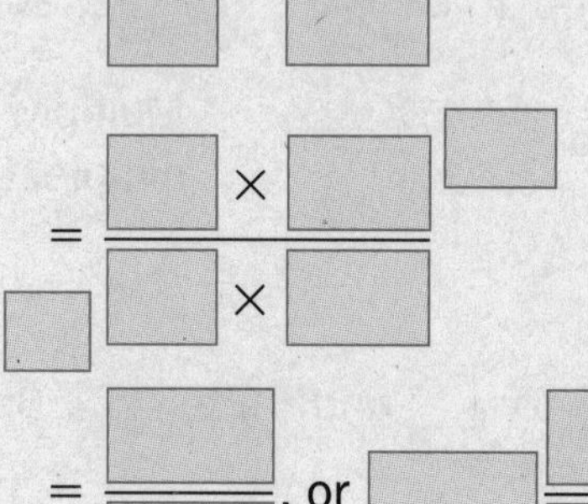

Write and as improper fractions.

Use the rule for multiplying fractions. Divide out common factors.

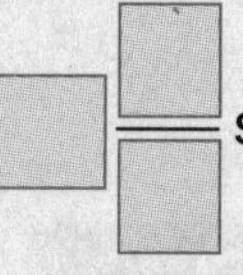

= , or

Multiply. The answer is in simplest form.

Answer: The area of the field is square feet.

LESSON 7.4

Dividing Fractions

Goal: Use reciprocals to divide fractions.

For Your Notebook

Vocabulary

Reciprocal:

EXAMPLE 1 Writing Reciprocals

	Original number	Fraction	Reciprocal	Check
a.	$\frac{2}{9}$			
b.	14	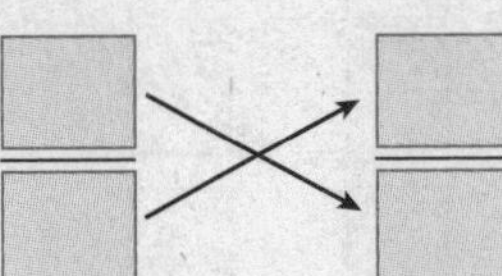		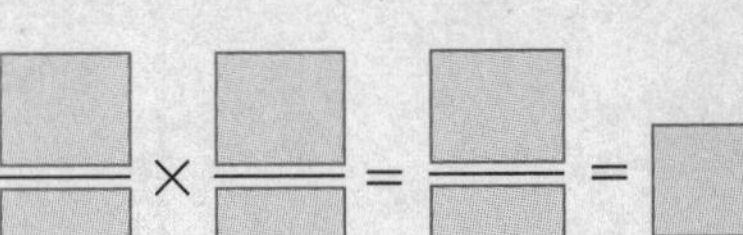
c.	$1\frac{3}{5}$	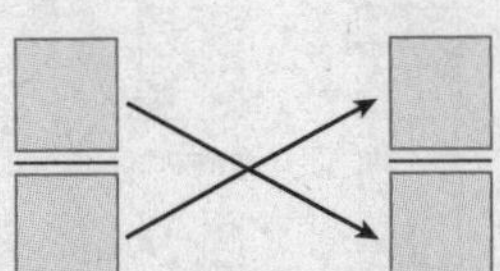		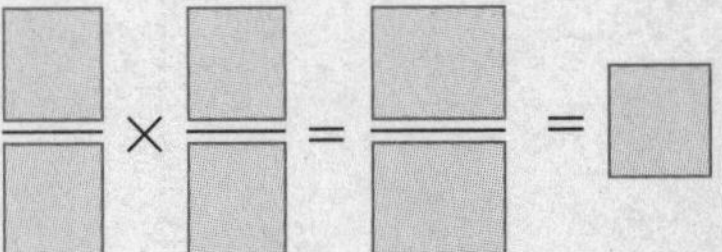

When writing the reciprocal of a mixed number, first write the mixed number as an improper fraction, then find the reciprocal of the improper fraction.

Your turn now **Write the reciprocal of the number.**

1. $\frac{1}{6}$	**2.** 7	**3.** 20	**4.** $1\frac{3}{8}$

Dividing Fractions

Words To divide by a fraction, multiply by ______.

Numbers $\frac{3}{7} \div \frac{4}{5} = \frac{\square}{\square} \times \frac{\square}{\square}$

Algebra $\frac{\square}{\square} \div \frac{\square}{\square} = \frac{a}{b} \cdot \frac{d}{c}$ $(b, c, d \neq 0)$

EXAMPLE 2 Dividing Two Fractions

Bees A honey bee is about $\frac{2}{3}$ inch long and a yellow jacket is about $\frac{1}{2}$ inch long. How many times longer is a honey bee than a yellow jacket?

Solution

Number of times longer $= \frac{\square}{\square} \div \frac{\square}{\square}$ Divide length of ______ by length of ______.

$= \frac{\square}{\square} \times \frac{\square}{\square}$ Multiply by the reciprocal of the divisor.

$= \frac{\square \times \square}{\square \times \square}$ Use the rule for multiplying fractions.

$= \frac{\square}{\square}$, or $\square\frac{\square}{\square}$ Multiply.

Answer: The length of a honey bee is $\square\frac{\square}{\square}$ times the length of a yellow jacket.

EXAMPLE 3 Dividing a Fraction and a Whole Number

a. If you cut a $\frac{5}{8}$-foot long piece of wood into 10 equally-sized pieces, how long is each of the ten pieces of wood?

b. If you divide a 10-foot long piece of wood into pieces that are each $\frac{5}{8}$ foot long, how many pieces do you have?

WATCH OUT!
When dividing, be sure to take the reciprocal of the divisor, not the dividend. You can multiply to check your work. In Example 3, check part (a) by multiplying your answer by 10 and check part (b) by multiplying your answer by $\frac{5}{8}$.

Solution

a. Divide $\frac{5}{8}$ by 10.

b. Divide 10 by $\frac{5}{8}$.

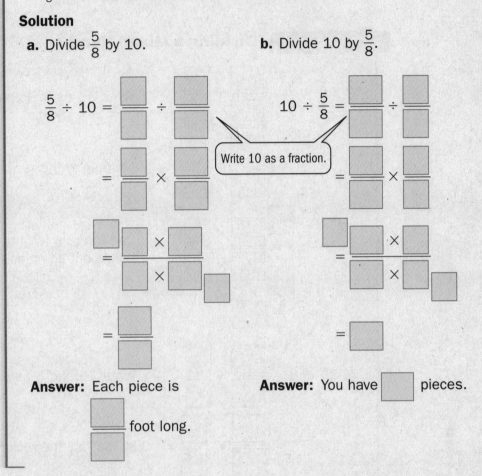

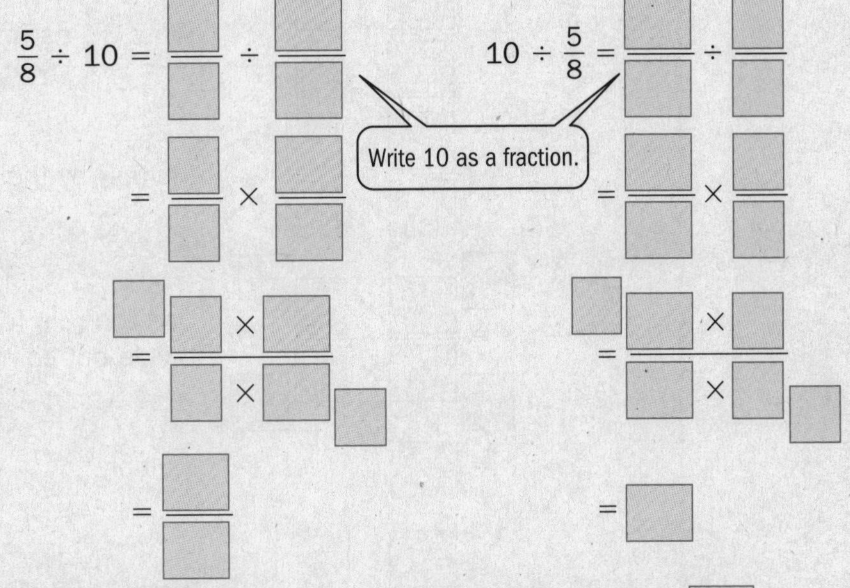

Answer: Each piece is ____ foot long.

Answer: You have ____ pieces.

Your turn now **Divide. Write the answer in simplest form.**

5. $\frac{7}{9} \div \frac{3}{8}$	**6.** $\frac{5}{6} \div \frac{1}{3}$	**7.** $\frac{8}{15} \div 4$	**8.** $18 \div \frac{3}{4}$

LESSON 7.5

Dividing Mixed Numbers

Goal: Divide mixed numbers.

EXAMPLE 1 Dividing a Mixed Number

a. $3\frac{3}{4} \div \frac{3}{8} = \frac{\square}{\square} \div \frac{\square}{\square}$ Write $3\frac{3}{4}$ as an improper fraction.

$= \frac{\square}{\square} \times \frac{\square}{\square}$ Multiply by the reciprocal of the divisor.

$= \frac{\square \times \square}{\square \times \square}$ Use the rule for multiplying fractions. Divide out common factors.

$= \square$ Multiply.

b. $2\frac{2}{5} \div 8 = \frac{\square}{\square} \div \frac{\square}{\square}$ Write $2\frac{2}{5}$ and 8 as improper fractions.

$= \frac{\square}{\square} \times \frac{\square}{\square}$ Multiply by the reciprocal of the divisor.

$= \frac{\square \times \square}{\square \times \square}$ Use the rule for multiplying fractions. Divide out common factors.

$= \frac{\square}{\square}$ Multiply.

EXAMPLE 2 Dividing by a Mixed Number

$6\frac{1}{4} \div 1\frac{1}{9} = \frac{\square}{\square} \div \frac{\square}{\square}$ Write $6\frac{1}{4}$ and $1\frac{1}{9}$ as improper fractions.

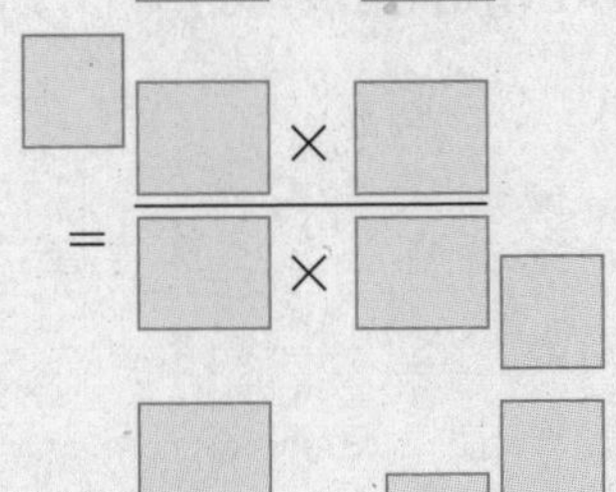

$= \frac{\square}{\square} \times \frac{\square}{\square}$ Multiply by the reciprocal of the divisor.

$= \frac{\square \times \square}{\square \times \square}$ Use the rule for multiplying fractions. Divide out common factors.

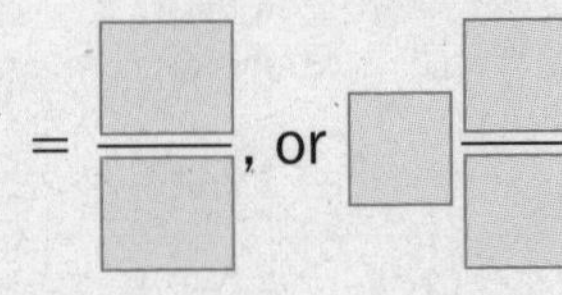

$= \frac{\square}{\square}$, or $\square\frac{\square}{\square}$ Multiply.

WATCH OUT!

When you divide by a mixed number, first you rewrite it as an improper fraction. Then don't forget to multiply by the *reciprocal* of the improper fraction.

✓ **Check** Round $6\frac{1}{4}$ to ☐ and replace $1\frac{1}{9}$ with the compatible number ☐. The answer is reasonable because it is close to the estimate ☐ ÷ ☐ = ☐.

Your turn now Divide. Use estimation to check your answer.

1. $5\frac{1}{4} \div 7$	**2.** $5\frac{3}{5} \div \frac{14}{15}$	**3.** $\frac{7}{8} \div 4\frac{2}{3}$	**4.** $3\frac{1}{8} \div 7\frac{1}{2}$

5. Which quotient in Exercises 1–4 is greater than 1?

EXAMPLE 3 Choosing an Operation

Peanuts A person working at a natural foods store is packaging peanuts from a 50-pound bag into $1\frac{1}{4}$-pound bags. How many bags will he need?

Solution

When solving division problems that involve whole numbers and fractions or mixed numbers, rewrite the whole number as an improper fraction.

1. Choose the operation by thinking about a similar whole number problem: If the peanuts in a 50-pound bag were being packaged into 2 pound bags, you would *divide* ____ by ____. So, *divide* ____ by ____.

2. Divide. ____ ÷ ____ = $\frac{\square}{\square} \div \frac{\square}{\square}$

$= \frac{\square}{\square} \times \frac{\square}{\square}$

$= \frac{\square \times \square}{\square \times \square}$

$= \square$

Answer: He will need ____ bags.

Weight and Capacity in Customary Units

Goal: Use customary units of weight and capacity.

For Your Notebook

Vocabulary

Ounce (oz):

Pound (lb):

Ton (T):

Fluid ounce (fl oz):

Cup (c):

Pint (pt):

Quart (qt):

Gallon (gal):

EXAMPLE 1 Choosing Units of Weight

Just as you did in Lesson 4.7 with metric units of mass and capacity, you should use your benchmarks for customary units of weight to choose appropriate units for measurement.

Choose an appropriate customary unit to measure the weight.

a. A ball of yarn weighs $2\frac{1}{2}$? . **b.** A book weighs $2\frac{1}{2}$? .

Solution

a. A ball of yarn weighs $2\frac{1}{2}$ ______, because it is heavier than ______ and lighter than ______.

b. A book weighs $2\frac{1}{2}$ ______, because it is heavier than ______ and much lighter than ______.

Your turn now **Choose an appropriate customary unit to measure the weight of the item.**

1. light bulb	2. school bus	3. refrigerator

EXAMPLE 2 Choosing Units of Capacity

Choose an appropriate customary unit to measure the capacity.

a. cereal bowl **b.** large flower vase

Solution

a. A cereal bowl holds about as much as ______

You can use ______ or one of the smaller units, ______

b. A large flower vase holds about as much as ______.

You can use ______, but you wouldn't use ______.

Notice that there are two types of ounces: the fluid ounce (fl oz) used for measuring capacity and the ounce (oz) used for measuring weight.

EXAMPLE 3 Choosing Customary Units

What does each measure describe about an empty sauce pot?

a. 5 qt **b.** 2 lb

Solution

a. A quart is a measure of ______, so 5 quarts describes ______.

b. A pound is a measure of ______, so 2 pounds describes ______.

Your turn now **Choose an appropriate customary unit to measure.**

4. capacity of a bucket	5. capacity of a kitchen garbage can	6. weight of a stapler

LESSON 7.7

Changing Customary Units

Goal: Change customary units of measure.

EXAMPLE 1 Changing Units Using Multiplication

Change 3 mi 540 yd to yards.

3 mi 540 yd = ____ + ____ — Write the measure as a sum.

= (3 ____ ____) yd + ____ yd — Change the miles to yards.

= ____ yd + ____ yd — ____.

= ____ yd — Add.

EXAMPLE 2 Changing Units Using Division

Change 43 fl oz to cups. Express the answer in two ways.

There are 8 fl oz in a cup, so ____ 43 by 8.

$8\overline{)43}$ = ____ R ____ ← You can interpret the remainder as ____ fl oz.

____

____ ← You can also interpret the remainder as ____ c, because the remaining division ____ ÷ ____ can be written as ____.

Answer: There are ____ c ____ fl oz in 43 fl oz. This can also be written as ____ c.

WATCH OUT!
There should always be more of the smaller unit and fewer of the larger unit. So, you *multiply* by 12 to change feet to inches and you *divide* by 16 to change ounces to pounds.

Your turn now **Copy and complete the statement.**

1. 2 ft 9 in. = _?_ in.	**2.** 52 oz = _?_ lb	**3.** $9\frac{1}{4}$ T = _?_ lb

EXAMPLE 3 Multiplying by a Form of 1

Change $4\frac{2}{3}$ oz to pounds.

To get the correct unit in the answer, choose the form of 1 that has the unit you are changing to in the numerator and the unit you are changing from in the denominator.

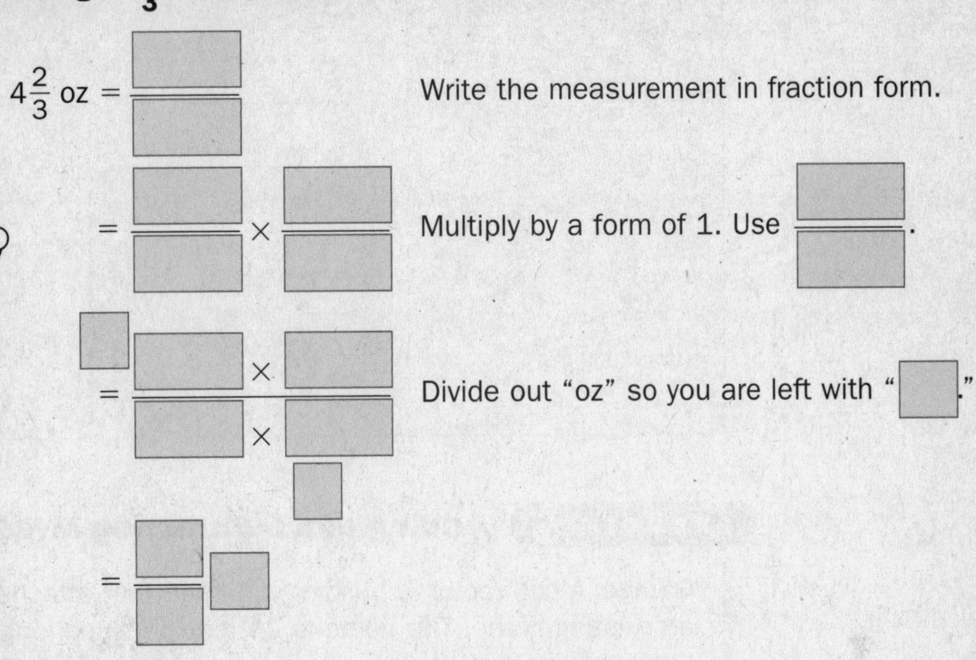

$4\frac{2}{3}$ oz =
Write the measurement in fraction form.
Multiply by a form of 1. Use
Divide out "oz" so you are left with " ."

EXAMPLE 4 Finding a Relationship

On a typical day, Sasha drinks 64 fluid ounces of water. How many gallons of water does Sasha drink on a typical day?

Solution

1. Find the relationship between gallons and fluid ounces. Use the four relationships 1 gal = 4 qt, 1 qt = 2 pt, 1 pt = 2 c, and 1 c = 8 fl oz.

$\frac{1\ \square}{4\ \square} \times \frac{1\ \square}{2\ \square} \times \frac{1\ \square}{2\ \square} \times \frac{1\ \square}{8\ \square}$

$= \frac{\square \times \square \times \square \times \square}{\square \times \square \times \square \times \square} = \frac{\square}{\square}$

So, 1 gallon = ☐ fluid ounces.

2. Multiply 64 fl oz by a form of 1 that relates gallons and fluid ounces.

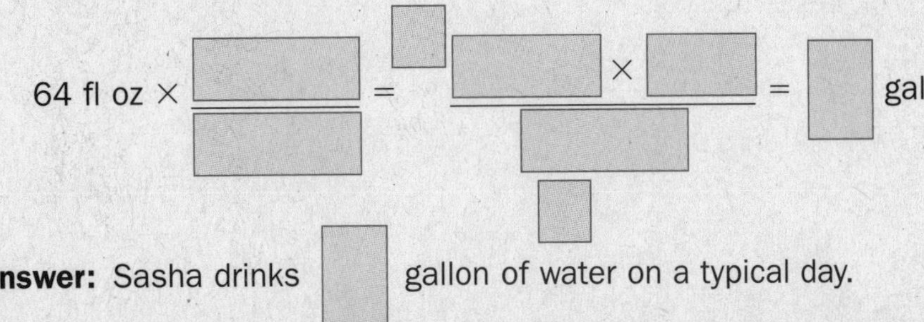

Answer: Sasha drinks ☐ gallon of water on a typical day.

Your turn now **Copy and complete the statement.**

4. $\frac{7}{10}$ yd = ? in.	5. $5\frac{3}{4}$ lb = ? oz	6. 20 fl oz = ? qt

EXAMPLE 5 Adding and Subtracting Measures

Garage A contractor is building a garage that attaches along the length of an existing home. The home is 24 feet 5 inches long and the garage will be 20 feet 8 inches long.

a. What is the sum of the lengths of the home and the garage?

b. What is the difference in the lengths of the home and the garage?

Solution

a. Add. Then rename the sum.

____ ft ____ in.

\+ ____ ft ____ in.

____ ft ____ in.

Rename ____ ft ____ in.

as ____ ft ____ in.

Answer: The sum of the lengths is ____ ft ____ in.

b. Rename. Then subtract.

Rename one of the feet as ____ in.

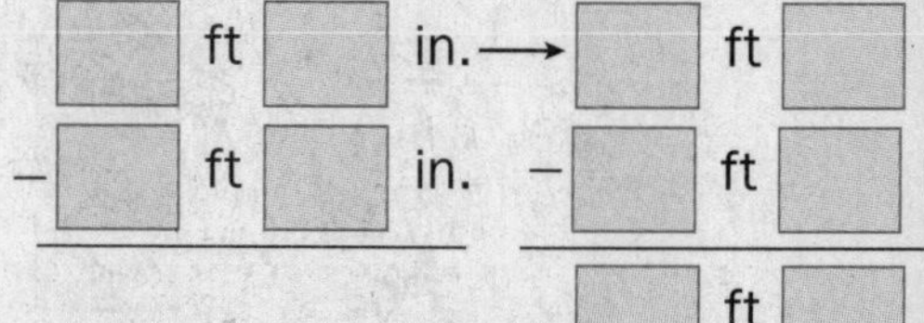

____ ft ____ in. → ____ ft ____ in.

− ____ ft ____ in. − ____ ft ____ in.

____ ft ____ in.

Answer: The difference in the lengths is ____ ft ____ in.

Words to Review

Give an example of the vocabulary word.

Reciprocal

Ounce

Pound

Ton

Fluid ounce

Cup

Pint

Quart

Gallon

Review your notes and Chapter 7 by using the Chapter Review on pages 358–359 of your textbook.

Ratios

Goal: Write ratios and equivalent ratios.

Vocabulary

Ratio: ______

Equivalent ratio: ______

EXAMPLE 1 **Writing a Ratio in Different Ways**

Baseball A baseball team is made up of nine players: three outfielders, four infielders, one pitcher, and one catcher. Write the ratio of the number of infielders to the total number of players.

Solution

Because four of the nine players are infielders, the ratio of the number of infielders to the total number of players,

$\frac{\text{Number of infielders}}{\text{Total number of players}}$, can be written as $\frac{\square}{\square}$, as $\square : \square$,

or as $\square$ to $\square$.

EXAMPLE 2 **Writing Ratios in Simplest Form**

Use the information in Example 1. Write the ratio of the number of outfielders to the total number of players in simplest form.

Solution

$$\frac{\text{Number of outfielders}}{\text{Total number of players}} = \frac{\square}{\square} = \frac{\square \times \square}{\square \times \square} = \frac{\square}{\square}$$

Answer: The ratio is $\frac{\square}{\square}$, or $\square$ to $\square$, so there is $\square$ outfielder for every $\square$ players.

Your turn now **In Exercises 1 and 2, write the ratio in three ways.**

1. catchers to infielders	**2.** outfielders to infielders
3. Write the ratio of the number of pitchers and catchers to the number of infielders in simplest form.	

EXAMPLE 3 **Writing an Equivalent Ratio**

Complete the statement $\frac{7}{12} = \frac{?}{48}$ to write equivalent ratios.

Solution

Think about the denominators of the two fractions.

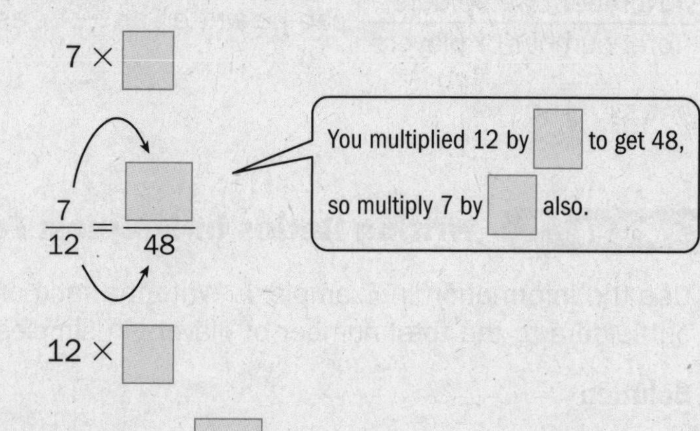

7 ×
7/12 = /48
12 ×
You multiplied 12 by to get 48,
so multiply 7 by also.

Need help with equivalent fractions? See page 228 of your textbook.

Answer: $\frac{7}{12} = \frac{\square}{48}$

EXAMPLE 4 Comparing Ratios Using Decimals

Homework Tara has completed $\frac{3}{5}$ of her history problems and 10 out of 16 of her biology problems. Which set of problems is closer to being completed?

Solution

Need help writing fractions as decimals? See page 253 of your textbook.

Write each ratio as a decimal. Then compare the decimals.

History: $\frac{3}{5} = \square$ Biology: 10 out of 16 $= \frac{\square}{\square} = \square$

Answer: Because $\square > \square$, Tara is closer to completing her $\square$ problems.

Your turn now **Copy and complete the statement.**

4. $\frac{3}{4} = \frac{?}{20}$	**5.** $\frac{8}{?} = \frac{48}{54}$	**6.** $\frac{20}{35} = \frac{4}{?}$

Copy and complete the statement using <, >, or =.

7. $\frac{11}{30}$ __?__ $\frac{7}{15}$	**8.** $\frac{3}{7}$ __?__ 12 out of 28	**9.** 4 : 6 __?__ 5 : 30

Rates

Goal: Write rates, equivalent rates, and unit rates.

Vocabulary

Rate:

Unit Rate:

EXAMPLE 1 **Writing an Equivalent Rate**

Swimming Pool A machine that pours concrete used to form the bottom and sides of an inground swimming pool pumps the concrete into the ground at a rate of 540 gallons every 60 minutes. How long will it take to pump 1080 gallons?

Solution

Write an *equivalent rate* that has 1080 gallons in the numerator.

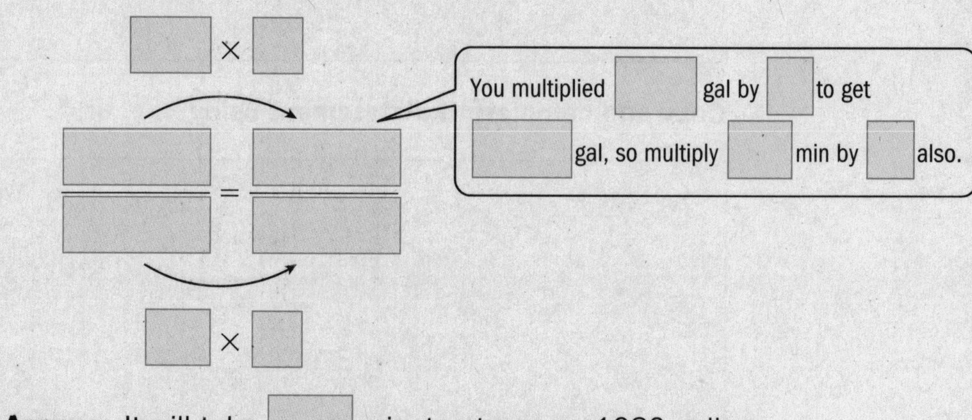

You multiplied gal by to get
gal, so multiply min by also.

Answer: It will take minutes to pump 1080 gallons.

EXAMPLE 2 Writing a Unit Rate

Write the machine's pumping rate from Example 1 as a unit rate.

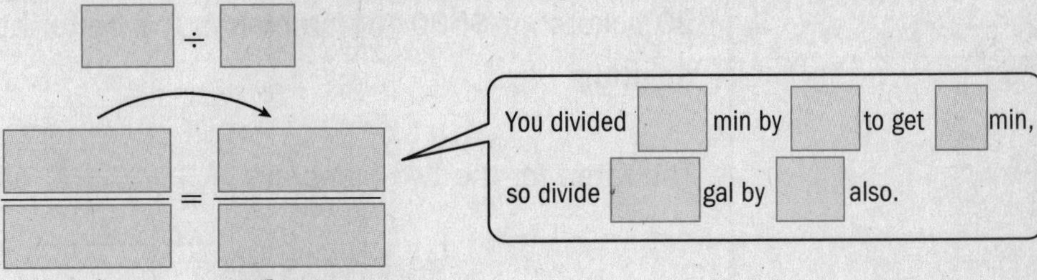

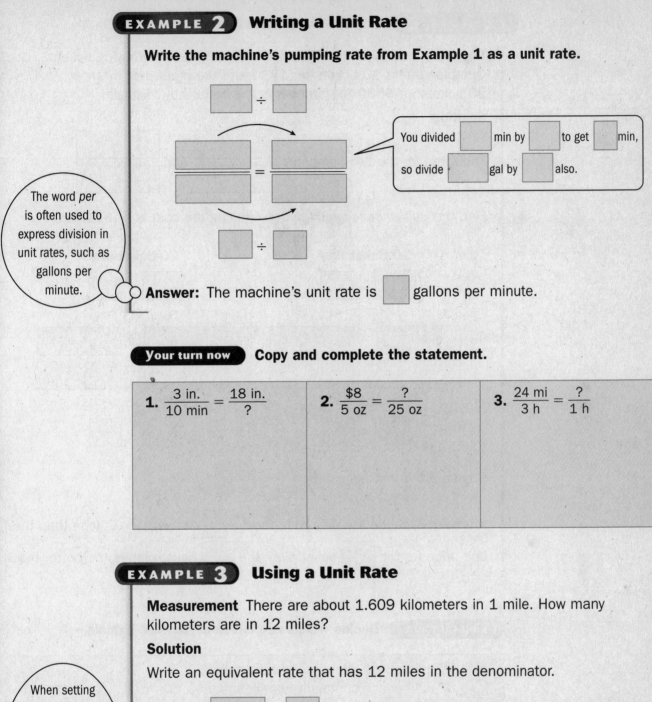

The word *per* is often used to express division in unit rates, such as gallons per minute.

Answer: The machine's unit rate is ☐ gallons per minute.

Your turn now **Copy and complete the statement.**

1. $\frac{3 \text{ in.}}{10 \text{ min}} = \frac{18 \text{ in.}}{?}$	**2.** $\frac{\$8}{5 \text{ oz}} = \frac{?}{25 \text{ oz}}$	**3.** $\frac{24 \text{ mi}}{3 \text{ h}} = \frac{?}{1 \text{ h}}$

EXAMPLE 3 Using a Unit Rate

Measurement There are about 1.609 kilometers in 1 mile. How many kilometers are in 12 miles?

Solution

Write an equivalent rate that has 12 miles in the denominator.

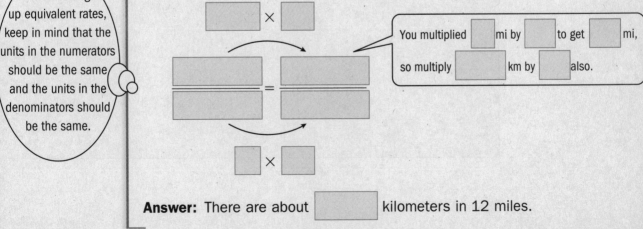

×

=

×

You multiplied ☐ mi by ☐ to get ☐ mi, so multiply ☐ km by ☐ also.

When setting up equivalent rates, keep in mind that the units in the numerators should be the same and the units in the denominators should be the same.

Answer: There are about ☐ kilometers in 12 miles.

EXAMPLE 4 Comparing Unit Rates

Hockey A hockey team offers two different plans for buying tickets. One plan offers 10 tickets for $330 and the other plan offers 20 tickets for $560. Which plan is the better buy? Explain.

Solution

The rates for the two plans are ______ and ______.

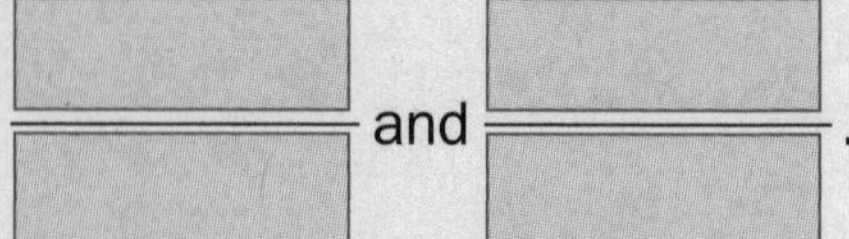

Find the *unit price* for each plan by finding the cost of one ticket.

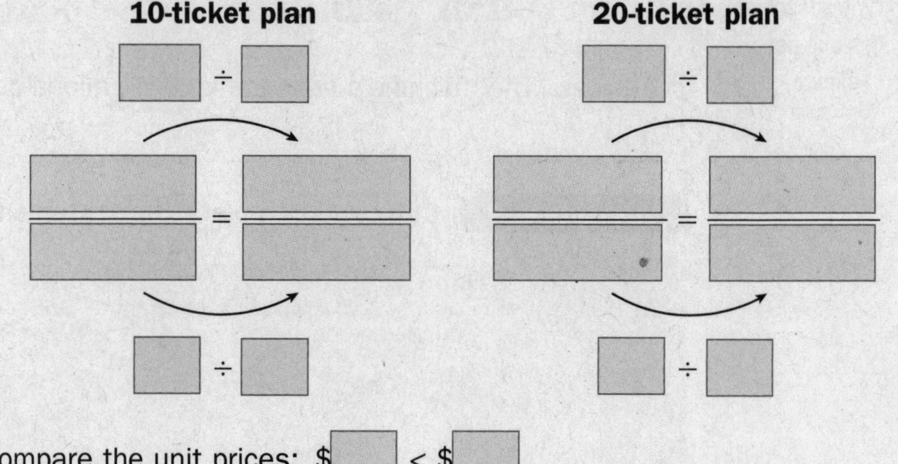

Compare the unit prices: $ ____ < $ ____.

Answer: Because the unit price for the ____-ticket plan is less than the unit price for the ____-ticket plan, the ____-ticket plan is the better buy.

Your turn now **Decide which size is the better buy. Explain.**

4. A 16-fluid ounce container of milk costs $1.28.
A 32-fluid ounce container of milk costs $1.60.

Solving Proportions

Goal: Write and solve proportions.

Vocabulary

Proportion:

Cross products:

Cross Products Property

Words In a proportion, the cross products are equal.

Algebra

$\frac{p}{q} = \frac{r}{s}$, where q and s are nonzero.

$\square \cdot \square = \square \cdot \square$

Numbers

$\frac{2}{3} = \frac{8}{12}$

$\square \cdot \square = \square \cdot \square$

EXAMPLE 1 Checking a Proportion

Use cross products to decide whether the ratios form a proportion.

The proportion $\frac{5}{12} = \frac{20}{48}$ in part (a) of Example 1 is read "5 is to 12 as 20 is to 48."

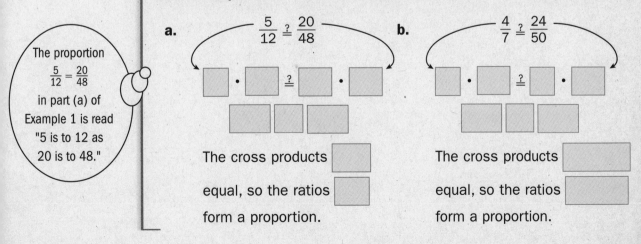

a. $\frac{5}{12} \stackrel{?}{=} \frac{20}{48}$

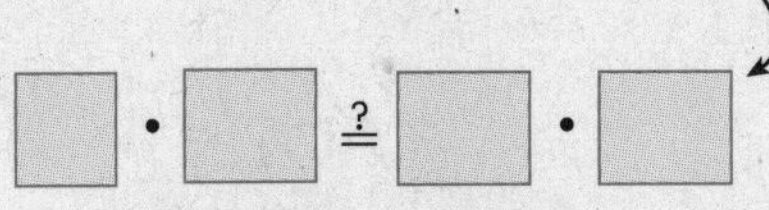

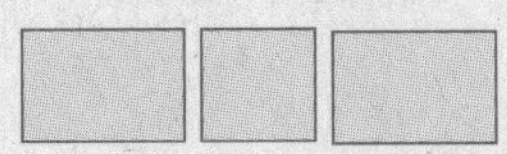

The cross products ___ equal, so the ratios ___ form a proportion.

b. $\frac{4}{7} \stackrel{?}{=} \frac{24}{50}$

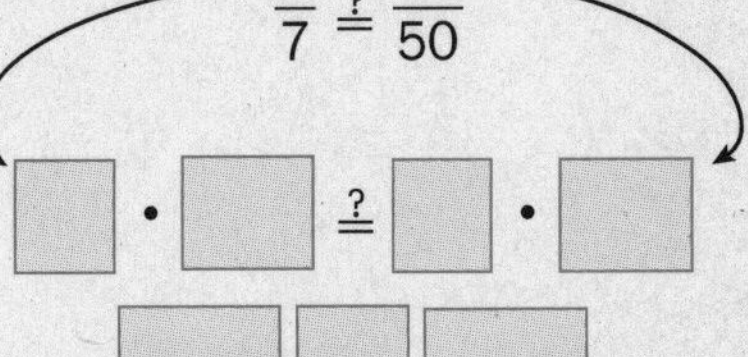

The cross products ___ equal, so the ratios ___ form a proportion.

EXAMPLE 2 Solving Using Mental Math

Solve the proportion $\frac{3}{15} = \frac{30}{x}$.

Solution

Method 1 Use equivalent ratios.

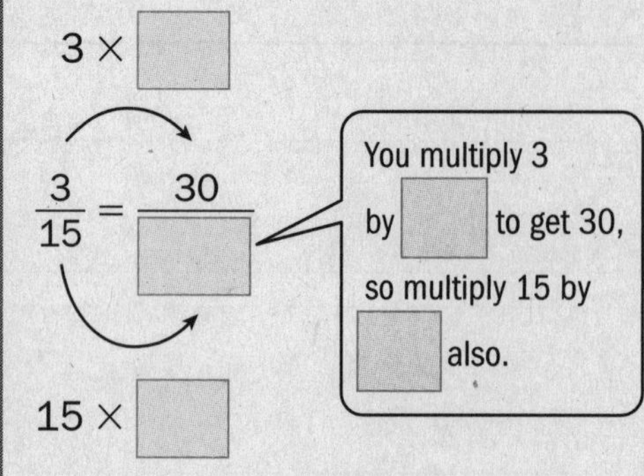

3 ×
$\frac{3}{15} = \frac{30}{\square}$
15 ×
You multiply 3 by to get 30, so multiply 15 by also.

Method 2 Use cross products.

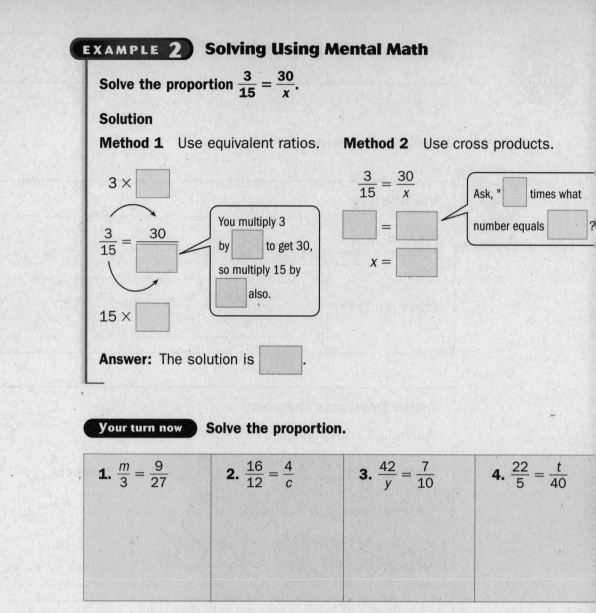

$\frac{3}{15} = \frac{30}{x}$

$\square = \square$

$x = \square$

Ask, " times what number equals ?"

Answer: The solution is ____.

Your turn now **Solve the proportion.**

1. $\frac{m}{3} = \frac{9}{27}$	2. $\frac{16}{12} = \frac{4}{c}$	3. $\frac{42}{y} = \frac{7}{10}$	4. $\frac{22}{5} = \frac{t}{40}$

EXAMPLE 3 Solving Using a Verbal Model

Trains A passenger train has traveled 180 miles in 3 hours. At that same rate, how long will it take to travel the total distance of 300 miles?

Solution

Use a proportion. Let t represent the total time it will take to travel 300 miles.

$\frac{\text{Distance traveled}}{\text{Time traveled}} = \frac{\text{Total distance}}{\text{Total time}}$ Write a verbal model.

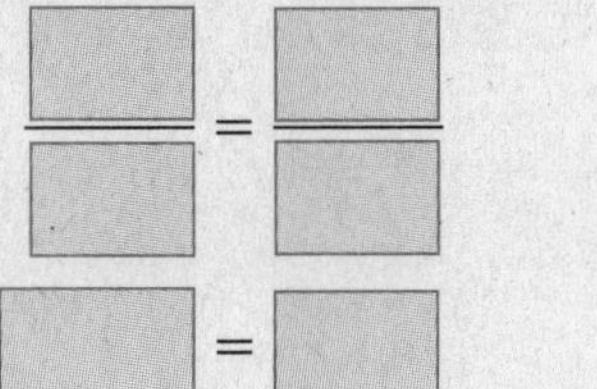

Substitute values.

Rewrite proportion without units.

Write the cross products. They are equal.

Solve using mental math.

Answer: It will take ____ hours to travel 300 miles.

EXAMPLE 4 Solving Using a Related Equation

Solve the proportion $\frac{35}{10} = \frac{x}{8}$.

Solution

$\frac{35}{10} = \frac{x}{8}$ Write original proportion.

____ = ____ Write the cross products. They are equal.

____ ÷ ____ = ____ Write the related division equation.

____ = ____ Divide.

Answer: The solution is ____.

Need help writing a related equation? See page 687 of your textbook.

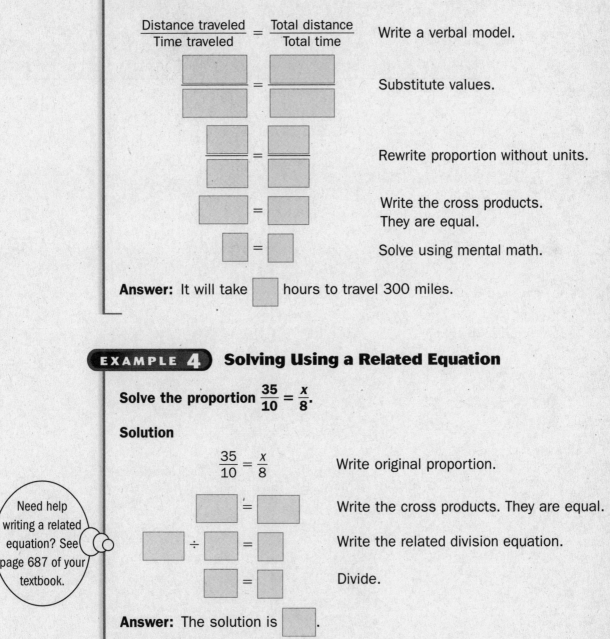

Your turn now **Solve the proportion.**

5. $\frac{x}{12} = \frac{20}{8}$	6. $\frac{18}{y} = \frac{30}{50}$	7. $\frac{40}{15} = \frac{b}{9}$	8. $\frac{36}{30} = \frac{42}{s}$

LESSON 8.4

Proportions and Scale Drawings

Goal: Use proportions to find measures of objects.

EXAMPLE 1 Using a Scale Drawing

Toy Box You are building a toy box for your brother. In the scale drawing of the toy box, the box has a length of 2.6 inches. What is the actual length of the toy box?

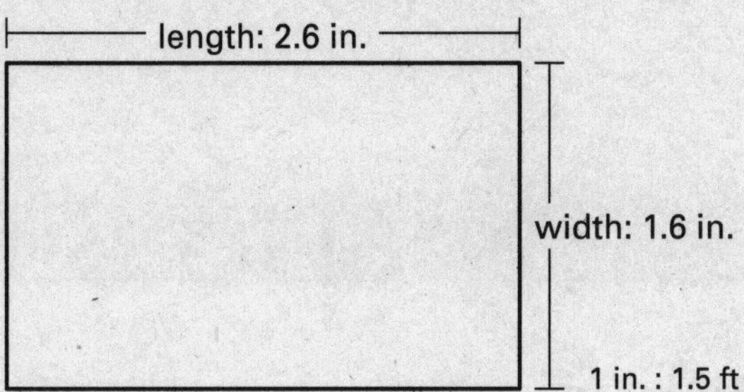

Solution

To solve the problem, write and solve a proportion. Let x represent the actual length of the toy box in feet.

When setting up a proportion, make sure that the numerators are the scale dimensions and the denominators are the actual dimensions or vice-versa.

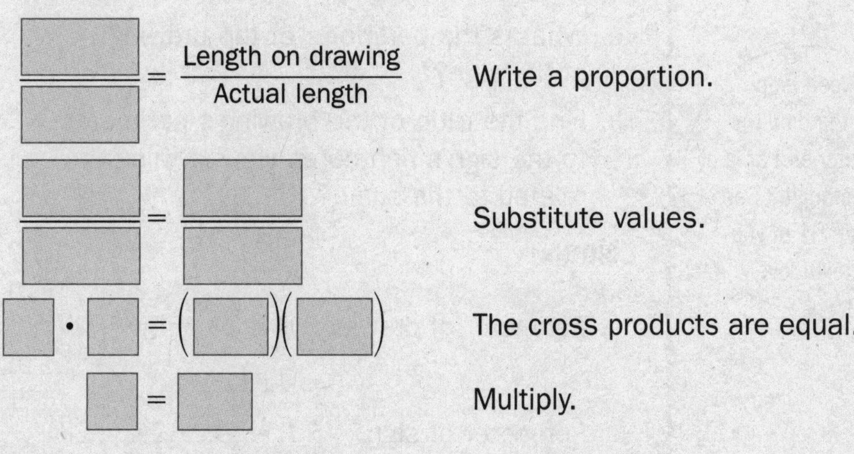

Answer: The actual length of the toy box is ______ feet.

Your turn now **Use the scale drawing shown in Example 1.**

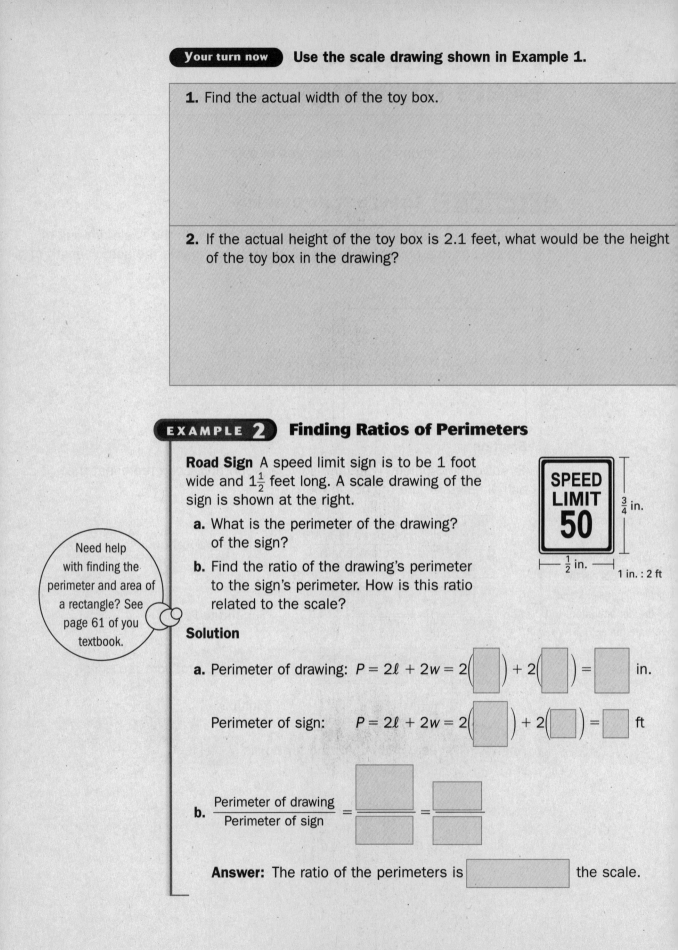

1. Find the actual width of the toy box.

2. If the actual height of the toy box is 2.1 feet, what would be the height of the toy box in the drawing?

EXAMPLE 2 Finding Ratios of Perimeters

Road Sign A speed limit sign is to be 1 foot wide and $1\frac{1}{2}$ feet long. A scale drawing of the sign is shown at the right.

a. What is the perimeter of the drawing? of the sign?

b. Find the ratio of the drawing's perimeter to the sign's perimeter. How is this ratio related to the scale?

Need help with finding the perimeter and area of a rectangle? See page 61 of you textbook.

Solution

a. Perimeter of drawing: $P = 2\ell + 2w = 2(\quad) + 2(\quad) = \quad$ in.

Perimeter of sign: $P = 2\ell + 2w = 2(\quad) + 2(\quad) = \quad$ ft

b. $\dfrac{\text{Perimeter of drawing}}{\text{Perimeter of sign}} = \dfrac{\quad}{\quad} = \dfrac{\quad}{\quad}$

Answer: The ratio of the perimeters is ______ the scale.

EXAMPLE 3 Finding Ratios of Areas

Use the information from Example 2. Find the ratio of the drawing's area to the sign's area. How is this ratio related to the scale?

Solution

Area of drawing: $A = \ell w =$ ___ • ___ = ___ in.^{2}

Area of sign: $A = \ell w =$ ___ • ___ = ___ ft^2

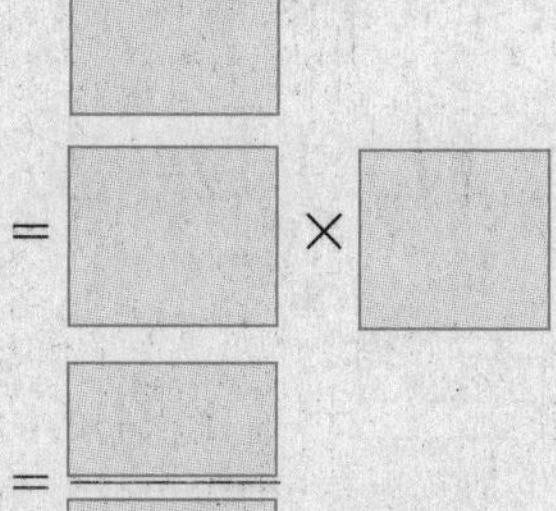

$\frac{\text{Area of drawing}}{\text{Area of sign}} = \frac{\_\_\_}{\_\_\_}$ Substitute values.

$= \frac{\_\_\_}{\_\_\_}$ Write the mixed number as an improper fraction.

$= \_\_\_ \times \_\_\_$ Multiply by the reciprocal of the divisor.

$= \frac{\_\_\_}{\_\_\_}$ Simplify.

$= \frac{\_\_\_}{\_\_\_}$ Write ratio in terms of scale.

Answer: The ratio of the areas, ___ : ___, is ___ the scale.

Your turn now **A rectangular road sign is 120 centimeters long and 90 centimeters wide. A scale drawing of the road sign has a length of 40 millimeters and a width of 30 millimeters. The scale of the drawing is 1 mm : 3 cm.**

3. What is the ratio of the perimeters of the drawing and the sign?	**4.** What is the ratio of the areas of the drawing and the sign?

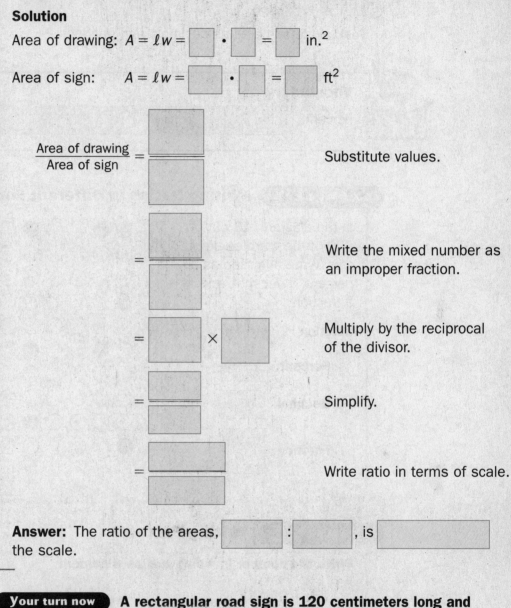

LESSON 8.5

Understanding Percent

Goal: Write percents as decimals and fractions.

Vocabulary

Percent:

EXAMPLE 1 Writing Ratios in Different Forms

In the diagram, 13 out of 100 of the marbles are grey. Write this ratio as a percent, a decimal, and a fraction.

Solution

Percent:

Decimal:

Fraction:

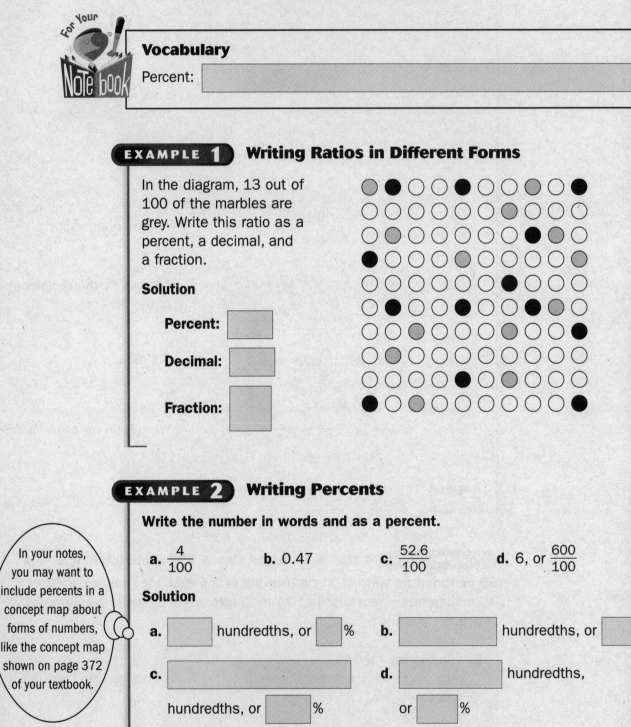

EXAMPLE 2 Writing Percents

Write the number in words and as a percent.

a. $\frac{4}{100}$ **b.** 0.47 **c.** $\frac{52.6}{100}$ **d.** 6, or $\frac{600}{100}$

Solution

a. hundredths, or %

b. hundredths, or

c. hundredths, or %

d. hundredths, or %

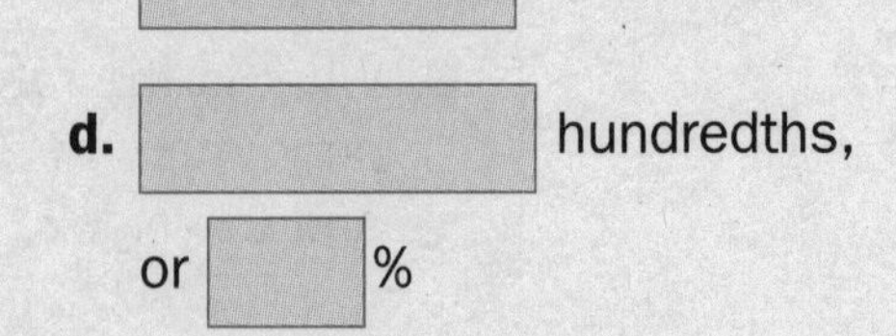

In your notes, you may want to include percents in a concept map about forms of numbers, like the concept map shown on page 372 of your textbook.

Your turn now **Write the number as a percent, decimal, and fraction.**

1. 71 hundredths	**2.** 1 hundredth	**3.** 200 hundredths

Writing Percents as Decimals and Fractions

To write a percent as a *decimal*:

[ ] the value by [ ].   29% = [ ] [ ] [ ] = [ ]

To write a percent as a *fraction*:

Rewrite the percent using a denominator of [ ]. Simplify if possible.   84% = $\frac{[\ ]}{[\ ]} = \frac{[\ ]}{[\ ]}$

EXAMPLE 3 **Writing Percents in Different Forms**

Remember that when dividing a number by 100, the decimal point in the number moves 2 places to the left.

a. Write 36.5% as a decimal.

36.5% = [ ] [ ] [ ] = [ ]

b. Write 60% as a fraction.

60% = $\frac{[\ ]}{[\ ]} = \frac{[\ ]}{[\ ]}$

EXAMPLE 4 Circle Graphs with Percents

Survey In a survey, 100 people were asked where they read books at home. The results are shown as percents.

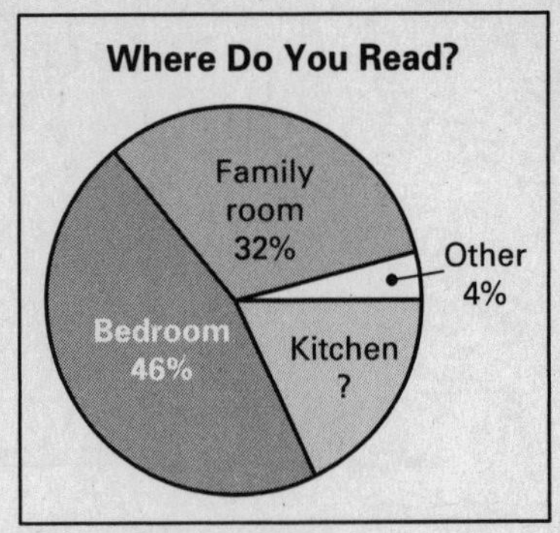

a. What percent of the people responded "Kitchen"?

b. What percent of the people did *not* respond "Family room"?

Solution

a. The circle graph represents ____ %. The sum of the percents given is ____ % + ____ % + ____ % = ____ %, so the percent of the people who responded "Kitchen" is ____ % − ____ % = ____ %.

b. The percent of people who did not respond "Family room" is ____ % − ____ % = ____ %.

Your turn now Write the percent as a decimal and a fraction.

4. 4%	5. 15%	6. 80%	7. 4.6%

Percents, Decimals, and Fractions

Goal: Write fractions and decimals as percents.

EXAMPLE 1 Writing Fractions as Percents

Restaurants A waitress has been keeping track of the number of items she has sold. She recorded that six of the last ten potato orders were for French fries, and eighteen of the last twenty-five beverage orders were for soft drinks. What percent of the last ten potato orders were for French fries and what percent of the last twenty-five beverage orders were for soft drinks?

Solution

To answer the questions, first write each record as a fraction. Then write an equivalent fraction with a denominator of 100 to find the percent.

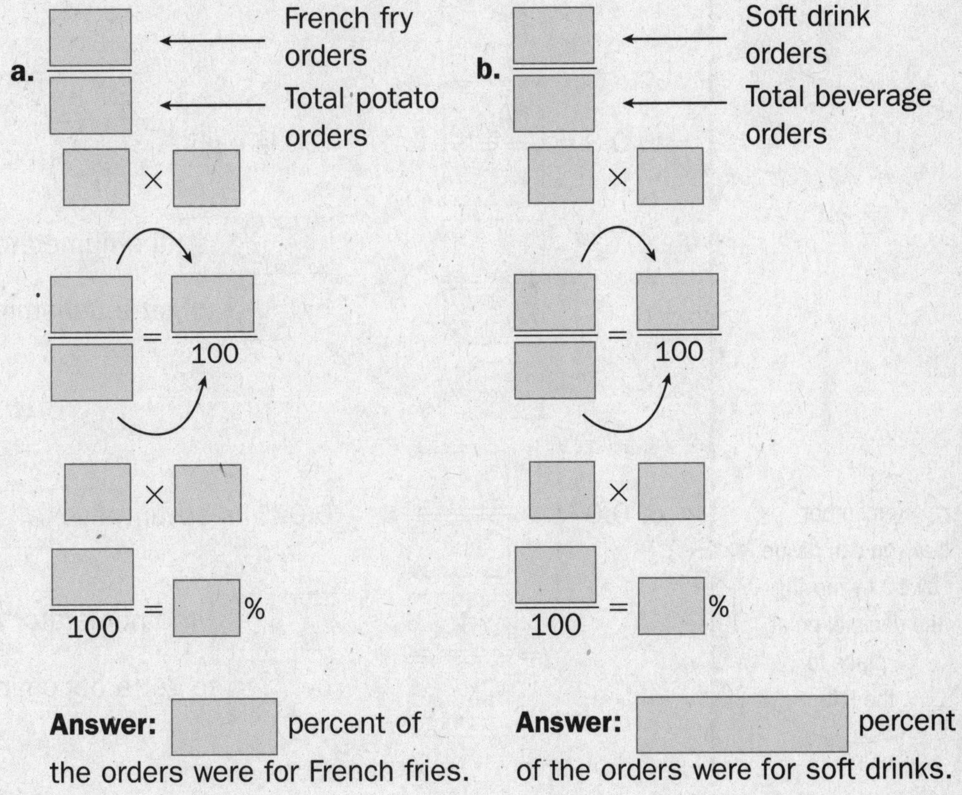

Answer: ______ percent of the orders were for French fries.

Answer: ______ percent of the orders were for soft drinks.

Your turn now **Write the fraction as a percent.**

1. $\frac{1}{4}$	2. $\frac{9}{10}$	3. $\frac{11}{20}$	4. $\frac{7}{50}$

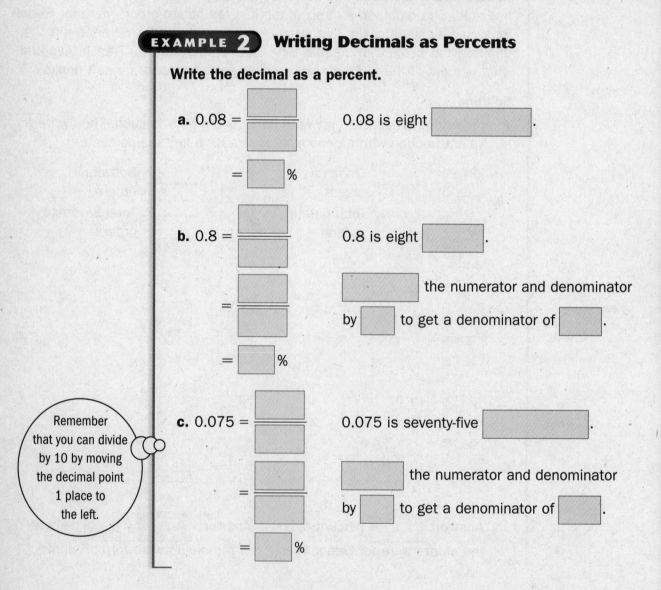

EXAMPLE 2 Writing Decimals as Percents

Write the decimal as a percent.

a. $0.08 = \frac{\square}{\square}$ 0.08 is eight ______.

$= \square\%$

b. $0.8 = \frac{\square}{\square}$ 0.8 is eight ______.

$= \frac{\square}{\square}$ ______ the numerator and denominator by ______ to get a denominator of ______.

$= \square\%$

c. $0.075 = \frac{\square}{\square}$ 0.075 is seventy-five ______.

$= \frac{\square}{\square}$ ______ the numerator and denominator by ______ to get a denominator of ______.

$= \square\%$

Remember that you can divide by 10 by moving the decimal point 1 place to the left.

EXAMPLE 3 Using Decimals to Write Percents

Defective Parts The machine used to manufacture a plastic part occasionally needs to be adjusted. The machine is adjusted when 3% of the parts made contain some kind of defect. During a recent run, 125 parts were made and only 3 were defective. Does the machine need to be adjusted?

Use decimals to write fractions as percents when you cannot easily write the equivalent form of the fraction with a denominator of 100.

Solution

$\frac{\square}{\square} = \square$ Divide $\square$ by $\square$ to write the fraction as a decimal.

$= \frac{\square}{\square}$ $\square$ is $\square$.

$= \frac{\square}{\square}$ $\square$ the numerator and denominator by $\square$ to get a denominator of $\square$.

$= \square\%$

Answer: Because $\square$ % $\square$ 3%, the machine $\square$ need to be adjusted.

Your turn now **Write the decimal or fraction as a percent.**

5. 0.9	**6.** 0.108	**7.** $\frac{5}{8}$	**8.** $\frac{17}{40}$

Common Percents, Decimals, and Fractions

Fifths	Fourths	Thirds
$20\% = 0.2 = \frac{\square}{\square}$	$\square\% = 0.25 = \frac{1}{4}$	$33\frac{1}{3}\% = 0.\overline{3} = \frac{\square}{\square}$
$\square\% = 0.4 = \frac{2}{5}$	$50\% = 0.5 = \frac{\square}{\square}$	$66\frac{2}{3}\% = \square = \frac{2}{3}$
$60\% = \square = \frac{3}{5}$	$75\% = \square = \frac{3}{4}$	
$80\% = 0.8 = \frac{\square}{\square}$		

EXAMPLE 4 **Using Common Relationships**

Order the numbers $\frac{3}{5}$, 40%, and 0.54 from least to greatest.

Write the number as decimals and graph them on a number line.

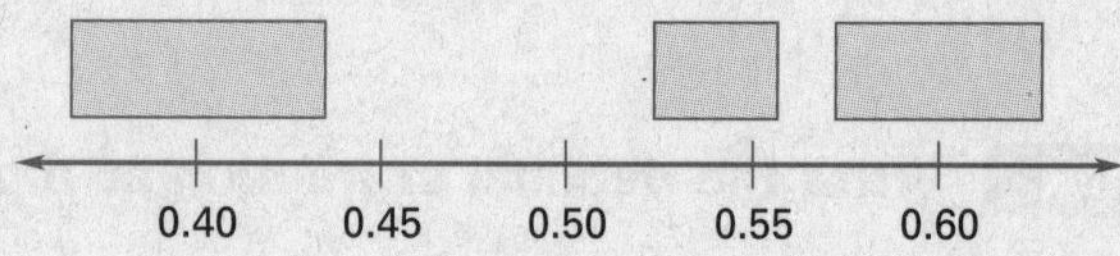

Answer: An ordered list of the numbers is ____, ____, and ____.

Finding a Percent of a Number

Goal: Multiply to find a percent of a number.

For Your Notebook

Vocabulary

Interest:

Principal:

Annual interest rate:

Simple interest:

You may want to include Example 1 in your notes to illustrate when a fraction or when a decimal may be the more convenient form of a percent to use. In part (a), the fraction form of 25% is compatible with 80. In part (b), you can multiply by the decimal form of 40% easily using mental math.

EXAMPLE 1 **Finding a Percent of a Number**

a. Find 25% of 80. Use a fraction.

25% of 80 = $\frac{\square}{\square}$ × ☐

= $\frac{\square}{\square}$

= ☐

Answer: 25% of 80 is ☐.

b. Find 40% of 32. Use a decimal.

40% of 32 = ☐ × ☐

= ☐

Answer: 40% of 32 is ☐.

Your turn now **Find the percent of the number. Explain your method.**

1. 20% of 48	**2.** 60% of 75	**3.** 8% of 30	**4.** 10% of 97

EXAMPLE 2 Finding a Discount

Inline Skates The regular price of a pair of inline skates is \$80. The sale price is 35% off the regular price. What is the sale price?

1. Find the discount. ____% of \$____ = ____ × \$____ = \$____

2. Subtract the discount from the regular price. \$____ − \$____ = \$____

Answer: The sale price of the skates is \$____.

EXAMPLE 3 Finding the Sales Tax

Buying a CD You are buying a CD that costs \$12. There is a 7% sales tax. What is the total amount of your purchase?

1. Find the sales tax. ____% of \$____ = ____ × \$____ = \$____

2. Add the sales tax to the cost of the item. \$____ + \$____ = \$____

Answer: The total amount of your purchase is \$____.

EXAMPLE 4 Solving a Simpler Problem

Haircut You get your hair cut and the bill is \$18.50. You want to leave a tip of about 15%. Use simpler percents and mental math to estimate the amount of the tip.

1. Round the bill to the nearest dollar. \$18.50 ≈ \$____

2. Find 10% of the bill. ____ × \$____ = \$____

3. Find 5% of the bill. It is half of 10% of the bill. ____ × \$____ = \$____

4. Add the partial tips. \$____ + \$____ = \$____

Answer: A 15% tip for a \$18.50 bill is about \$____.

Your turn now **Find the cost described.**

5. A ski jacket's regular price is $110. Find the cost after a 30% discount.

6. The price of a pack of guitar strings is $10.50. Find the cost with a sales tax of 8%.

Simple Interest Formula

Interest paid only on the principal is **simple interest.**

Words

Simple interest = ______ • ______ • ______

Algebra $I = Prt$

EXAMPLE 5 Finding Simple Interest

Savings You deposit $55 in an account. The annual interest rate is 2%. How much simple interest will you earn on that money in 3 years?

Solution

$I =$ ______ Write the simple interest formula.

$=$ ______ (______)(______) Substitute values. Write 2% as a decimal.

$=$ ______ Multiply.

Answer: You will earn $______ in simple interest in 3 years.

Words to Review

Give an example of the vocabulary word.

Ratio

Equivalent ratio

Rate

Unit rate

Proportion

Cross products

Percent

Interest

Principal

Annual interest rate

Simple interest

Review your notes and Chapter 8 by using the Chapter Review on pages 414–415 of your textbook.

Introduction to Geometry

Goal: Identify lines, rays, and segments.

Vocabulary

Point:

Line:

Ray:

Endpoint:

Segment:

Plane:

Intersecting lines:

Parallel lines:

EXAMPLE 1 Identifying Lines, Rays, and Segments

Identify and name the *line*, *ray*, or *segment*.

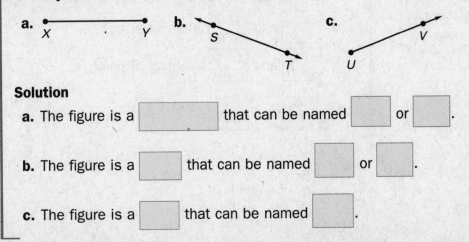

a. X Y

b. S T

c. U V

Solution

a. The figure is a ______ that can be named ______ or ______.

b. The figure is a ______ that can be named ______ or ______.

c. The figure is a ______ that can be named ______.

Your turn now **Identify and name the *line*, *ray*, or *segment*.**

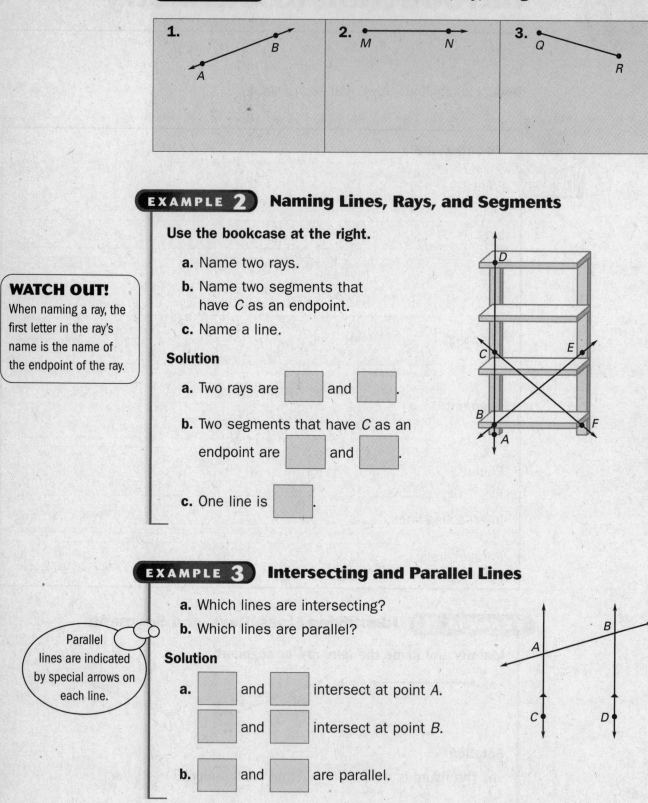

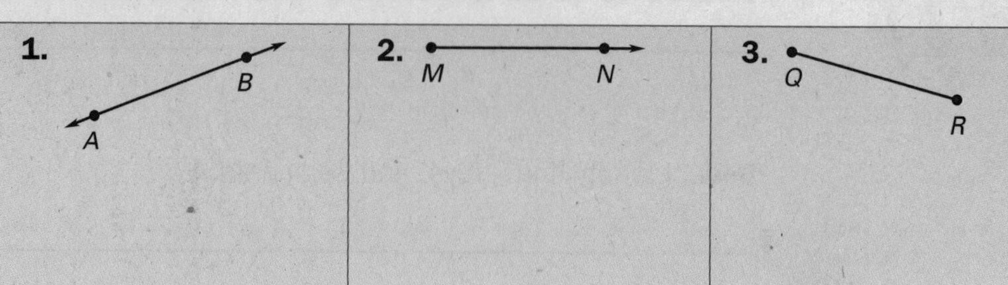

EXAMPLE 2 Naming Lines, Rays, and Segments

Use the bookcase at the right.

a. Name two rays.

b. Name two segments that have *C* as an endpoint.

c. Name a line.

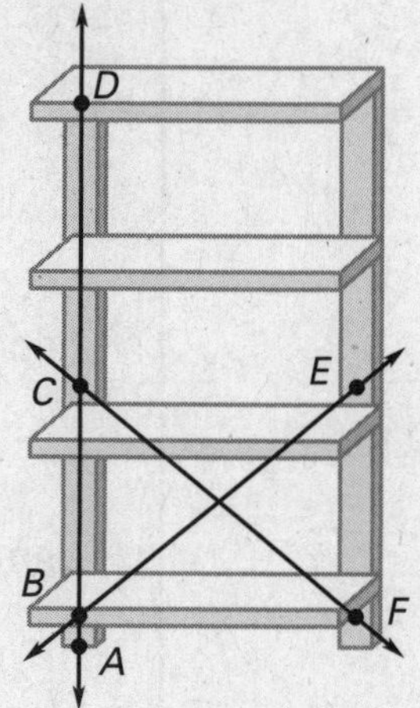

> **WATCH OUT!**
> When naming a ray, the first letter in the ray's name is the name of the endpoint of the ray.

Solution

a. Two rays are ______ and ______.

b. Two segments that have *C* as an endpoint are ______ and ______.

c. One line is ______.

EXAMPLE 3 Intersecting and Parallel Lines

a. Which lines are intersecting?

b. Which lines are parallel?

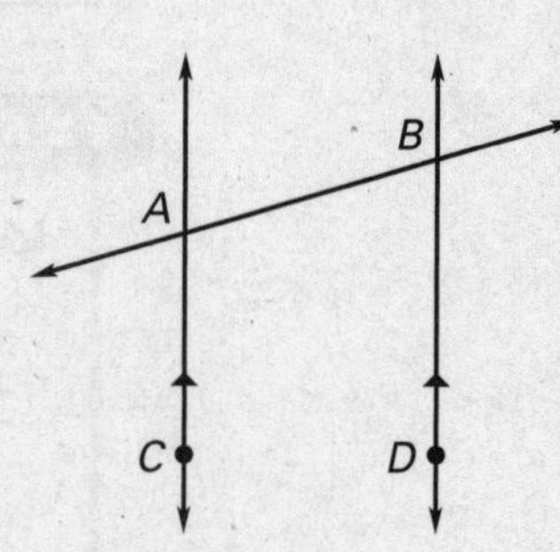

> Parallel lines are indicated by special arrows on each line.

Solution

a. ______ and ______ intersect at point *A*.

______ and ______ intersect at point *B*.

b. ______ and ______ are parallel.

Your turn now **Use the diagram below.**

4. What is another way to write $\overrightarrow{LO}$? $\overrightarrow{PL}$?

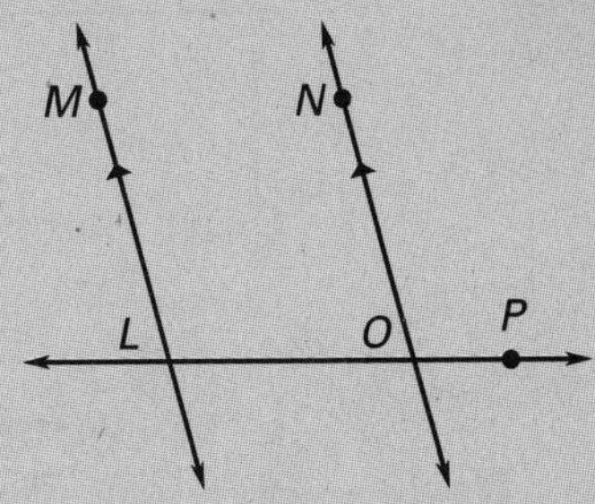

5. Which lines are intersecting? parallel?

Angles

Goal: Name, measure, and draw angles.

For Your Notebook

Vocabulary

Angle:

Vertex:

Degrees (°):

EXAMPLE 1 Naming Angles

Lamp The arms of an adjustable lamp form an angle. Name the angle formed by the arms of the lamp in three different ways.

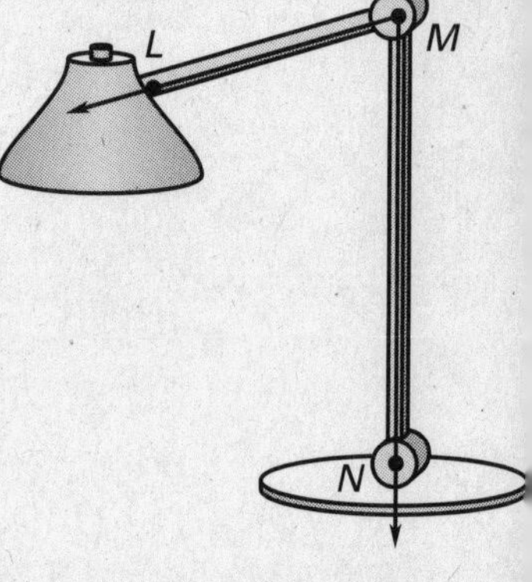

Solution

Name the angle by its vertex alone: ______.

Name the angle by its vertex and two points, with the vertex as the middle point: ______.

Name the angle by its vertex and two points, but switch the order of the two points: ______.

Your turn now **Name the angle in three ways.**

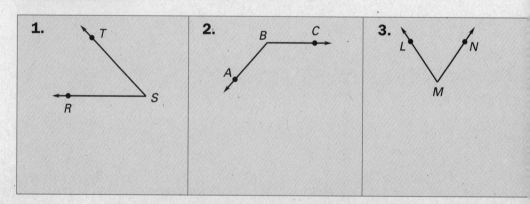

1. (T, S, R)	2. (A, B, C)	3. (L, M, N)

EXAMPLE 2 Drawing Angles

Some protractors have an inner scale and an outer scale. You read one scale when measuring clockwise and the other scale when measuring counterclockwise. Make sure you use the same scale for each ray of the angle.

Use a protractor to draw an angle that has a measure of 116°.

Solution

1. Draw and label a ray $\overrightarrow{BC}$.
2. Place the center of the protractor at the endpoint of the ray. Line up the ray with the 0° line. Then draw and label a point at the 116° mark on the ______ scale.
3. Remove the protractor and draw $\overrightarrow{BA}$ to complete the angle.

Your turn now **Use a protractor to draw an angle that has the given measure.**

4. 35°	**5.** 50°	**6.** 125°	**7.** 160°

EXAMPLE 3 Estimating Angle Measures

Use estimation to name the angle whose measure is closest to the given measure.

a. 160°

b. 75°

c. 90°

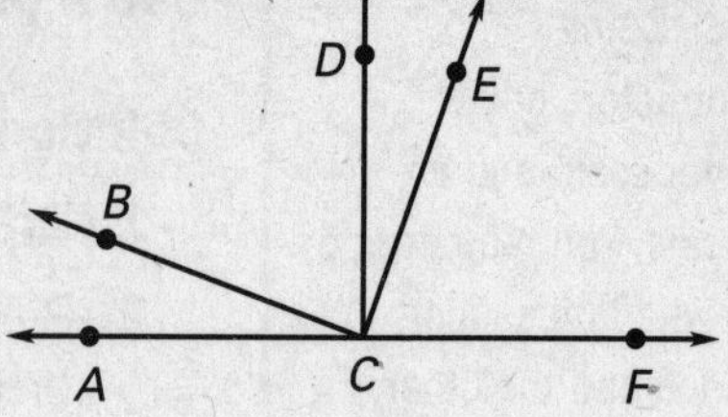

WATCH OUT!

When two or more angles share a vertex, each angle must be named using three points.

Solution

Imagine that C is at the center and that $\overrightarrow{CA}$ and $\overrightarrow{CF}$ are on the 0° line.

a. A 160° angle is close to ____° and greater than ____°, so ____ has the measure that is closest to 160°.

b. A 75° angle is close to ____° and less than ____°, so ____ and ____ both have measures that are close to 75°.

c. A 90° angle is ____, so ____, ____, and ____ all have measures that are close to 90°.

Classifying Angles

Goal: Classify angles and find angle measures.

Vocabulary

Right angle:

Acute angle:

Obtuse angle:

Straight angle:

Vertical angles:

Complementary angles:

Supplementary angles:

Classifying Angles	
A ______ **angle** is an angle whose measure is ______.	An ______ **angle** is an angle whose measure is ______.
An ______ **angle** is an angle whose measure is ______.	A ______ **angle** is an angle whose measure is ______.

EXAMPLE 1 Classifying Angles

Estimate to classify the angles in the figure as *acute*, *right*, or *obtuse*.

$\angle R$ is an ______ angle because $m\angle R$ is ______.

$\angle S$ is an ______ angle because $m\angle S$ is ______.

$\angle T$ is a ______ angle because $\angle T$ is ______.

$\angle U$ is an ______ angle because $m\angle U$ is ______.

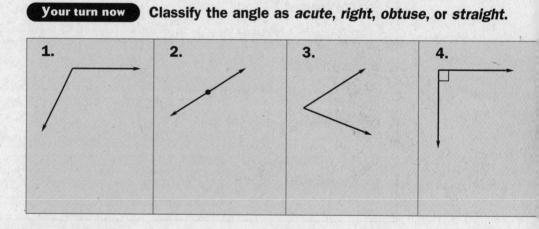

Your turn now **Classify the angle as *acute*, *right*, *obtuse*, or *straight*.**

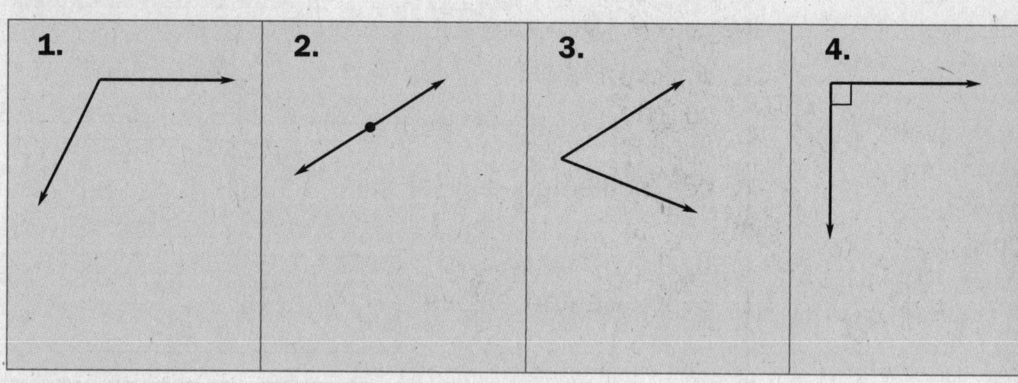

EXAMPLE 2 Using Vertical Angles

Find the measure of $\angle CBE$.

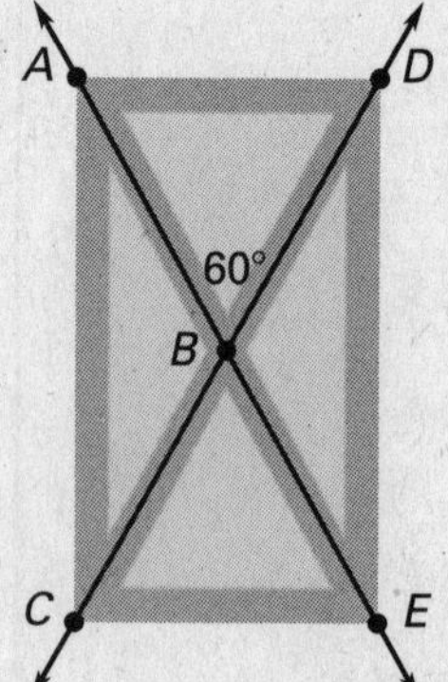

Because $\angle CBE$ and ______ are vertical angles,

$m\angle CBE =$ ______ $=$ ______.

Answer: The measure of $\angle CBE$ is ______.

Complementary and Supplementary Angles

Complementary angles Two angles are complementary if the ____ of their measures is ____.

$m\angle 1$ ____ $m\angle 2 =$ ____

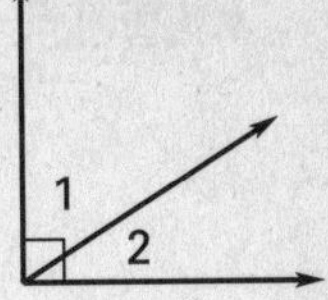

Supplementary angles Two angles are supplementary if the ____ of their measures is ____.

$m\angle 3$ ____ $m\angle 4 =$ ____

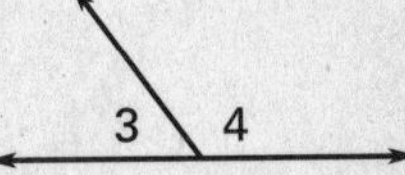

EXAMPLE 3 Classifying Pairs of Angles

To associate complementary angles with 90° and supplementary angles with 180°, remember that "c" is before "s" in the alphabet and 90 is before 180 on a number line.

Decide whether the angles are *complementary* or *supplementary*.

a.

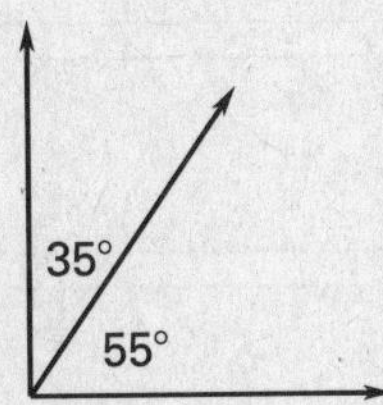

b.

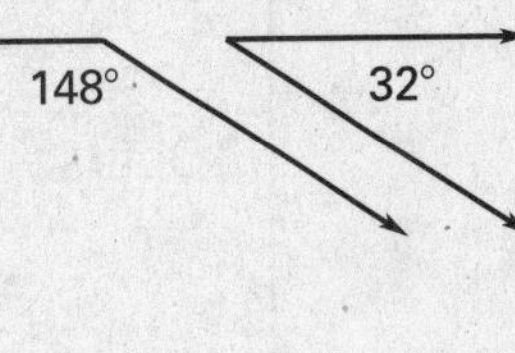

Solution

a. The angles are ____ because ____ ____.

b. The angles are ____ because ____ ____.

EXAMPLE 4 Solving for an Unknown Measure

When solving for an unknown measure, it can be helpful to draw a diagram before you set up an equation to solve the problem.

Recliner The back of a recliner can tilt back 125°. What is the angle between the back of the recliner and the floor?

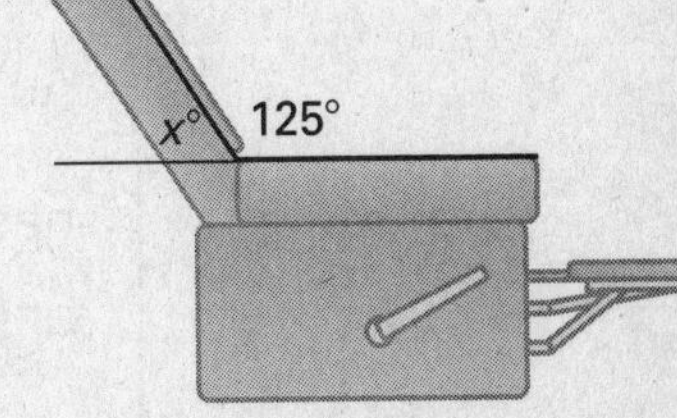

Solution

Start by drawing a diagram. Then find the angle that is ____ to 125°.

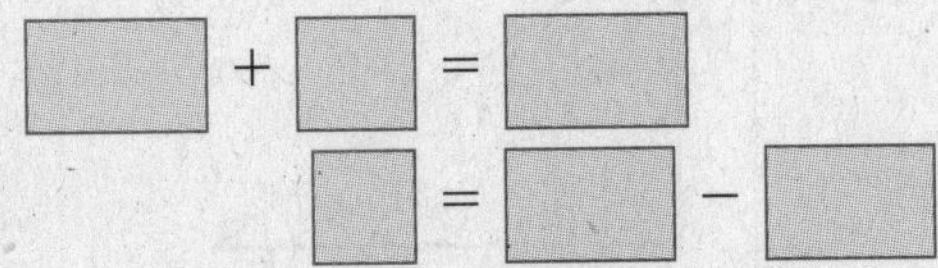

____ + ____ = ____ Write an equation that models the situation.

____ = ____ − ____ Write a related subtraction equation.

____ = ____ Subtract.

Answer: The angle between the back of the recliner and the floor is ____.

Classifying Triangles

Goal: Classify triangles by their angles and by their sides.

For Your Notebook

Vocabulary

Triangle:

Acute triangle:

Right triangle:

Obtuse triangle:

Equilateral triangle:

Isosceles triangle:

Scalene triangle:

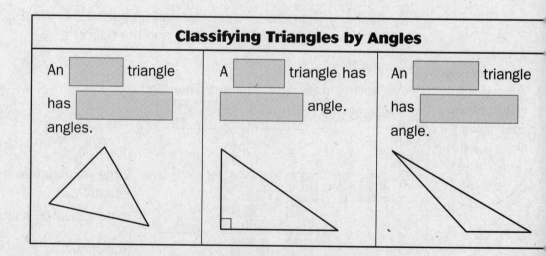

Classifying Triangles by Angles		
An ____ triangle has ____ angles.	A ____ triangle has ____ angle.	An ____ triangle has ____ angle.

EXAMPLE 1 Classifying Triangles by Angles

When classifying a triangle by its angles, it is helpful to identify the largest angle first.

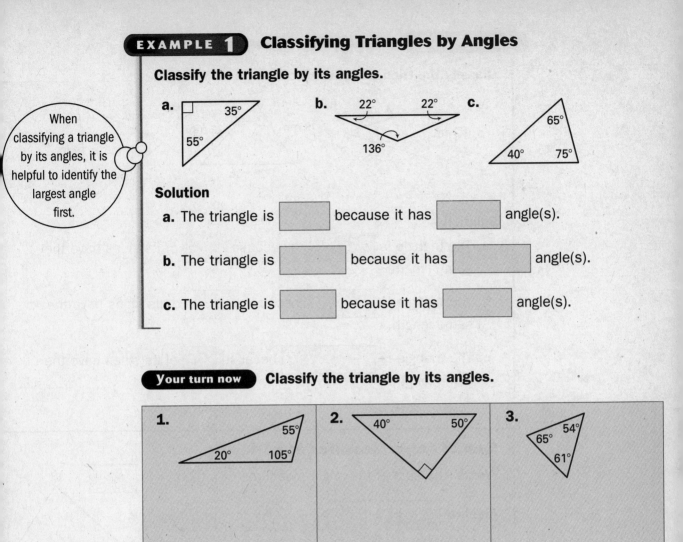

Classify the triangle by its angles.

a. 35°, 55° (right angle)

b. 22°, 22°, 136°

c. 65°, 40°, 75°

Solution

a. The triangle is ______ because it has ______ angle(s).

b. The triangle is ______ because it has ______ angle(s).

c. The triangle is ______ because it has ______ angle(s).

Your turn now **Classify the triangle by its angles.**

1. 55°, 20°, 105°	**2.** 40°, 50° (right angle)	**3.** 54°, 65°, 61°

Classifying Triangles by Sides		
An ______ triangle has ______ sides of ______ length.	An ______ triangle has ______ sides of ______ length.	A ______ triangle has ______ sides of ______ lengths.

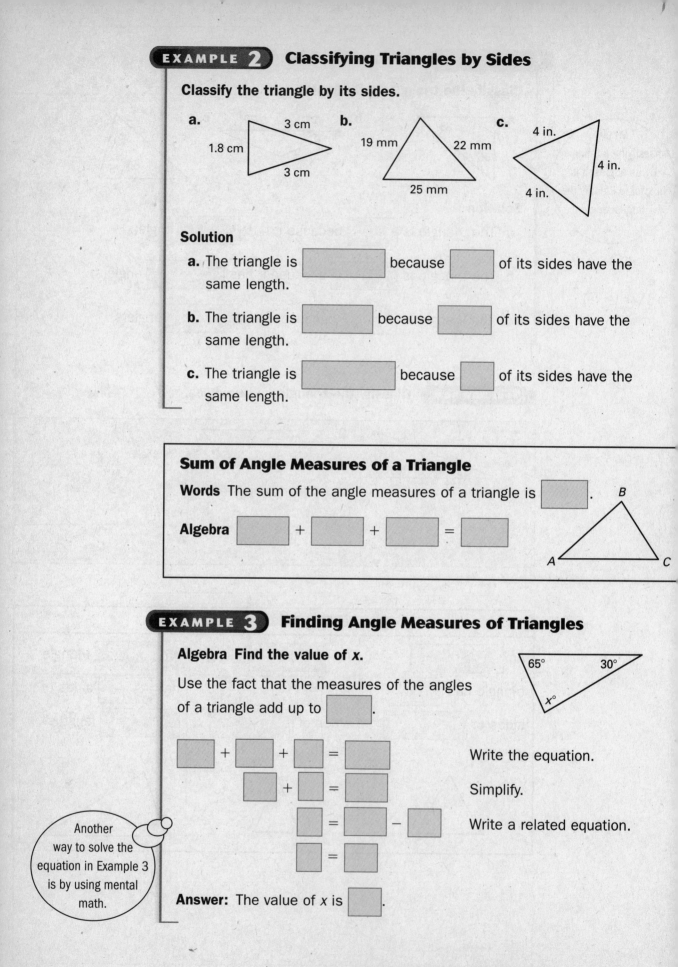

EXAMPLE 2 Classifying Triangles by Sides

Classify the triangle by its sides.

a. **b.** **c.**

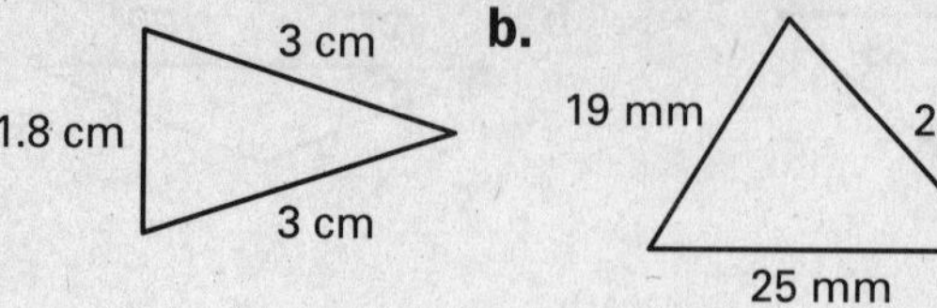

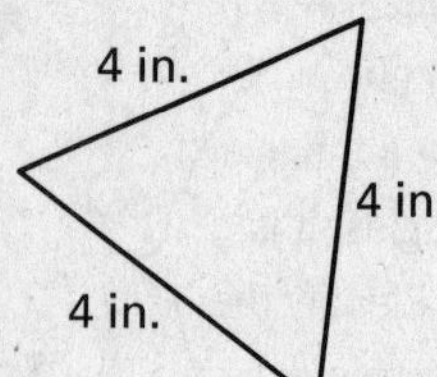

Solution

a. The triangle is ______ because ______ of its sides have the same length.

b. The triangle is ______ because ______ of its sides have the same length.

c. The triangle is ______ because ______ of its sides have the same length.

Sum of Angle Measures of a Triangle

Words The sum of the angle measures of a triangle is ______.

Algebra ______ + ______ + ______ = ______

B

A C

EXAMPLE 3 Finding Angle Measures of Triangles

Algebra Find the value of *x*.

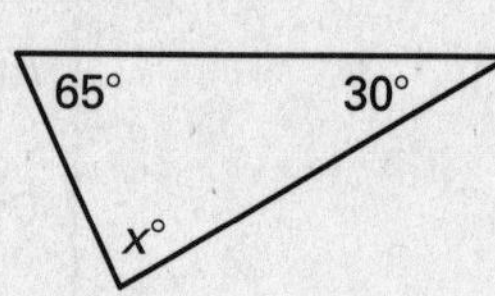

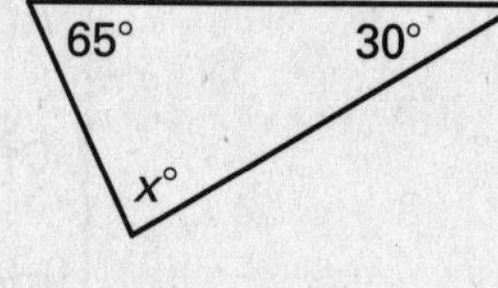

Use the fact that the measures of the angles of a triangle add up to ______.

______ + ______ + ______ = ______ Write the equation.

______ + ______ = ______ Simplify.

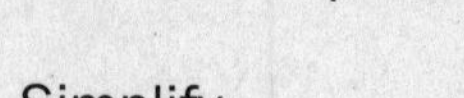

______ = ______ − ______ Write a related equation.

______ = ______

Answer: The value of *x* is ______.

Another way to solve the equation in Example 3 is by using mental math.

Classifying Quadrilaterals

Goal: Classify quadrilaterals by their angles and sides.

For Your Notebook

Vocabulary

Quadrilateral:

Parallelogram:

Rectangle:

Rhombus:

Square:

Special Quadrilateral	Diagram
A ______ is a quadrilateral with ______.	
A ______ is a parallelogram with ______.	
A ______ is a parallelogram with ______.	
A ______ is a parallelogram with ______ and ______ ______.	

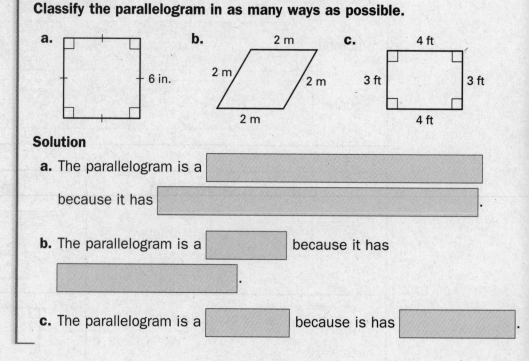

EXAMPLE 1 Classifying Quadrilaterals

Tell whether the statement is *true* or *false*. Explain your reasoning.

a. All rhombuses are squares.

b. Some parallelograms are rectangles.

Try making a Venn diagram in your notebook to help you organize the different types of quadrilaterals. For help with Venn diagrams, see page 703 of your textbook.

Solution

a.

b.

EXAMPLE 2 Classifying Parallelograms

Classify the parallelogram in as many ways as possible.

a.

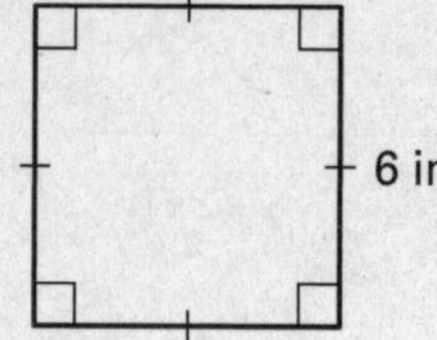

b.

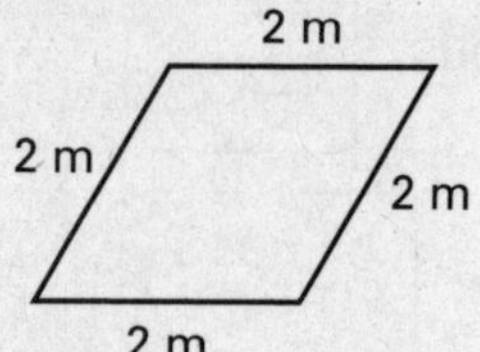

c.

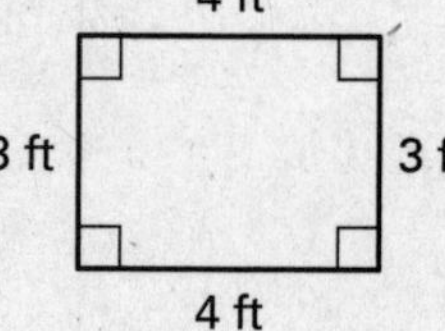

Solution

a. The parallelogram is a ______ because it has ______.

b. The parallelogram is a ______ because it has ______.

c. The parallelogram is a ______ because is has ______.

EXAMPLE 3 Drawing a Quadrilateral

Before drawing the quadrilateral in Example 3, identify what properties a square has that a rhombus isn't required to have.

Draw a quadrilateral that is a rhombus but not a square.

1. Draw one side.

2. Draw an angle that isn't a 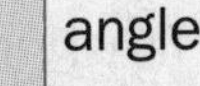 angle.

Then draw a side with the ______ length.

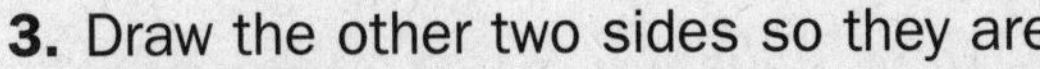

3. Draw the other two sides so they are ______ to the sides you've already drawn and all the ______ length.

Your turn now **Classify the quadrilateral in as many ways as possible.**

1.

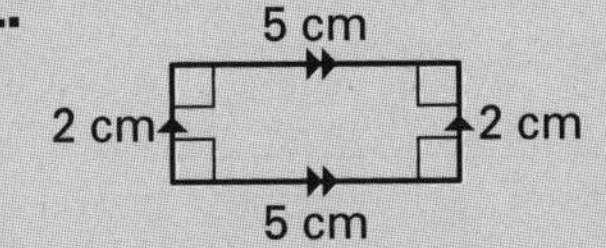

2.

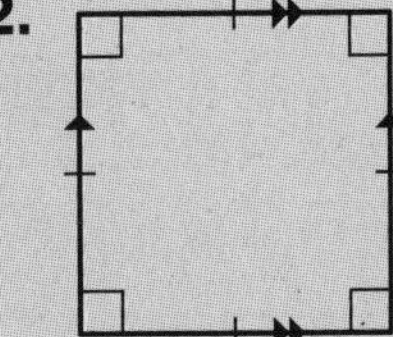

3.

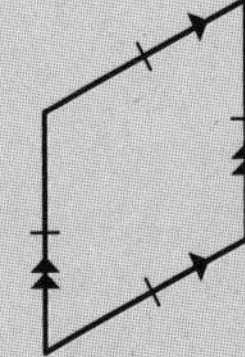

4. Draw a parallelogram that is not a rectangle, a rhombus, or a square.

Polygons

Goal: Classify polygons by their sides.

Vocabulary

Polygon:

Vertex:

Pentagon:

Hexagon:

Octagon:

Regular polygon:

Diagonal:

Classifying Polygons

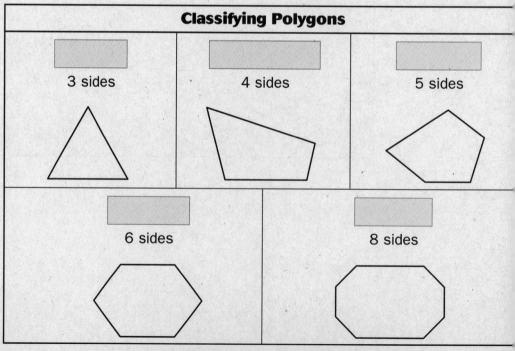

3 sides	4 sides	5 sides
6 sides	8 sides	

EXAMPLE 1 Classifying Polygons

To help remember how many sides a polygon has, use the following. "tri" means 3. "quad" means 4. "penta" means 5. "hexa" means 6. "octa" means 8.

Patio The pattern for a patio floor is shown. Describe the figures found in the pattern.

Solution

To describe the figures in the pattern, count the number of sides of each figure.

Answer: The figures are ______ and ______.

Your turn now **Classify the polygon.**

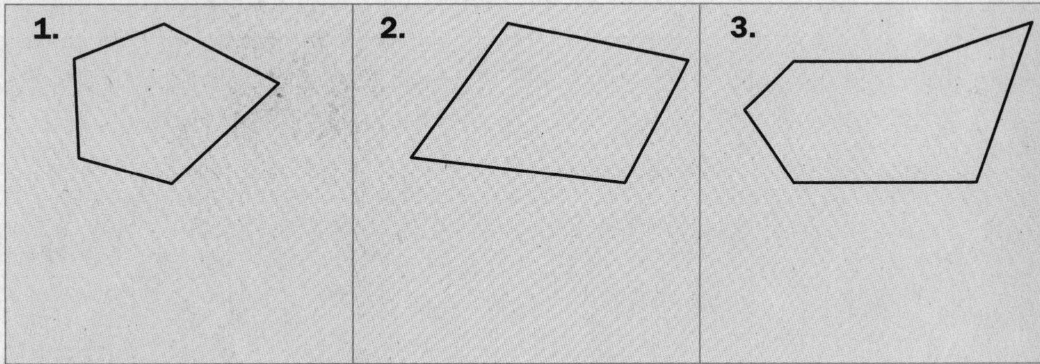

EXAMPLE 2 Classifying Regular Polygons

Classify the polygon and tell whether it is regular.

Matching angle marks indicate that the angles have equal measures.

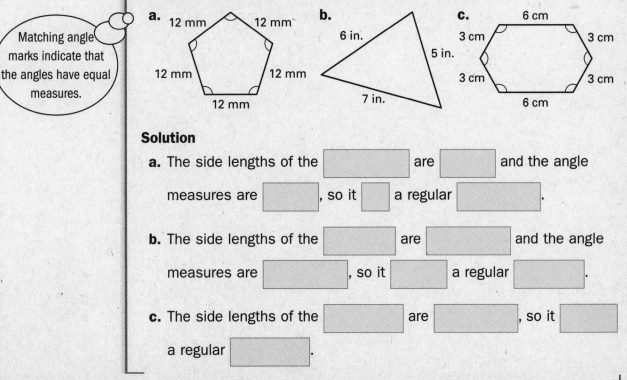

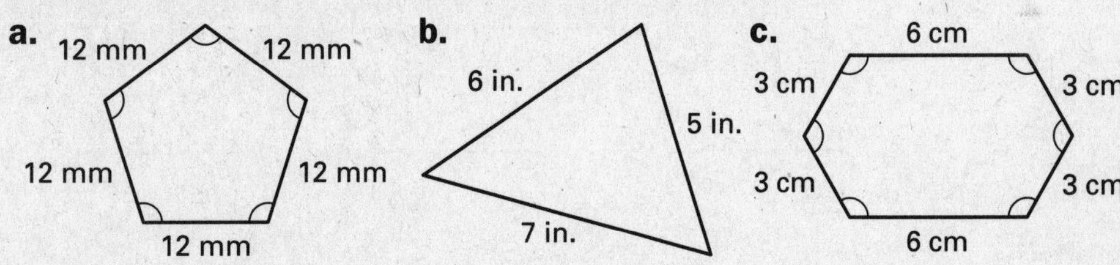

Solution

a. The side lengths of the ______ are ______ and the angle measures are ______, so it ______ a regular ______.

b. The side lengths of the ______ are ______ and the angle measures are ______, so it ______ a regular ______.

c. The side lengths of the ______ are ______, so it ______ a regular ______.

EXAMPLE 3 Diagonals of a Regular Polygon

How many diagonals can be drawn from one vertex of a regular octagon? How many triangles do the diagonals form?

Solution

Sketch a regular octagon and draw all the possible diagonals from one vertex.

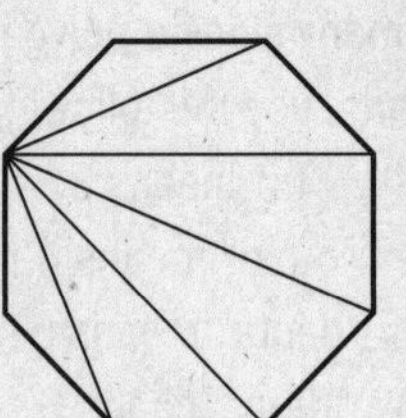

Answer: There are ______ diagonals and ______ triangles.

Your turn now **Tell how many triangles are formed by the diagonals from one vertex of the figure.**

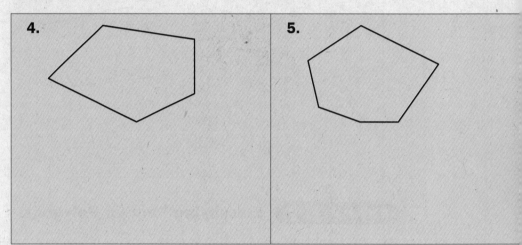

4.

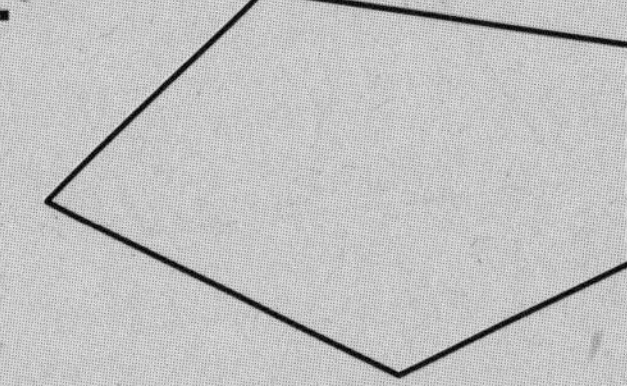

5.

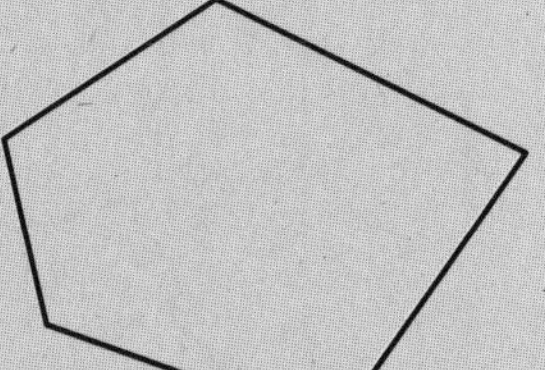

Congruent and Similar Figures

Goal: Identify similar and congruent figures.

Vocabulary

Congruent: ______

Similar: ______

Corresponding parts: ______

EXAMPLE 1 Congruent and Similar Triangles

Tell whether the triangles are *similar*, *congruent*, or *neither*.

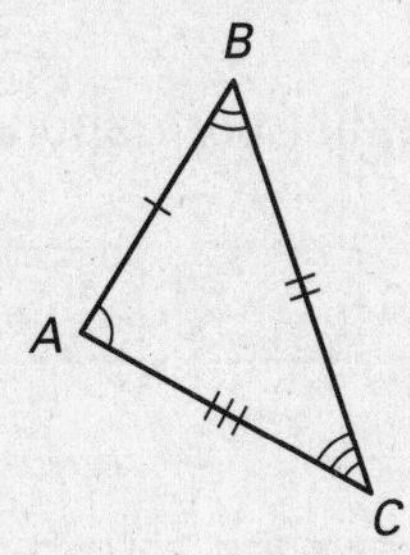

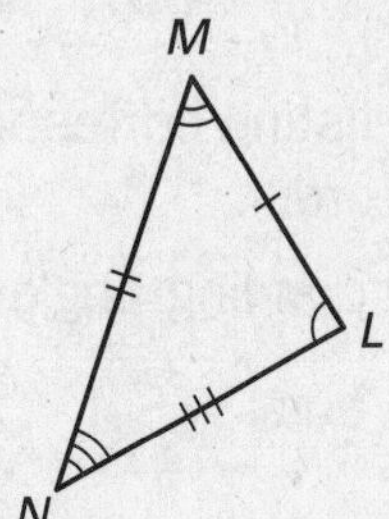

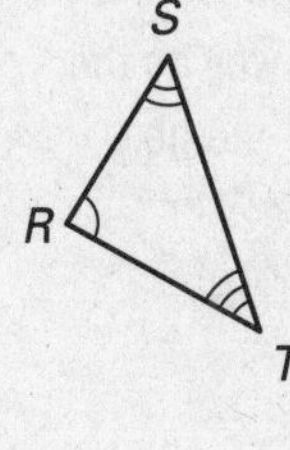

Solution

______ are similar because they have the same ______.

______ are congruent because they have the same ______.

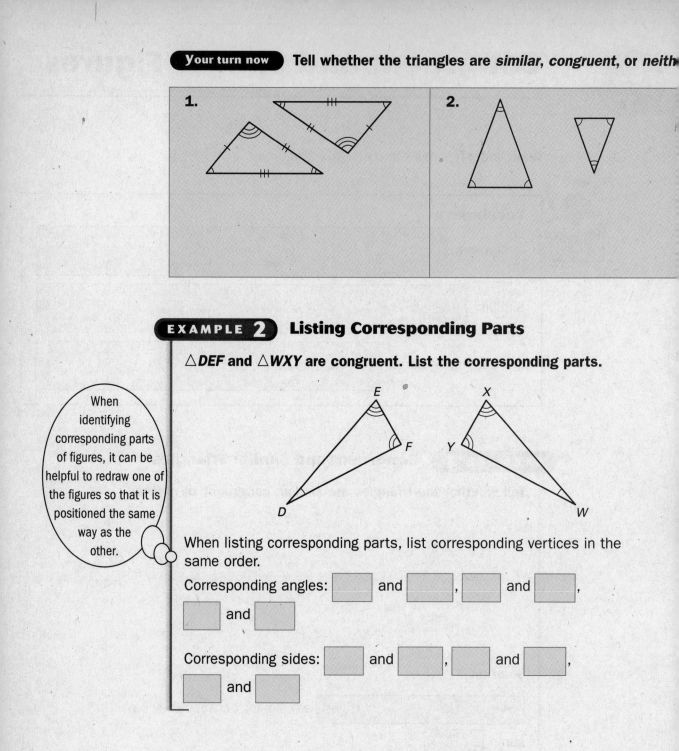

Your turn now **Tell whether the triangles are *similar*, *congruent*, or *neith***

1. 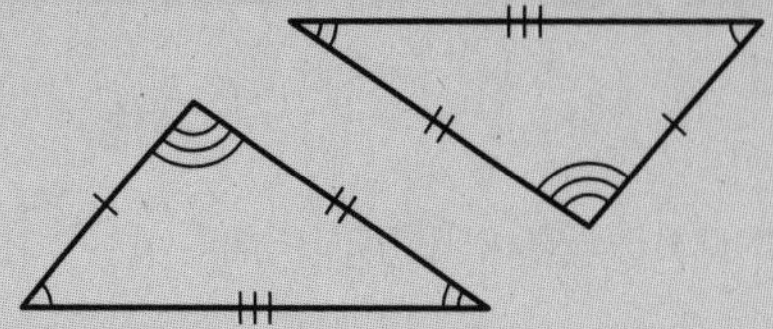

2. 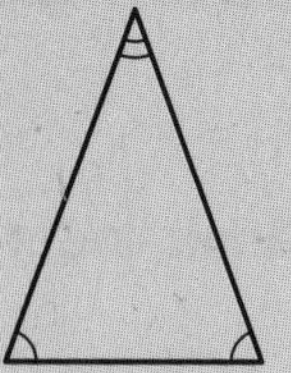 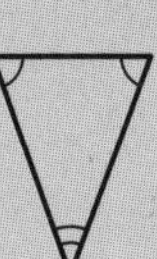

EXAMPLE 2 Listing Corresponding Parts

$\triangle DEF$ and $\triangle WXY$ are congruent. List the corresponding parts.

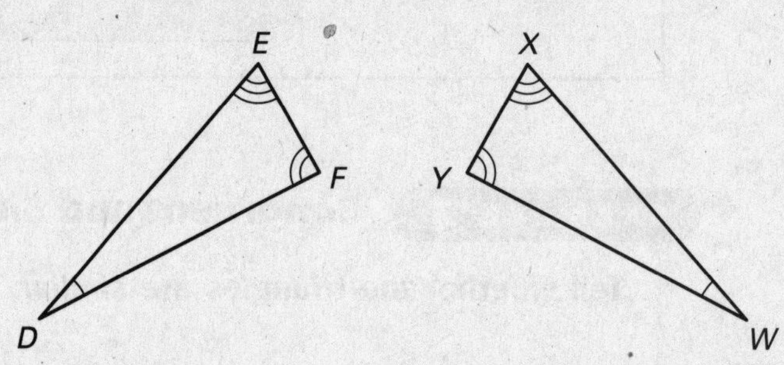

When identifying corresponding parts of figures, it can be helpful to redraw one of the figures so that it is positioned the same way as the other.

When listing corresponding parts, list corresponding vertices in the same order.

Corresponding angles: ______ and ______, ______ and ______, ______ and ______

Corresponding sides: ______ and ______, ______ and ______, ______ and ______

EXAMPLE 3 Using Corresponding Parts

In Example 3, you may want to draw each parallelogram as a separate figure to help you identify the corresponding parts.

Quilt Pattern In the quilt block shown, *ABCD* and *EFCD* are congruent.

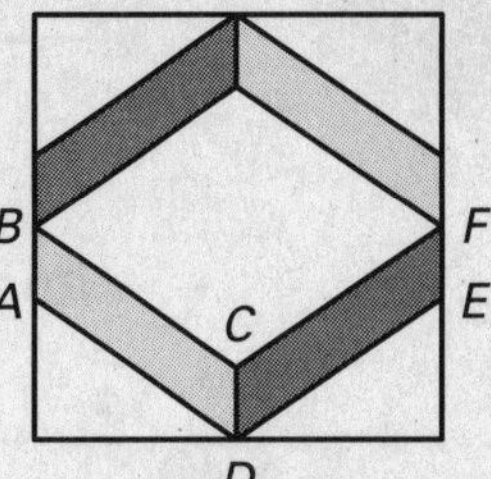

a. If $\overline{AD}$ is 5.5 inches long, how long is $\overline{ED}$? Why?

b. If $m\angle CFE = 56°$, what is $m\angle CBA$? Why?

Solution

a. $\overline{ED}$ has a length of ______ inches because ______________________.

b. $m\angle CBA =$ ______ because ______________________.

Your turn now $\triangle ABC$ and $\triangle QRS$ are similar. List the corresponding parts. Then find $m\angle A$ and $m\angle S$.

3.

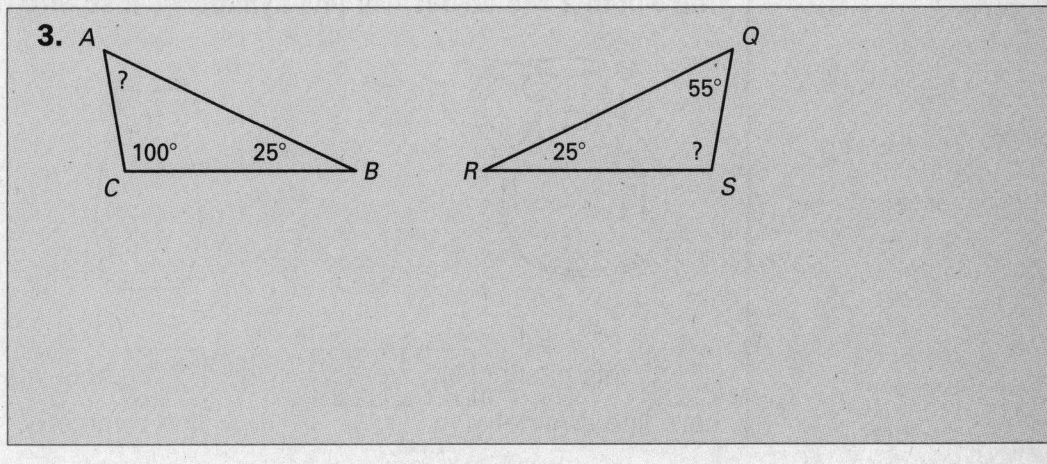

Line Symmetry

Goal: Identify lines of symmetry.

For Your Notebook

Vocabulary

Line symmetry:

Line of symmetry:

EXAMPLE 1 **Identifying Lines of Symmetry**

Tell whether the object has line symmetry. If so, draw the line of symmetr

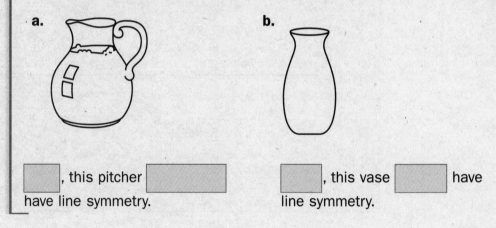

a.

____, this pitcher ____ have line symmetry.

b.

____, this vase ____ have line symmetry.

Your turn now **Tell whether the figure has line symmetry. If so, draw the line(s) of symmetry.**

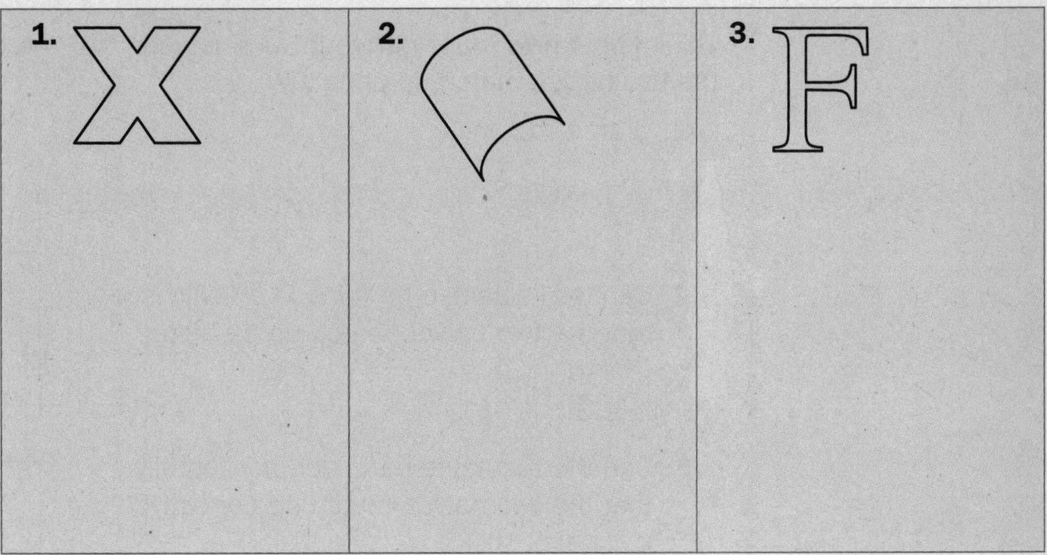

Lines of Symmetry

A figure can have zero, one, or multiple lines of symmetry.

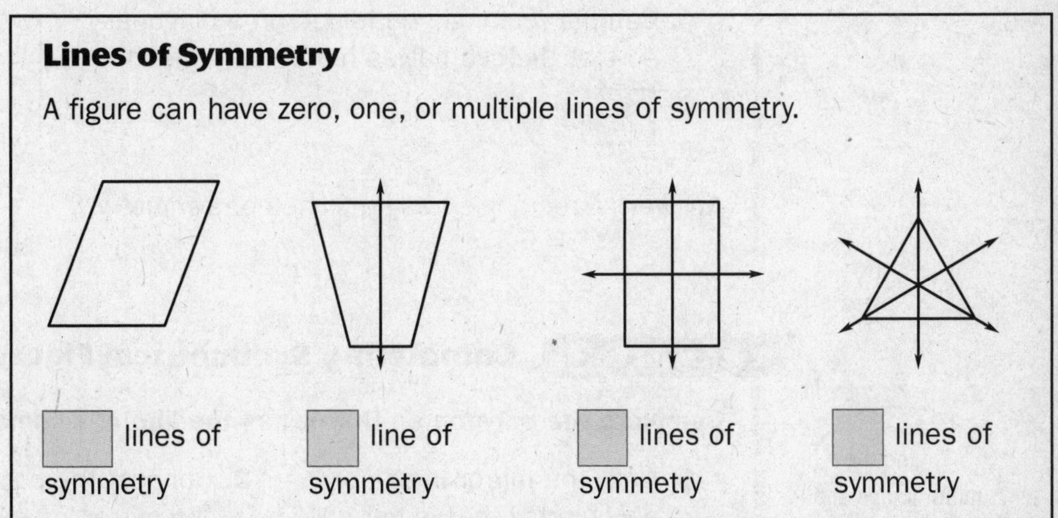

☐ lines of symmetry ☐ line of symmetry ☐ lines of symmetry ☐ lines of symmetry

EXAMPLE 2 Multiple Lines of Symmetry

Find the number of lines of symmetry in a rectangle.

Think about how many different ways you can fold a rectangle in half so tha the two halves match up perfectly.

1. Draw a rectangle.

2. Can the rectangle be folded vertically so that the two halves match up perfectly?

3. Can the rectangle be folded horizontally so that the two halves match up perfectly?

4. Can the rectangle be folded on a diagonal so that the two halves match up perfectly?

Answer: A rectangle has ____ lines of symmetry.

EXAMPLE 3 Completing Symmetrical Figures

To find the mirror image of a point in Example 3, find the distance between the point and the line of symmetry. Place the mirror image point the same distance from the line of symmetry, but on the opposite side.

Complete the polygon so that it has the line of symmetry shown.

1. Draw the mirror image of each vertex that is not on the line of symmetry.

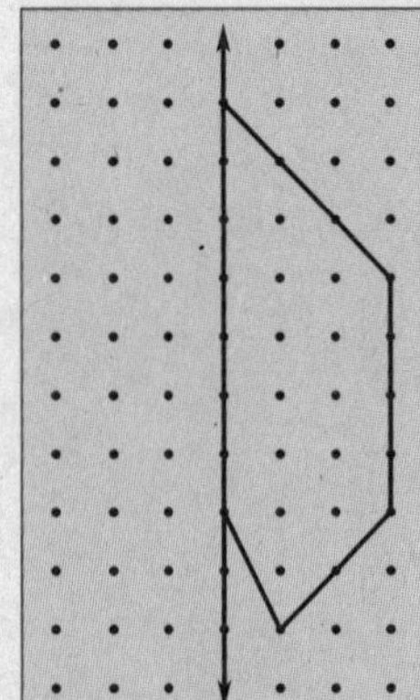

2. Connect the points to complete the mirror image so that the two halves are congruent.

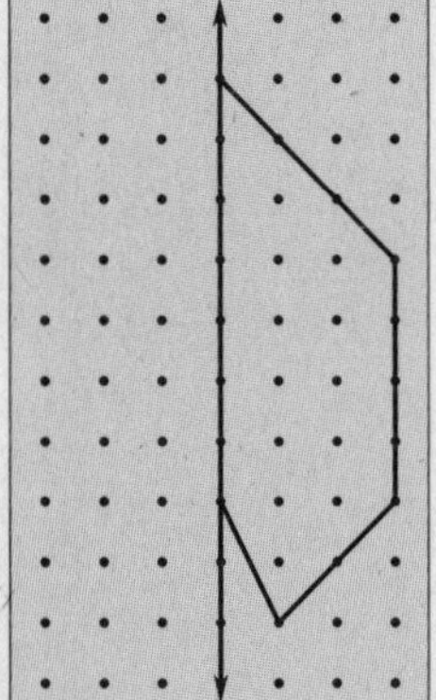

Words to Review

Give an example of the vocabulary word.

Ray

Endpoint

Segment

Intersecting lines

Parallel lines

Angle

Vertex

Degrees (°)

Acute angle

Right angle

Obtuse angle

Straight angle

Vertical angles

Complementary

Supplementary

Acute triangle

Right triangle

Obtuse triangle

Equilateral triangle

Isosceles triangle

Scalene triangle

Quadrilateral

Parallelogram

Rectangle

Rhombus

Square

Pentagon

Hexagon

Octagon

Regular polygon

Diagonal

Congruent figures

Similar figures

Review your notes and Chapter 9 by using the Chapter Review on pages 466–467 of your textbook.

Area of a Parallelogram

Goal: Find the area of a parallelogram.

For Your Notebook

Vocabulary

Base of parallelogram:

Height of a parallelogram:

Perpendicular:

Area of a Parallelogram

Words Area = ___ • ___

Algebra $A =$ ___

h

b

Include the formula for the area of a parallelogram in your notebook. Include an example like the one shown in Example 1.

EXAMPLE 1 **Finding the Area of a Parallelogram**

Find the area of the parallelogram shown at the right.

3 cm

8 cm

Solution

$A =$ ___ Write the formula for the area of a parallelogram.

$=$ ___ • ___ Substitute ___ for b and ___ for h.

$=$ ___ Simplify.

Answer: The area of the parallelogram is ___ square centimeters.

Your turn now **Find the area of the parallelogram described.**

1. base = 4 ft, height = 9 ft	2. base = 11 in., height = 5 in.

EXAMPLE 2 Finding an Unknown Dimension

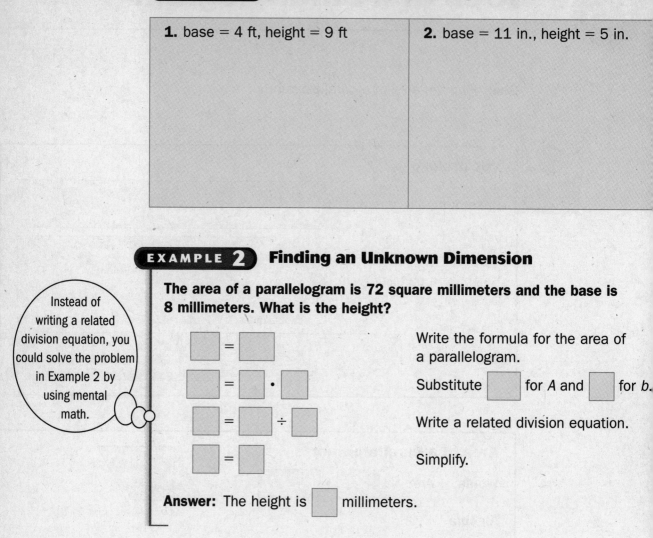

Instead of writing a related division equation, you could solve the problem in Example 2 by using mental math.

The area of a parallelogram is 72 square millimeters and the base is 8 millimeters. What is the height?

☐ = ☐	Write the formula for the area of a parallelogram.
☐ = ☐ • ☐	Substitute ☐ for *A* and ☐ for *b*.
☐ = ☐ ÷ ☐	Write a related division equation.
☐ = ☐	Simplify.

Answer: The height is ☐ millimeters.

EXAMPLE 3 Estimating Area

Geography The shape of a certain island can be approximated by a parallelogram. Use the map and the scale to estimate the area of the island.

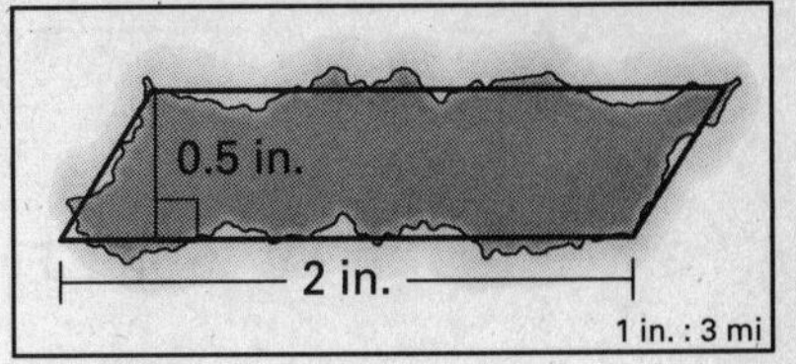

Solution

1. Use the scale to find the base, b, and the height, h, in miles.

Base

$\frac{\square \text{ in.}}{\square \text{ mi}} = \frac{\square \text{ in.}}{\square \text{ mi}}$

$\square \cdot \square = \square \cdot \square$

$\square = \square$

Height

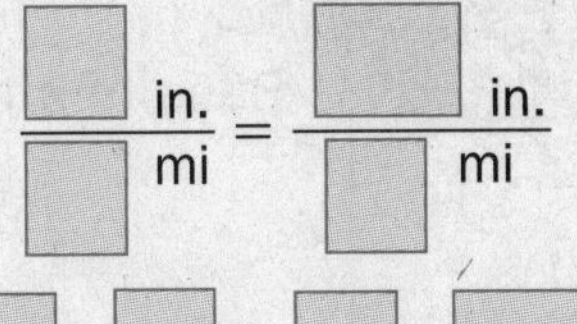

$\frac{\square \text{ in.}}{\square \text{ mi}} = \frac{\square \text{ in.}}{\square \text{ mi}}$

$\square \cdot \square = \square \cdot \square$

$\square = \square$

2. Estimate the island's area.

$A = \square$ Write the formula for the area of a parallelogram.

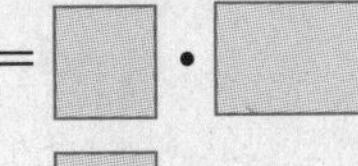

$= \square \cdot \square$ Substitute $\square$ for b and $\square$ for h.

$= \square$ Simplify.

Answer: The area of the island is about $\square$ square miles.

Your turn now **Find the unknown length.**

3. Area of parallelogram = 48 cm^2, base = __?__, height = 6 cm

4. Area of parallelogram = 18 ft^2, base = 6 ft, height = __?__

Area of a Triangle

Goal: Find the area of a triangle.

Vocabulary

Base of a triangle:

Height of a triangle:

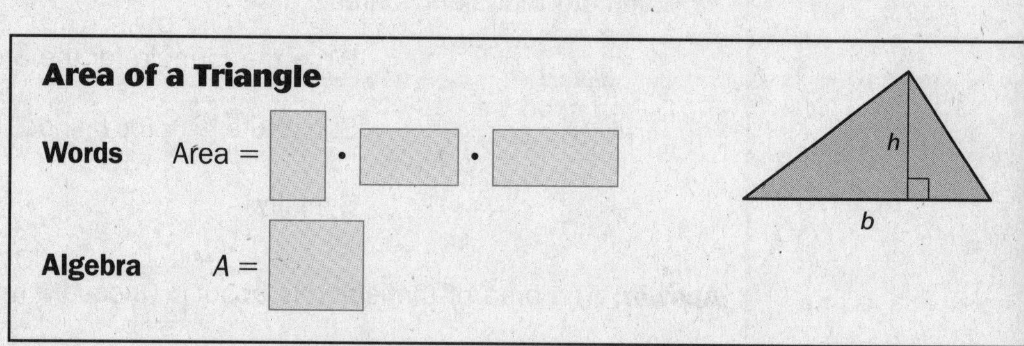

Area of a Triangle

Words Area = ___ • ___ • ___

Algebra $A =$ ___

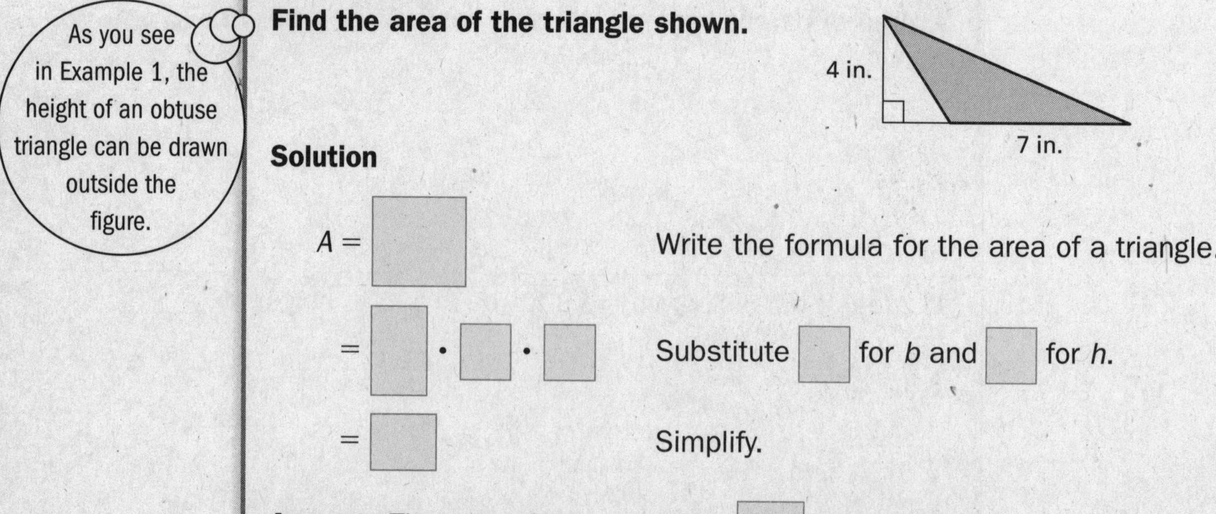

EXAMPLE 1 Finding the Area of a Triangle

As you see in Example 1, the height of an obtuse triangle can be drawn outside the figure.

Find the area of the triangle shown.

Solution

$A =$ ___ Write the formula for the area of a triangle.

$=$ ___ • ___ • ___ Substitute ___ for b and ___ for h.

$=$ ___ Simplify.

Answer: The area of the triangle is ___ square inches.

Your turn now **Find the area of the triangle described.**

1. base = 15 centimeters, height = 6 centimeters

2. base = 8 feet, height = 13 feet

EXAMPLE 2 Finding the Area of Combined Figures

Checkout Counter The layout for a checkout counter at a store is shown. How much glass, in square feet, is needed for the countertop?

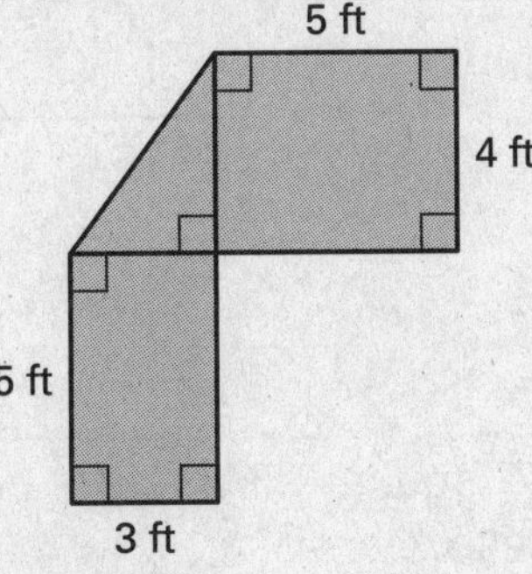

WATCH OUT!
Before finding the area of the triangle, label the lengths of the triangle's legs to make sure you use the correct dimensions.

Solution

1. Find the area of each shape.

Area of the triangle:

$A = \square \cdot \square \cdot \square = \square$

Area of smaller rectangle:

$A = \square \cdot \square = \square$

Area of larger rectangle:

$A = \square \cdot \square = \square$

2. Add the areas to find the total area.

$\square + \square + \square = \square$

Answer: You will need $\square$ square feet of glass for the countertop.

EXAMPLE 3 Finding the Height of a Triangle

The area of a triangle is 54 square meters and the base is 12 meters. What is the height of the triangle?

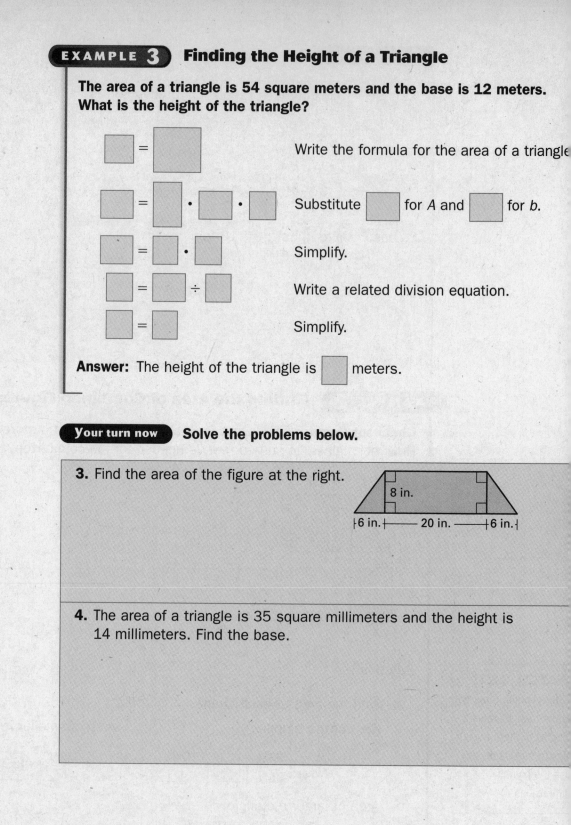

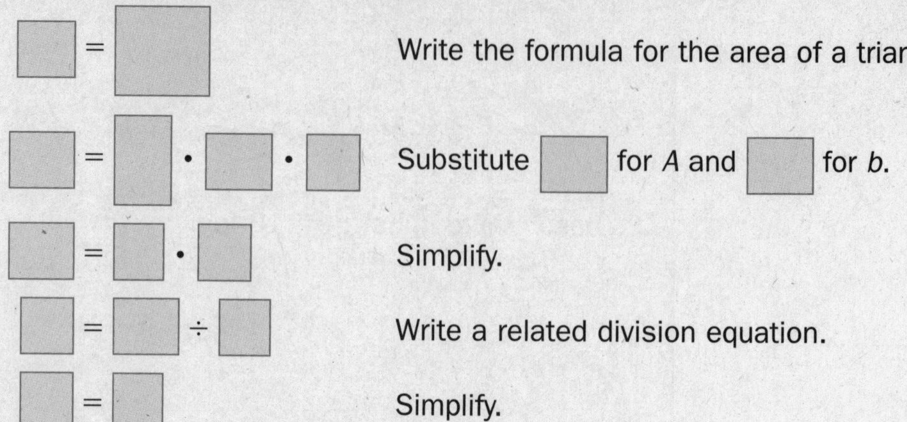

Write the formula for the area of a triangle
Substitute for *A* and for *b*.
Simplify.
Write a related division equation.
Simplify.

Answer: The height of the triangle is ____ meters.

Your turn now **Solve the problems below.**

3. Find the area of the figure at the right.

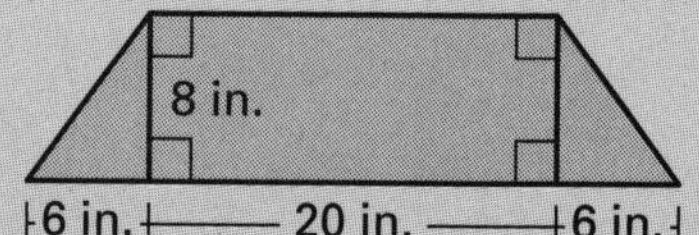

4. The area of a triangle is 35 square millimeters and the height is 14 millimeters. Find the base.

Circumference of a Circle

Goal: Find the circumference of a circle.

For Your Notebook

Vocabulary

Circle:

Center:

Radius:

Diameter:

Circumference:

Pi (π):

Circumference of a Circle

Words

Circumference = ___ • ___

Circumference = ___ • ___ • ___

Algebra

$C =$ ___ d

$C =$ ___ r

EXAMPLE 1 Finding the Circumference of a Circle

Wall Clock The diameter of the wall clock shown is 15 inches. About how far does the car on the second hand go in one minute? Round your answer to the nearest inch.

Solution

The distance that the car travels in one minute is equal to the circumference of the clock.

$C =$ ____	Write the formula for the circumference of a circle.
$\approx$ (____)(____)	Substitute ____ for π and ____ for d.
$=$ ____	Simplify.

Answer: The car will travel about ____ inches in one minute.

EXAMPLE 2 Using Radius to Find Circumference

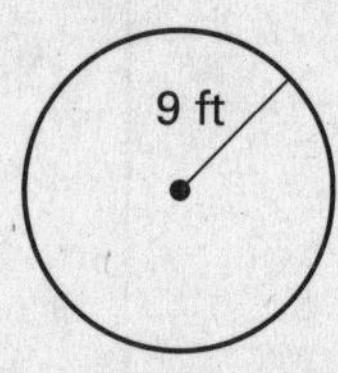

Find the circumference of the circle shown.

The diameter of a circle is twice the radius. Use $C =$ ____ to find the circumference when you know the radius of a circle.

$C =$ ____	Write the formula for the circumference of a circle.
$\approx$ ____(____)(____)	Substitute ____ for π and ____ for r.
$=$ ____	Simplify.

Answer: The circumference of the circle is about ____ feet.

Your turn now **Find the circumference of the circle.**

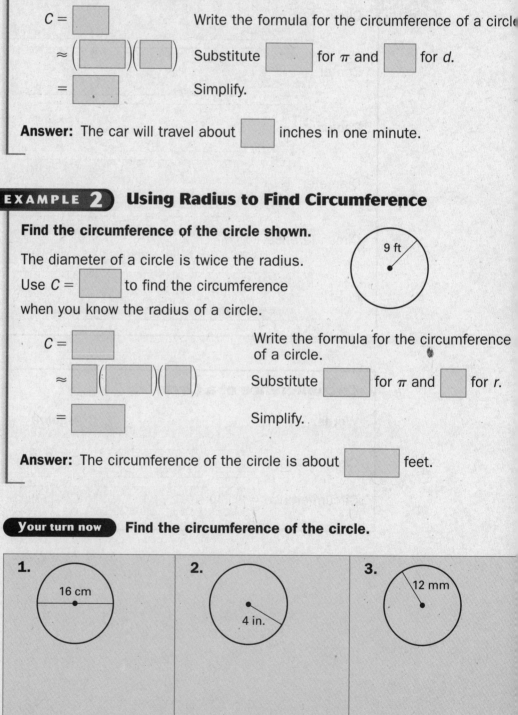

1. 16 cm

2.

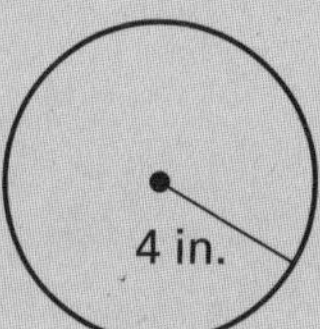

3.

EXAMPLE 3 Choosing an Approximation of Pi

When the diameter or radius of a circle is a multiple of 7, use $\frac{22}{7}$ for π.

Find the circumference of a circle with a diameter of 21 meters.

Because the diameter is a multiple of ____, use ____ for π.

$C =$ ____ Use the formula for the circumference of a circle.

$\approx$ ____ $\cdot$ ____ Substitute ____ for π and ____ for d.

$=$ $\frac{\_\_\_\_ \cdot \_\_\_\_^{\_\_\_\_}}{\_\_\_\__{\_\_\_\_}}$ Multiply. Divide out the common factor.

$=$ ____ Simplify.

Answer: The circumference of the circle is about ____ meters.

Your turn now **Find the circumference of the circle described. Tell what value you used for π. Explain your choice.**

4. $d = 18$ in.	**5.** $d = 28$ mm	**6.** $r = 56$ cm

EXAMPLE 4 Applying Circumference

Garden You are making the circular garden shown. The garden will be bordered by bricks that are 6 inches long. Estimate how many bricks you will need for the garden.

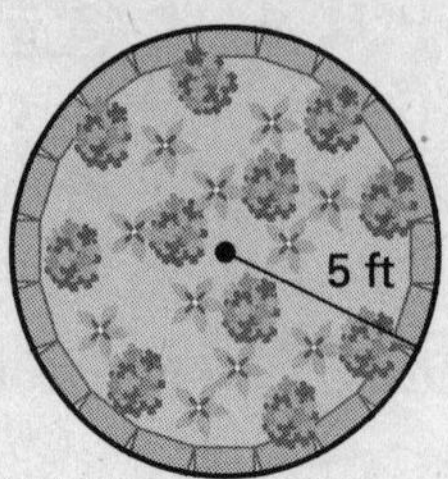

WATCH OUT!
Make sure that you are using the correct units when solving a problem. In Example 4, you can convert the length of the brick from inches to feet so that the brick length and the circumference of the garden are in the same units.

Solution

1. Find the circumference of the garden.

$C =$ ______ Write the formula for the circumferenc of a circle.

$\approx$ ______(______)(______) Substitute ______ for π and ______ for r.

$=$ ______ Simplify.

2. Estimate the number of bricks that you will need.

To estimate the number of bricks, divide the circumference by the bric length in feet.

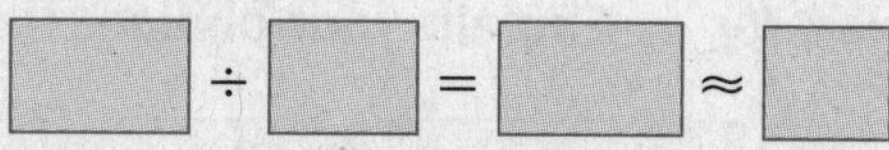

______ $\div$ ______ $=$ ______ $\approx$ ______

Answer: You will need about ______ bricks for the garden.

Area of a Circle

Goal: Find the area of a circle.

Area of a Circle

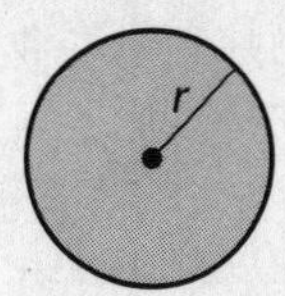

Words Area = (___) • (___)^2

Algebra $A =$ ___

EXAMPLE 1 Finding the Area of a Circle

Swimming Pool A cover is being made for the top of the swimming pool shown. How many square feet of material will you need to cover the pool?

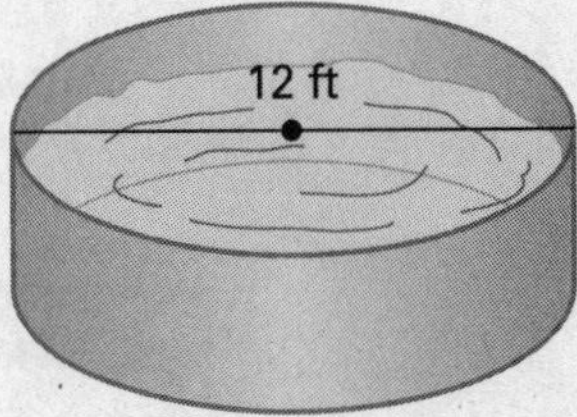

Solution

To answer the question, find the area of a circle with a diameter of 12 feet. Round to the nearest square foot.

Because the diameter is 12 feet, the radius is 12 ___ 2 = ___ feet.

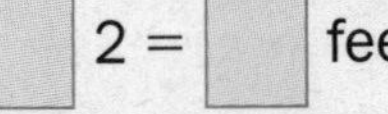

$A =$ ___ Write the formula for the area of a circle.

$\approx$ (___) • (___)^2 Substitute ___ for π and ___ for r.

$=$ ___ Simplify.

Answer: You will need about ___ square feet of material to cover the top of the pool.

Your turn now **Find the area of the circle.**

1. 22 ft

2. 9 cm

3. 5 m

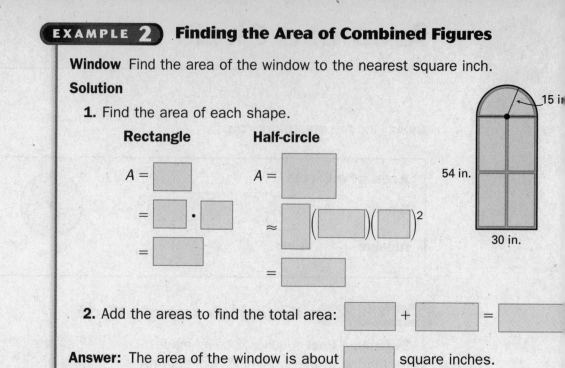

EXAMPLE 2 Finding the Area of Combined Figures

Window Find the area of the window to the nearest square inch.

Solution

1. Find the area of each shape.

Rectangle

$A =$ ____

$=$ ____ $\cdot$ ____

$=$ ____

Half-circle

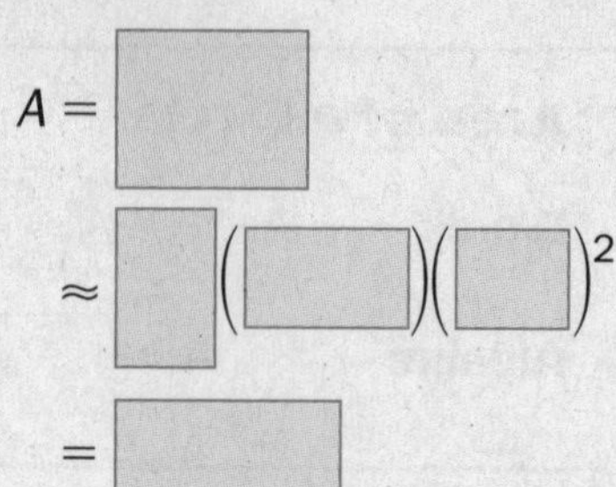

$A =$ ____

$\approx$ ____ (____)(____)^2

$=$ ____

2. Add the areas to find the total area: ____ + ____ = ____

Answer: The area of the window is about ____ square inches.

EXAMPLE 3 Comparing Areas

Drums How many times as great as the area of the top of a drum with a 10-inch diameter is the area of the top of a drum with a 14-inch diameter?

Solution

WATCH OUT!
Be sure to read diagrams carefully. The diagrams in Example 3 give the diameters of the drums. To find the area of the top of each drum, you must first find its *radius*.

1. Find the area of the top of each drum.

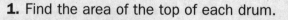

10-inch diameter

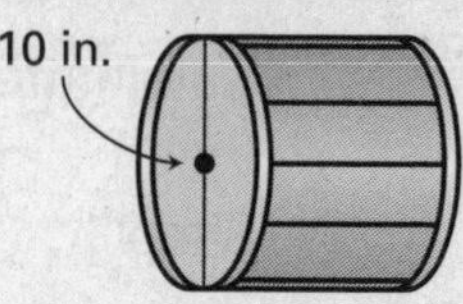

$A =$ ____

$\approx$ (____)(____)^2

$=$ ____ in.^{2}

14-inch diameter

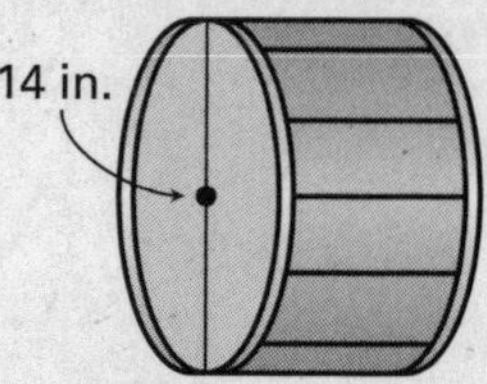

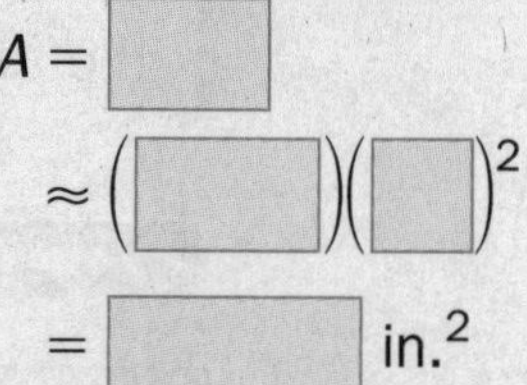

$A =$ ____

$\approx$ (____)(____)^2

$=$ ____ in.^{2}

2. Divide the area of the top of the drum with a 14-inch diameter by the area of the top of the drum with the 10-inch diameter.

$\frac{\text{____}}{\text{____}} =$ ____

Answer: The area of the top of the drum with a 14-inch diameter is about ____ times the area of the top of the drum with a 10-inch diameter.

Your turn now **Find the area of the figure to the nearest whole unit.**

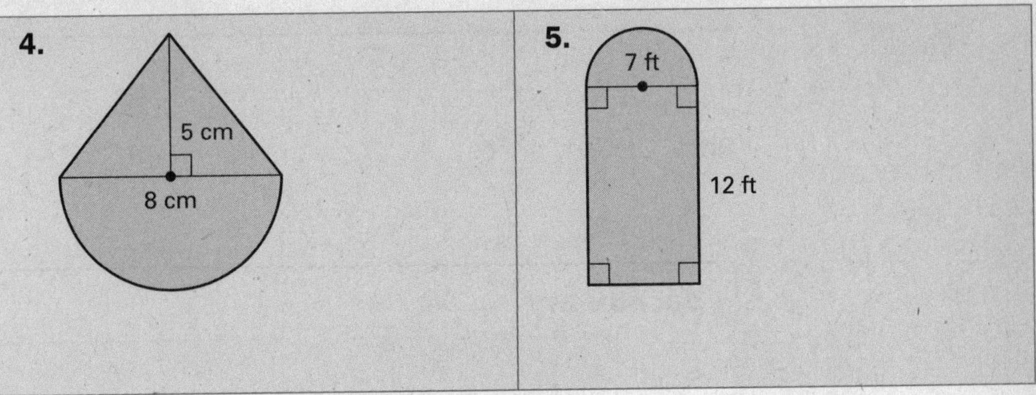

EXAMPLE 4 Making a Circle Graph

Arts Fair The table shows what fraction of the booths at an arts fair contain paintings, pottery, and clothing. Make a circle graph to represent the data.

Booth Contents	Paintings	Pottery	Clothing
Fraction of Booths	$\frac{3}{5}$	$\frac{1}{4}$	$\frac{3}{20}$

Solution

1. Find the angle measure of each sector. Each sector's angle measure is a fraction of 360°. Multiply each fraction in the table by 360° to get the angle measure for each sector.

Paintings

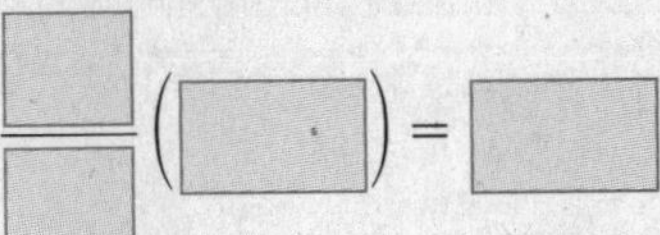

Pottery

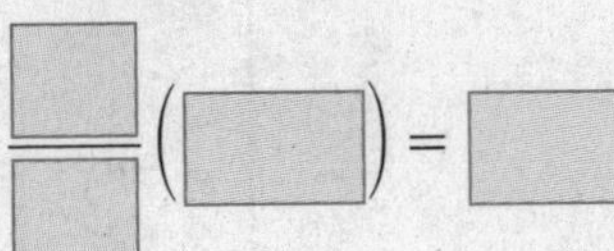

Clothing

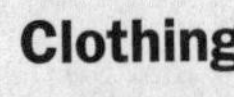

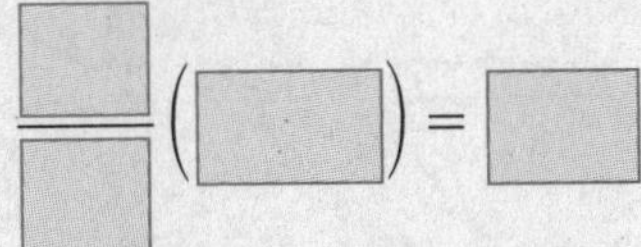

Need help with reading and interpreting circle graphs? See page 88 of your textbook.

2. Draw the circle graph.
   a. Use a compass to draw a circle.
   b. Use a protractor to draw the angle for each sector.
   c. Label each sector and give your graph a title.

Solid Figures

Goal: Classify solids.

For Your Notebook

Vocabulary

Solid:

Prism:

Cylinder:

Pyramid:

Cone:

Sphere:

Face:

Edge:

Vertex:

Classifying Solids

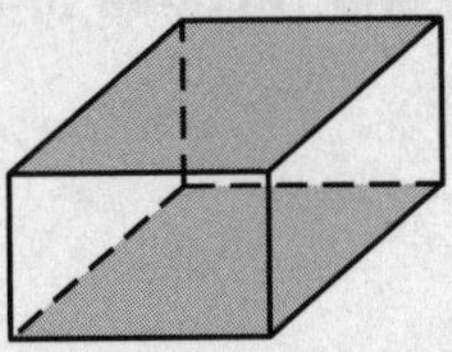

Rectangular prism

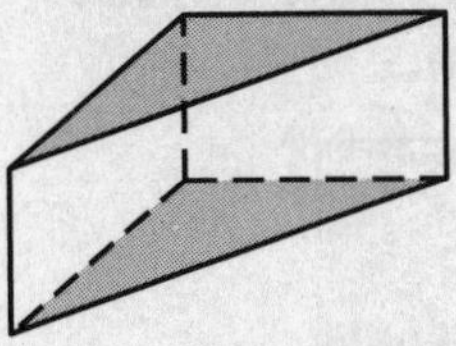

Triangular prism

A ______ is a solid with two ______ bases that are ______ polygons.

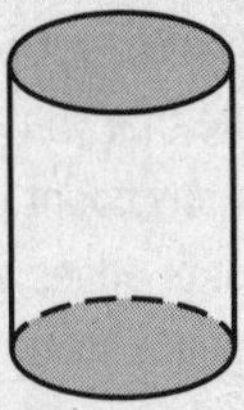

A ______ is a solid with two ______ bases that are ______ circles.

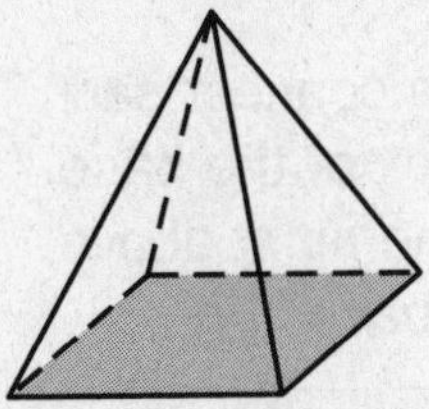

A ______ is a solid made up of ______. The base can be any ______, and the other polygons are ______ that share a common ______.

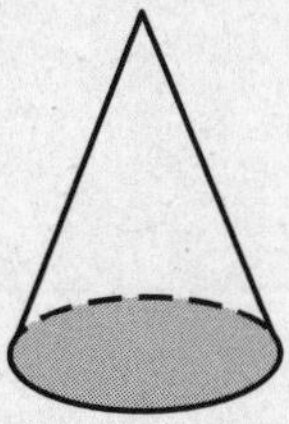

A ______ is a solid that has one ______ base and a ______ that is not in the same plane.

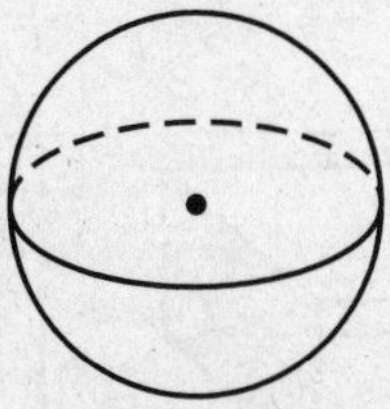

A ______ is the set of all points that are the same ______ from a point called the ______.

EXAMPLE 1 **Classifying Solids**

WATCH OUT!
The base(s) of a prism do not have to be on the top or bottom of the solid. They can be on the left- or right-hand side of the solid as in Example 1(c).

Classify the solid.

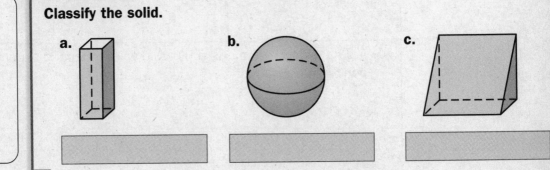

a.

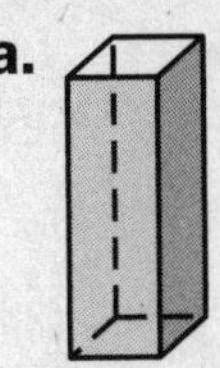

______

b.

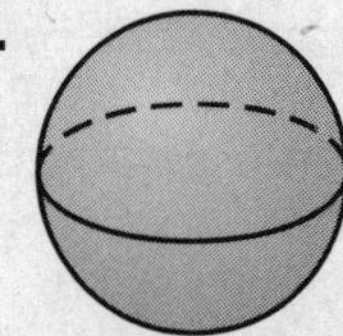

______

c.

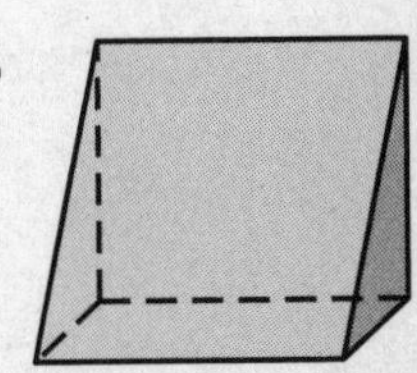

______

EXAMPLE 2 Counting Faces, Edges, and Vertices

To make sure that you accurately count the number of edges and vertices in a solid, you can make a mark on each edge and vertex as you are counting.

Count the number of faces, edges, and vertices of the triangular prism shown.

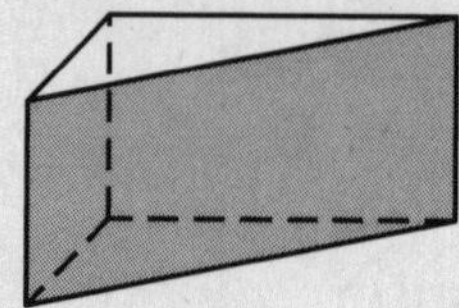

Answer: There are ____ rectangular faces and ____ triangular base(s) for a total of ____ faces. There are ____ edges. There are ____ vertices.

EXAMPLE 3 Drawing a Solid

1. To draw a rectangular pyramid, first draw the base and a point above the base.
2. Then connect each vertex of the base to the point above the base.
3. Partially erase hidden lines to create dashed lines.

Your turn now **Classify the solid. Then count the number of faces, edges and vertices.**

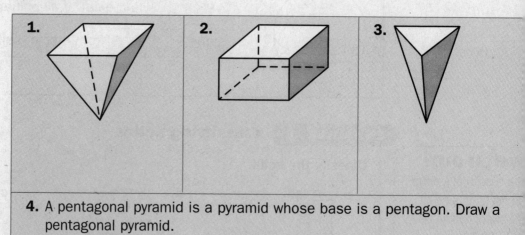

1. 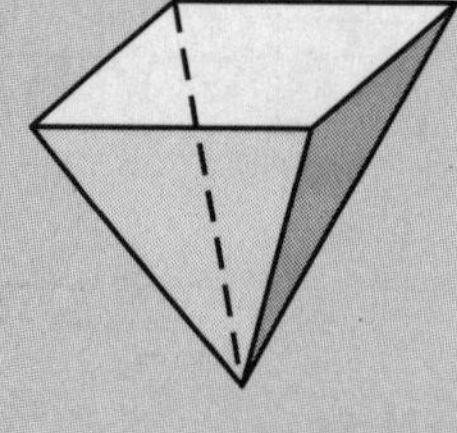

2. 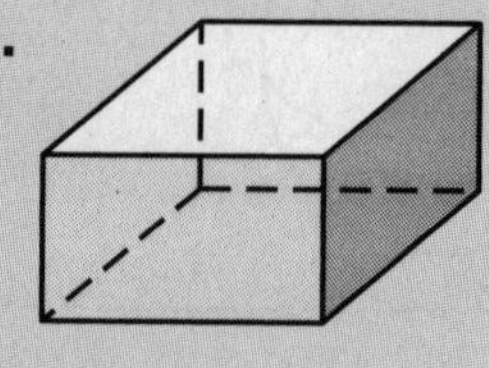

3. 

4. A pentagonal pyramid is a pyramid whose base is a pentagon. Draw a pentagonal pyramid.

Surface Area of a Prism

Goal: Find the surface area of a prism.

Vocabulary

Surface area: ______

EXAMPLE 1 Finding the Surface Area of a Prism

Find the surface area of the rectangular prism.

9 in.
4 in.
6 in.

1. Find the area of each face.

Area of the top or bottom face:

___ × ___ = ___

Area of the front or back face:

___ × ___ = ___

Area of the left or right face:

___ × ___ = ___

2. Add the areas of all six faces to find the surface area.

$S =$ ___ + ___ + ___ + ___ + ___ + ___

= ___

Answer: The surface area is ___ square inches.

EXAMPLE 2 Drawing a Diagram

Find the surface area of a rectangular prism that is 11 centimeters by 3 centimeters by 6 centimeters.

1. Draw a diagram of the prism and label the dimensions.
2. Find the area of each face. Then add these areas to find the surface area.

$S = (\square \times \square) + (\square \times \square) + (\square \times \square)$

$\quad + (\square \times \square) + (\square \times \square) + (\square \times \square)$

$\quad = \square + \square + \square + \square + \square + \square$

$\quad = \square$

Answer: The prism has a surface area of ☐ square centimeters.

EXAMPLE 3 Using Surface Area

Bookshelf A woodworker is putting a veneer, or a thin piece of expensive wood, on a less expensive board to make the bookshelf shown. The woodworker has 350 square inches of veneer. Is there enough veneer to complete the shelf?

Solution

Find the surface area of the shelf and compare it to the amount of veneer available.

$S = \square + \square + \square + \square + \square + \square$

$\quad = \square$

Answer: The surface area of the shelf is ☐ square inches. There are ☐ square inches of veneer available. The woodworker ☐ have enough veneer to complete the shelf.

Your turn now **In Exercises 2 and 3, you may want to draw a diagram.**

1. Find the surface area of the rectangular prism shown.

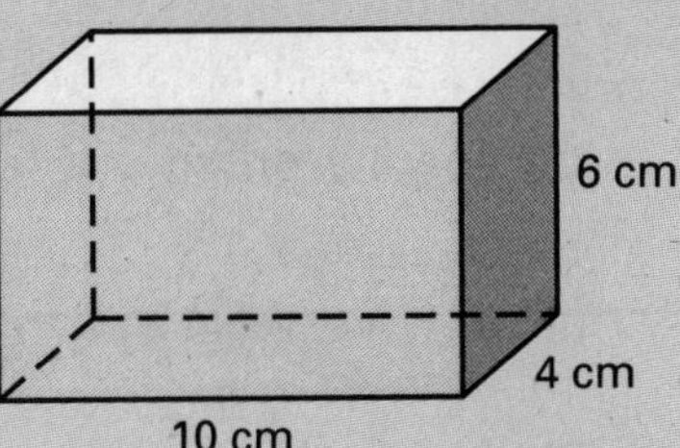

2. A rectangular prism is 2 meters by 5 meters by 5 meters. Find its surface area.

3. You want to paint a door that is 35 inches by 2 inches by 78 inches. The label on the can of paint says the paint covers a total area of 6000 square inches. Do you have enough paint to put 2 coats of paint on the door?

Volume of a Prism

Goal: Find the volume of a rectangular prism.

Vocabulary

Volume: ____

EXAMPLE 1 Counting Cubes in a Stack

Stacking Boxes A grocery store stocker is stacking cube-shaped boxes as shown. How many boxes are stacked?

Solution

To find the total number of boxes, multiply the number of boxes in one layer by the number of layers. The boxes are stacked in ____ layers. Each layer is a rectangle that is ____ boxes long and ____ boxes wide.

Boxes in one layer × Number of layers = Number of boxes

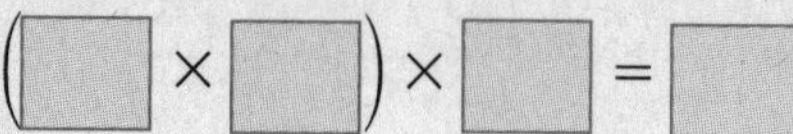

$(\_\_\_\_ \times \_\_\_\_) \times \_\_\_\_ = \_\_\_\_$

Answer: There are ____ boxes stacked so far.

If you have small building blocks, build a model of the figure shown in Example 1. Count the number of blocks you used in the model to check your answer.

Volume of a Rectangular Prism

Words Volume = ____ • ____ • ____

Algebra $V =$ ____

h ℓ w

EXAMPLE 2 Finding the Volume of a Prism

Find the volume of the rectangular prism.

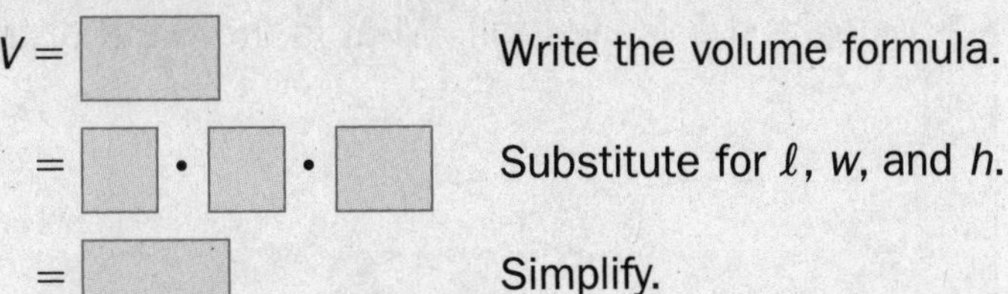

$V =$ ______ Write the volume formula.

$=$ ______ $\cdot$ ______ $\cdot$ ______ Substitute for ℓ, w, and h.

$=$ ______ Simplify.

20 cm

8 cm

7 cm

Answer: The volume is ______ cubic centimeters.

ATCH OUT!
urface area is
easured in square
its and volume is
easured in cubic
its.

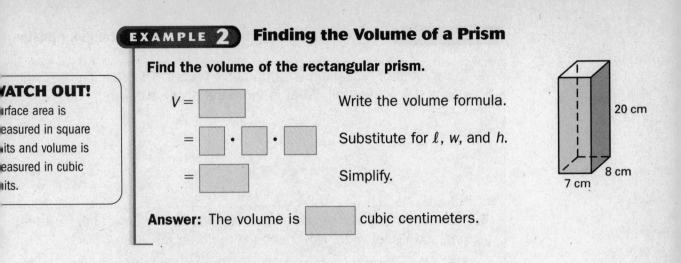

Your turn now **Find the volume of the rectangular prism.**

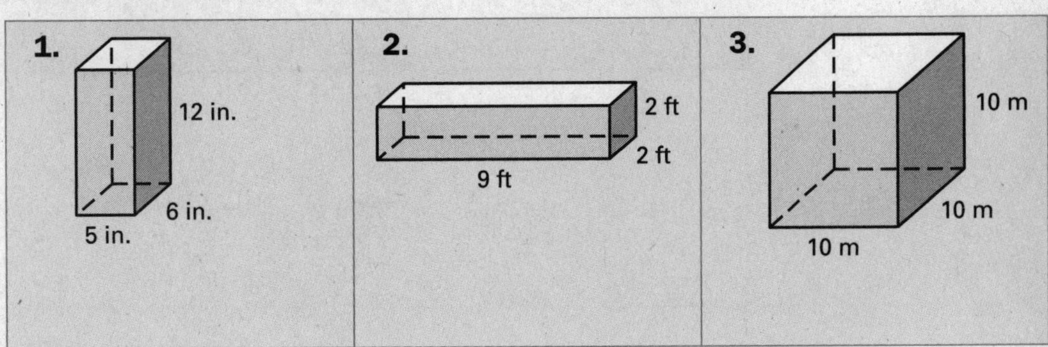

EXAMPLE 3 Using the Formula for Volume

Fish Hatchery A holding tank at a fish hatchery is 4 feet wide and 18 feet long. The volume of the tank is 576 cubic feet. How deep is the tank?

Solution

______ $=$ ______ Write the volume formula.

______ $=$ ______ $\cdot$ ______ $\cdot$ ______ Substitute for V, ℓ, and w.

______ $=$ ______ $\cdot$ ______ Simplify.

______ $=$ ______ $\div$ ______ Write a related division equation.

______ $=$ ______ Simplify.

Answer: The depth of the tank is ______ feet.

Your turn now **In Exercises 4 and 5, the solids are rectangular prisms.**

4. The volume of a cushion is 2000 cubic inches. The cushion is 20 inche long and 5 inches tall. What is the width of the cushion?

5. The volume of a flower box is 140 cubic feet. The flower box is 5 feet long and 7 feet wide. How deep is the flower box?

Words to Review

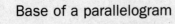

Give an example of the vocabulary word.

Base of a parallelogram

Height of a parallelogram

Perpendicular

Base of a triangle

Height of a triangle

Circle

Center

Radius

Diameter

Circumference

Pi (π)

Solid

Prism

Cylinder

Pyramid

Cone

Sphere

Face

Edge

Vertex

Surface area

Volume

Review your notes and Chapter 10 by using the Chapter Review on pages 518–519 of your textbook.

Comparing Integers

Goal: Compare and order integers.

For Your Notebook

Vocabulary

Integer:

Positive integers:

Negative integers:

Opposites:

EXAMPLE 1 Using Integers

In your notes, keep a list of words that could indicate a positive integer (increase, profit, above) and a list of words that could indicate a negative integer (loss, decrease, below).

Write the integer that represents the situation.

a. A fence post should reach a depth of 5 feet below ground level.

Answer: ☐ feet

b. A 14 point increase

Answer: ☐ points

Your turn now **Write the integer that represents the situation.**

1. a \$25 loss	**2.** an increase of 2 inches	**3.** 17 feet above sea level

EXAMPLE 2 Identifying Opposites

Find the opposite of −5.

The integer −5 is read as "negative 5" or as "the opposite of 5."

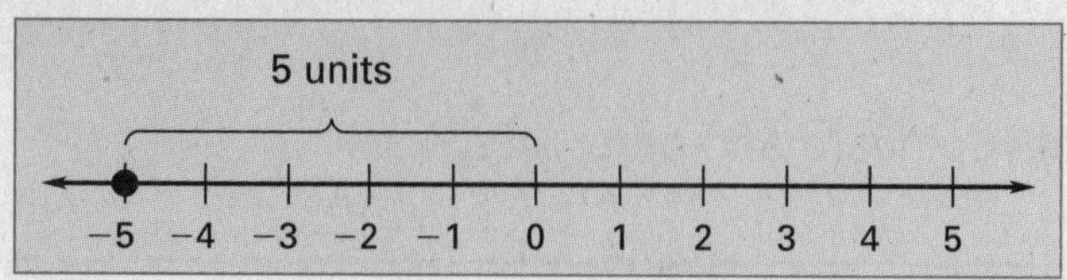

Answer: The opposite of −5 is ☐.

EXAMPLE 3 Comparing Integers

Compare −7 and −2.

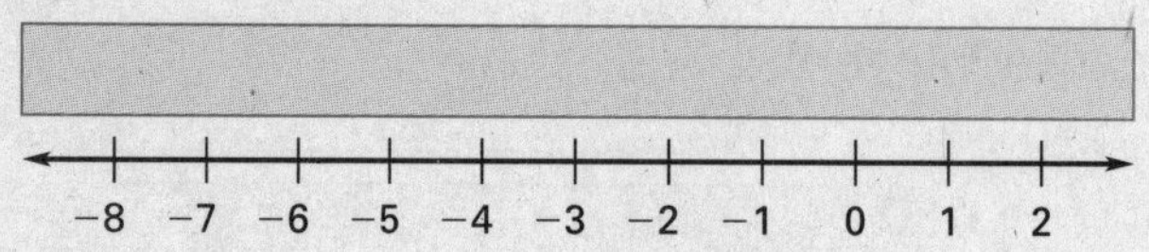

Answer: Because −7 is to the ☐ of −2 on the number line, −7 ☐ −2.

Your turn now **Find the opposite of the integer.**

4. 2	**5.** −6	**6.** −17	**7.** 1

Copy and complete the statement using < or >.

8. −8 ? 8	**9.** 0 ? −10	**10.** 6 ? −7	**11.** −3 ? −4

EXAMPLE 4 Ordering Integers

Lakes The table shows the elevations, with respect to sea level, of several natural lakes in the world. Which lake has the lowest elevation?

Lake	Elevation (with respect to sea level)
Caspian Sea	−92 feet
Lagoda	13 feet
Maracaibo	0 feet
Eyre	−52 feet
Nettilling	95 feet

Solution

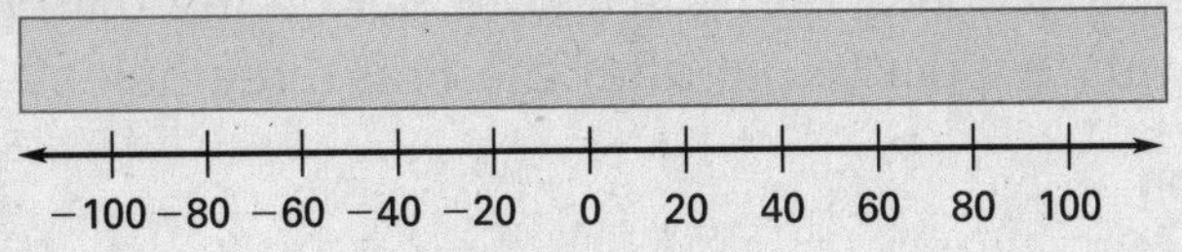

Answer: The ______ has the lowest elevation.

Adding Integers

Goal: Add integers.

Vocabulary

Absolute value: ______

EXAMPLE 1 **Modeling Integer Addition**

Golf During a game of golf, you score 4 over par on the first hole, 3 under par on the second hole, and 1 over par on the third hole. What is your total score with respect to par after the first three holes?

Solution

To understand the problem, read and organize the information.

First hole: ______ means 4 over par

Second hole: ______ means 3 under par

Third hole: ______ means 1 over par

Words like "over" and "under" can be used to indicate positive and negative integers respectively.

Start at ______ on a number line. Use arrows to represent over par and under par. Move ______ to add a positive number and ______ to add a negative number.

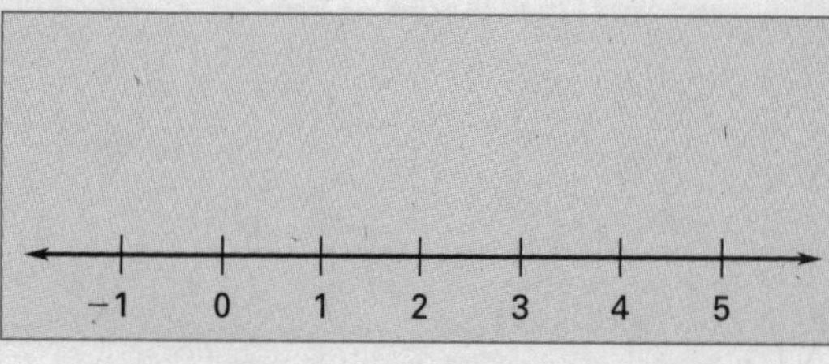

First hole: 0 + ______ = ______

Second hole: ______ + ______ = ______

Third hole: ______ + ______ = ______

Answer: Your total score after the first three holes is ______ ______ par.

Your turn now **Find the sum using a number line.**

1. $-7 + (-7)$

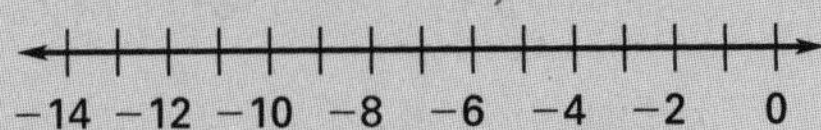

2. $-2 + 2$

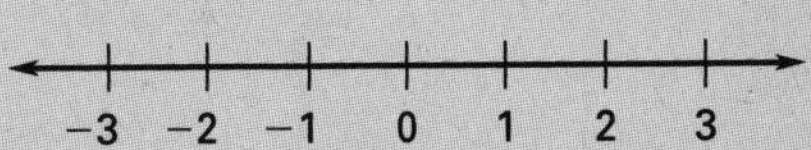

3. $-9 + 13$

−10 −8 −6 −4 −2 0 2 4

4. $4 + (-6)$

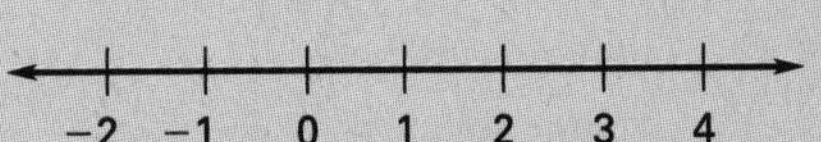

Adding Integers

Words	Numbers
Same Sign To add two integers with the same sign, add their ______ and write their ______.	$1 + 4 =$ ______ $-1 + (-4) =$ ______
Different Signs To add two integers with different signs, first subtract the ______ from the ______. Then write the sign of the number with the ______.	$-3 + 11 =$ ______ $3 + (-11) =$ ______

EXAMPLE 2 Adding Integers

a. In the sum $-2 + (-9)$, the numbers have ______. To find the sum, find | ___ | ___ | ___ | and write ______.

$-2 + (-9) =$ ___

b. In the sum $-5 + 2$, the numbers have ______ and ___ h the ___ absolute value. To find the sum, find | ___ | ___ | ___ and write ______.

$-5 + 2 =$ ___

When you find the sum of two numbers with different signs, you first find the number with the greater absolute value.

c. In the sum $-8 + 15$, the numbers have ______ and ___ h the greater absolute value. To find the sum, find | ___ | ___ | ___ |.

$-8 + 15 =$ ___

Your turn now **Find the absolute value of each number in the expression. Then find the sum.**

5. $-12 + (-3)$	**6.** $-8 + (-1)$	**7.** $6 + (-11)$	**8.** $32 + (-32)$

LESSON 11.3

Subtracting Integers

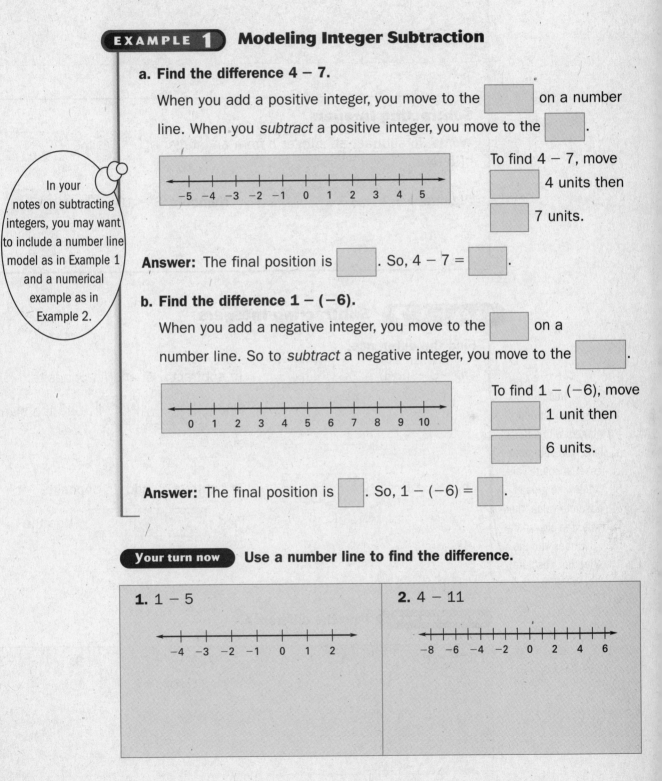

Goal: Subtract integers.

EXAMPLE 1 Modeling Integer Subtraction

a. Find the difference 4 − 7.

When you add a positive integer, you move to the ______ on a number line. When you *subtract* a positive integer, you move to the ______.

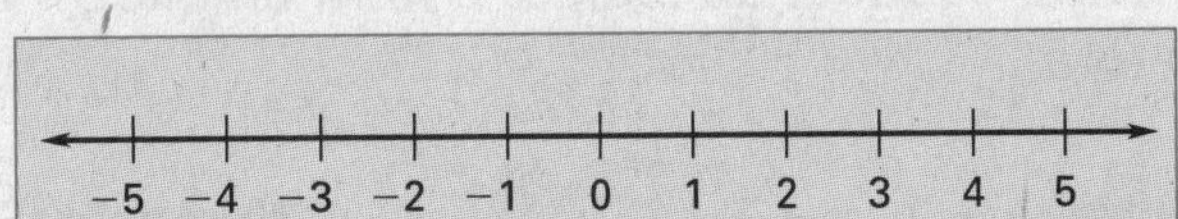

To find 4 − 7, move ______ 4 units then ______ 7 units.

Answer: The final position is ______. So, 4 − 7 = ______.

In your notes on subtracting integers, you may want to include a number line model as in Example 1 and a numerical example as in Example 2.

b. Find the difference 1 − (−6).

When you add a negative integer, you move to the ______ on a number line. So to *subtract* a negative integer, you move to the ______.

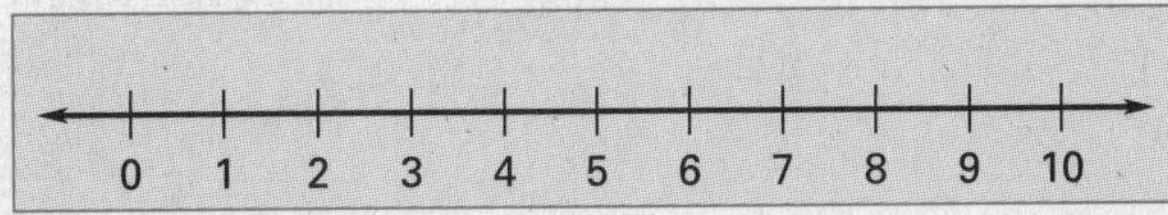

To find 1 − (−6), move ______ 1 unit then ______ 6 units.

Answer: The final position is ______. So, 1 − (−6) = ______.

Your turn now **Use a number line to find the difference.**

1. 1 − 5

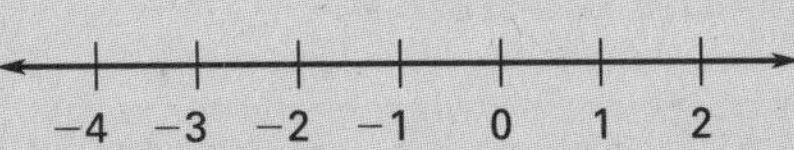

2. 4 − 11

3. $8 - (-2)$	**4.** $0 - (-6)$
 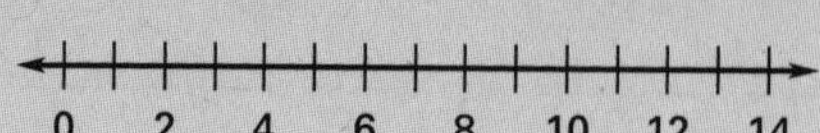	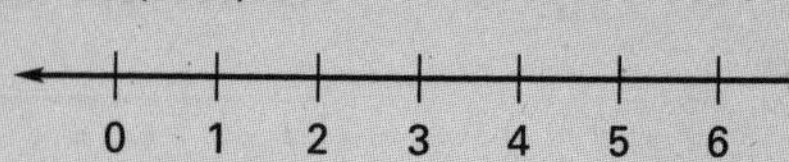

Subtracting Integers

Words To subtract an integer b from an integer a, ______ the ______ of b to a.

Algebra $a - b = a +$ ______

Numbers $8 - 10 = 8 +$ ______

$4 - (-9) = 4 +$ ______

EXAMPLE 2 Subtracting Integers

Find the difference.

a. $-3 - (-6) = -3$ ______ ______

$=$ ______

To subtract -6, add its opposite.

Find | ______ | | ______ | | ______ |. Use the sign of ______.

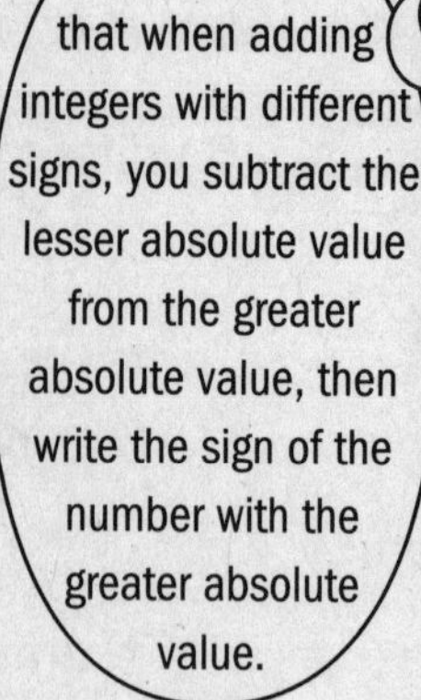

b. $-2 - 8 = -2$ ______ ______

$=$ ______

To subtract 8, add its opposite.

Find | ______ | | ______ | | ______ |. Use the ______ sign.

Your turn now **Find the difference.**

5. $5 - 8$	**6.** $-9 - 4$	**7.** $2 - (-7)$	**8.** $-1 - (-3)$

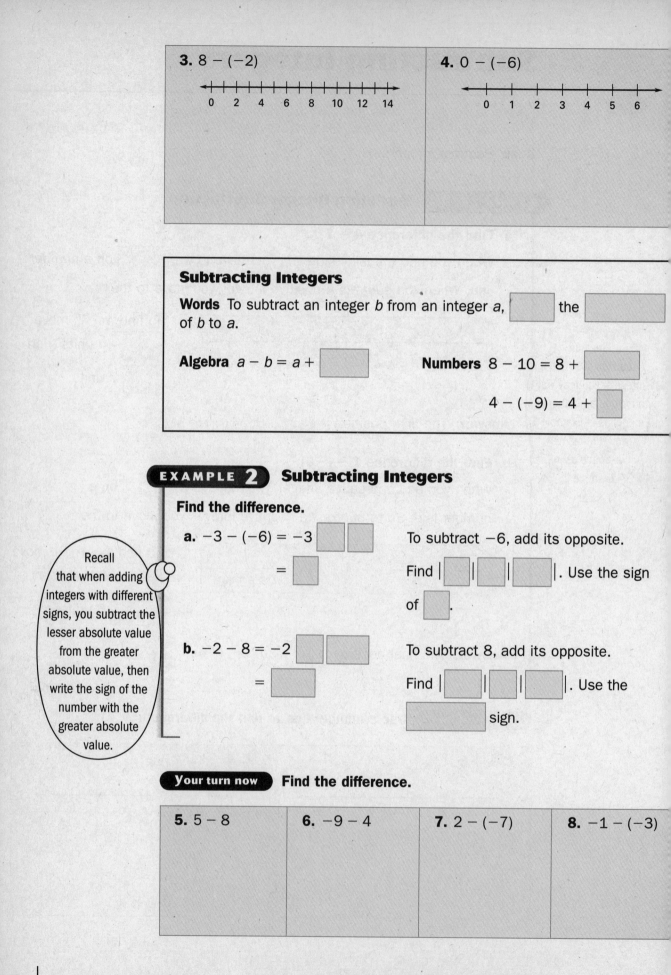

EXAMPLE 3 Using Integers to Solve Problems

Temperatures In the state of Washington, the highest recorded temperature was 118 degrees Fahrenheit above zero and the lowest recorded temperature was 48 degrees Fahrenheit below zero. What is the difference of the highest recorded temperature and the lowest recorded temperature?

Solution

1. Use integers to represent the two temperatures.

highest: ______ °F **lowest:** ______ °F

2. Subtract the lesser temperature from the greater.

______ − ______ = ______ + ______ To subtract ______, add its opposite.

= ______ Simplify.

Answer: The difference of the temperatures is ______ degrees Fahrenheit.

LESSON 11.4

Multiplying Integers

Goal: Multiply integers.

Multiplying Integers

Words	Numbers
The product of two positive integers is ______.	6(3) = ______
The product of two negative integers is ______.	−2(−7) = ______
The product of a positive integer and a negative integer is ______.	5(−4) = ______

EXAMPLE 1 **Multiplying Integers**

a. −9(−3) = ______ The product of two negative integers is ______

b. 6(−5) = ______ The product of a positive integer and a negative integer is ______.

c. −4(20) = ______ The product of a negative integer and a positive integer is ______.

Your turn now **Find the product.**

1. 6(7)	**2.** −3(−12)	**3.** 5(−5)	**4.** −2(8)

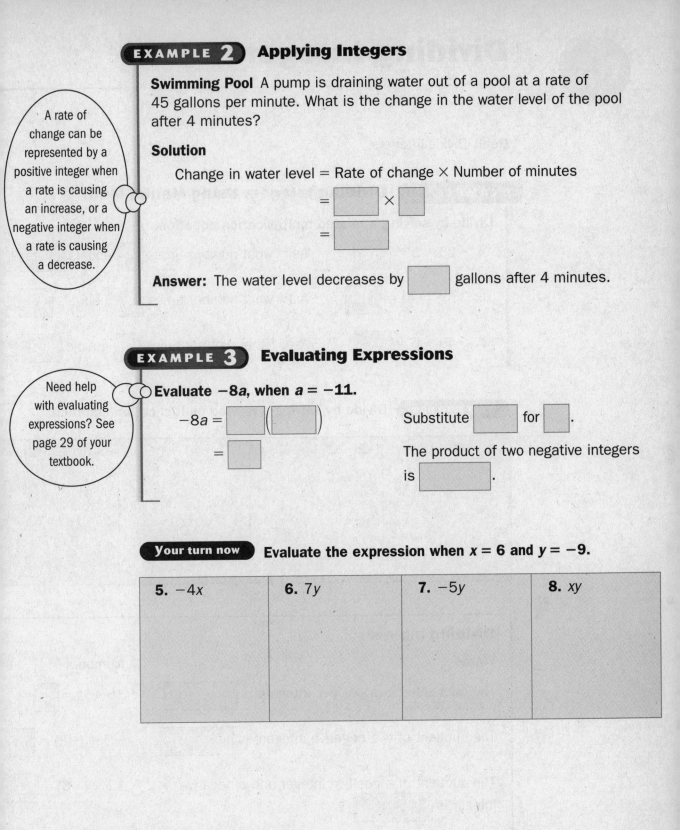

EXAMPLE 2 Applying Integers

Swimming Pool A pump is draining water out of a pool at a rate of 45 gallons per minute. What is the change in the water level of the pool after 4 minutes?

A rate of change can be represented by a positive integer when a rate is causing an increase, or a negative integer when a rate is causing a decrease.

Solution

Change in water level = Rate of change × Number of minutes

= ____ × ____

= ____

Answer: The water level decreases by ____ gallons after 4 minutes.

EXAMPLE 3 Evaluating Expressions

Need help with evaluating expressions? See page 29 of your textbook.

Evaluate $-8a$, when $a = -11$.

$-8a =$ ____ (____) Substitute ____ for ____.

= ____ The product of two negative integers is ____.

Your turn now **Evaluate the expression when $x = 6$ and $y = -9$.**

5. $-4x$	6. $7y$	7. $-5y$	8. xy

Dividing Integers

Goal: Divide integers.

EXAMPLE 1 **Dividing Integers Using Mental Math**

Divide by solving a related multiplication equation.

a. $-25 \div 5 =$ ☐ Ask "what number times ☐ equals ☐?"

b. $36 \div (-4) =$ ☐ Ask "what number times ☐ equals ☐?"

c. $-48 \div 6 =$ ☐ Ask, "what number times ☐ equals ☐?"

Your turn now **Divide by solving a related multiplication equation.**

1. $-21 \div 3$	**2.** $20 \div (-4)$	**3.** $-40 \div (-5)$	**4.** $0 \div (-2)$

Dividing Integers

Words	**Numbers**
The quotient of two positive integers is ☐.	$16 \div 4 =$ ☐
The quotient of two negative integers is ☐.	$-9 \div (-3) =$ ☐
The quotient of a positive integer and a negative integer is ☐.	$12 \div (-6) =$ ☐
The quotient of a negative integer and a positive integer is ☐.	$-18 \div 2 =$ ☐

EXAMPLE 2 Dividing Integers

a. $-72 \div (-8) =$ ☐ — The quotient of two negative integers is ☐.

b. $35 \div (-5) =$ ☐ — The quotient of a positive integer and a negative integer is ☐.

c. $-40 \div 4 =$ ☐ — The quotient of a negative integer and a positive integer is ☐.

EXAMPLE 3 Finding the Mean of Integers

Football A football team keeps track of the number of yards gained or lost during the first play of every game. The table shows the number of yards gained or lost during the first plays of the first three games of a season. Find the mean number of yards gained or lost during the first plays.

Game	Yards Gained or Lost During First Play
1	8 yard gain
2	2 yard loss
3	3 yard gain

Need help finding the mean? See page 93 of your textbook.

Solution

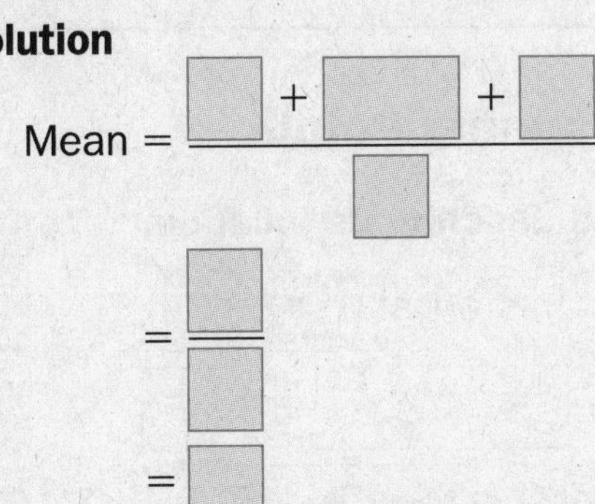

Answer: A mean of ☐ yards was gained during the first plays.

Your turn now **Find the quotient.**

5. $-39 \div 13$	**6.** $26 \div (-2)$	**7.** $8 \div (-8)$	**8.** $-42 \div (-6)$

Translations in a Coordinate Plane

Goal: Graph points with negative coordinates.

For Your Notebook

Vocabulary

Coordinate plane:

Quadrant:

Translation:

Image:

EXAMPLE 1 **Graphing Points**

Graph the point and describe its location.

a. To graph $A(-4, 0)$, start at (,).

Move units and units . Point A is .

b. To graph $B(5, -3)$, start at (,).

Move units and units . Point B is .

Need help graphing ordered pairs with positive coordinates? See page 83 of your textbook.

Graph the point and describe its location.

1. $A(0, -1)$	**2.** $B(-3, -2)$
3. $C(-4, 1)$	**4.** $D(2, -5)$

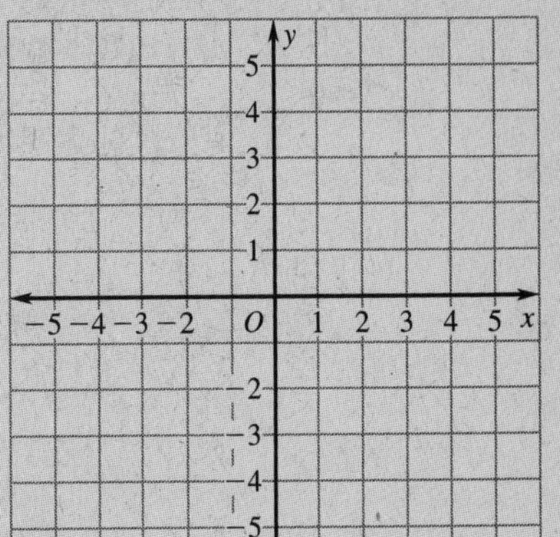

EXAMPLE 2 Translating a Figure

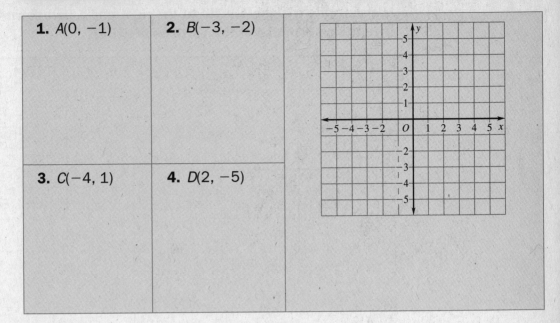

Stenciling You are creating a design on grid paper that will be used to make a stencil. In the design, $\triangle ABC$ will be translated 5 units to the right and 3 units down. The images of points A, B, and C will be points Q, R, and S respectively. Draw the image and give the coordinates of points Q, R, and S.

Solution

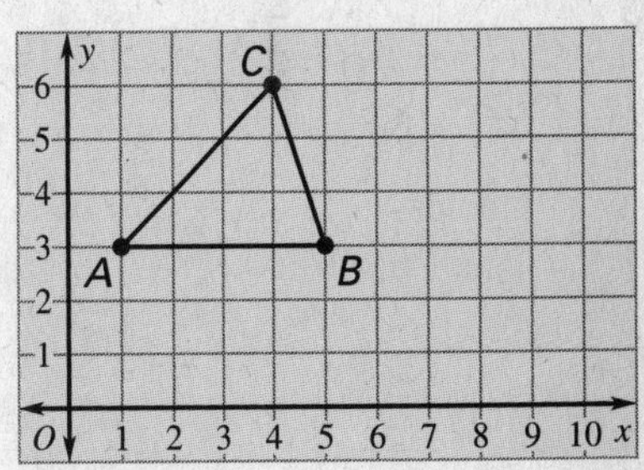

To draw the image, think of ______ the original figure 5 units to the right and 3 units down. You'll get the same image if you ______ the x-coordinates and ______ the y-coordinates.

$A(1, 3) \rightarrow (1\ \square\ \square, 3\ \square\ \square) \rightarrow Q(\square, \square)$

$B(5, 3) \rightarrow (5\ \square\ \square, 3\ \square\ \square) \rightarrow R(\square, \square)$

$C(4, 6) \rightarrow (4\ \square\ \square, 6\ \square\ \square) \rightarrow S(\square, \square)$

Answer: The coordinates are $Q(\square, \square)$, $R(\square, \square)$, and $S(\square, \square)$.

Your turn now **Graph the points and connect them to form $\triangle ABC$. Then translate the triangle 4 units to the right and 1 unit down to form $\triangle DEF$. Give the coordinates of the vertices of $\triangle DEF$.**

5. $A(-3, 3)$, $B(-1, -2)$, $C(2, 0)$	**6.** $A(1, -3)$, $B(4, -2)$, $C(-1, 1)$
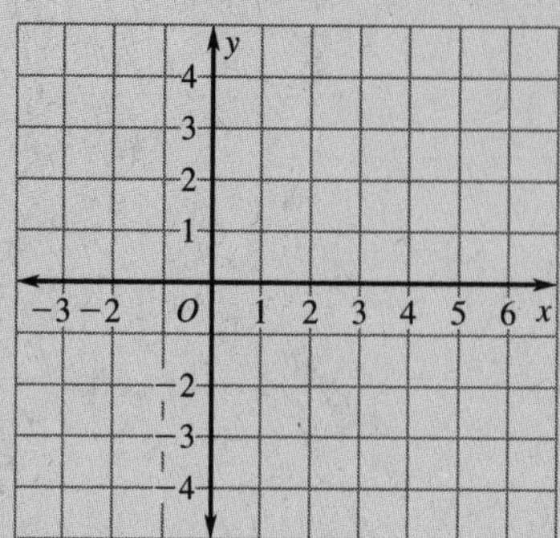	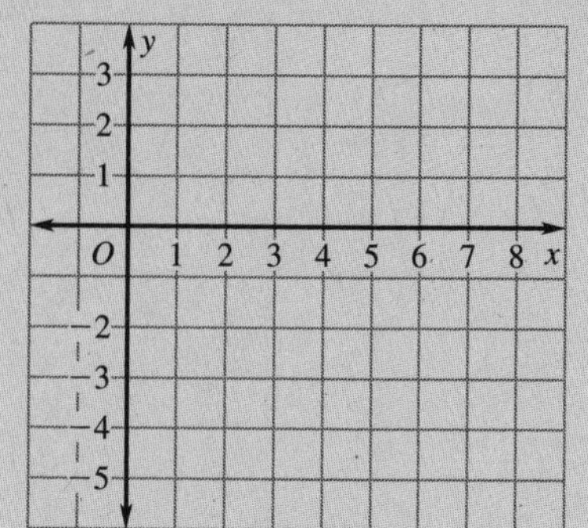

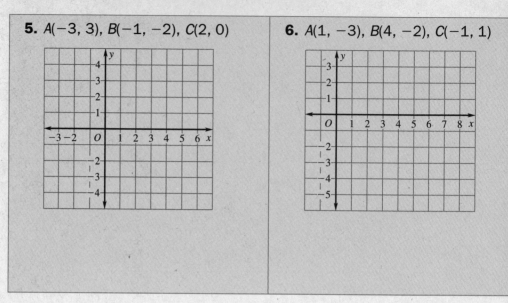

Reflections and Rotations

Goal: Recognize reflections and rotations.

For Your NoteBook

Vocabulary

Reflection:

Line of reflection:

Rotation:

Center of rotation:

Angle of rotation:

Transformation:

EXAMPLE 1 Identifying Reflections

Tell whether the solid figure is a reflection of the dashed figure. If it is a reflection, identify the line of reflection.

In Example 1, you can see that a figure that is not flipped or is not congruent to the original figure cannot be a reflection.

a.

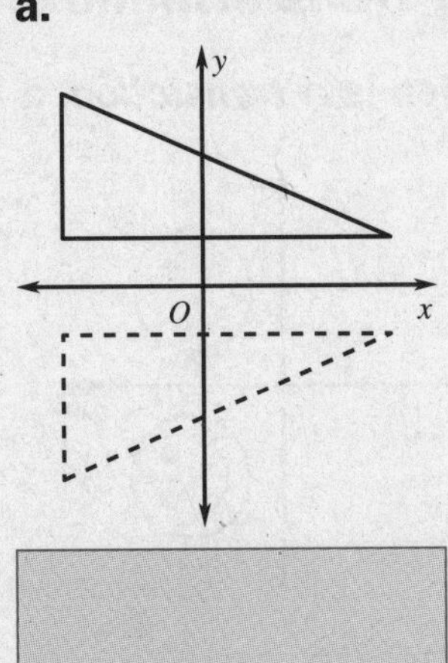

b.

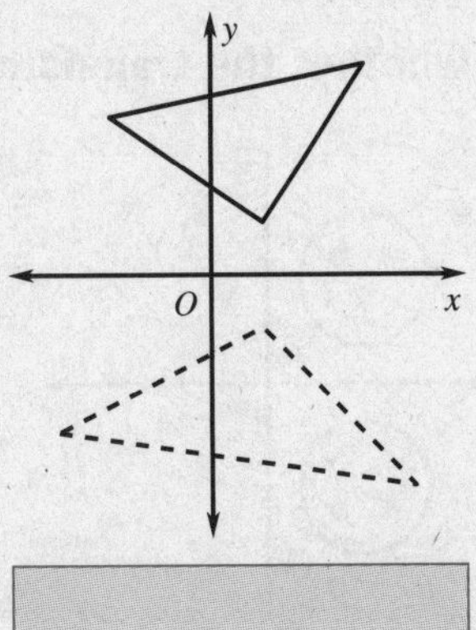

c.

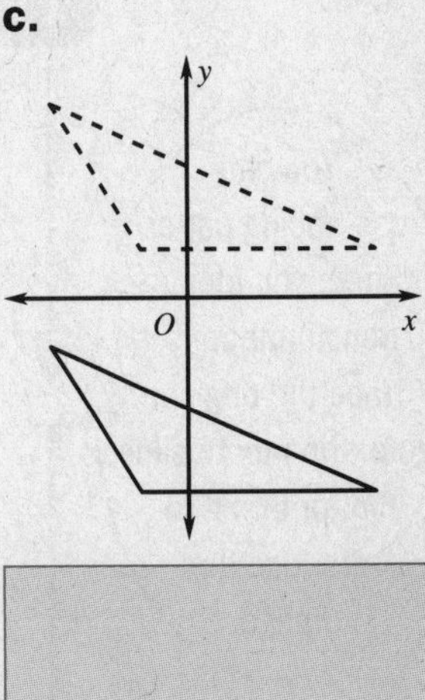

Your turn now Tell whether the outlined figure is a reflection of the solid figure. If it is a reflection, identify the line of reflection.

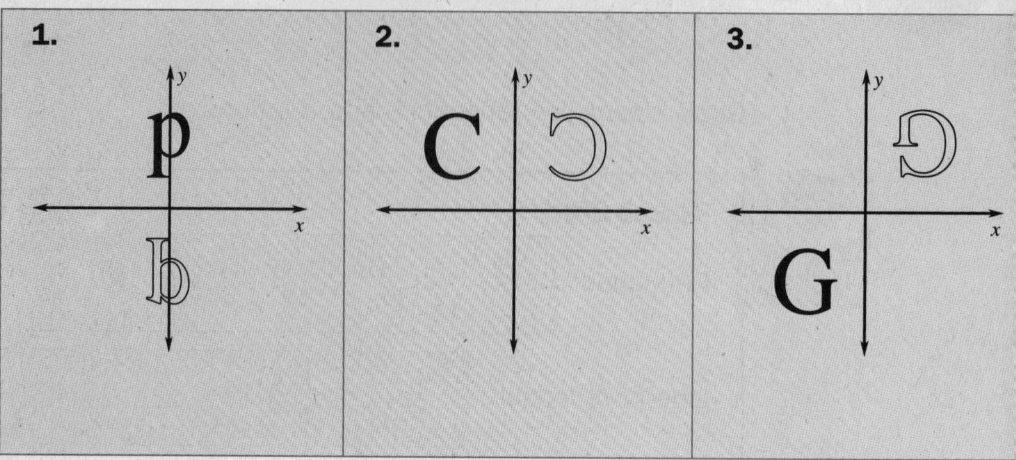

EXAMPLE 2 Identifying Rotations

Tell whether the outlined figure is a rotation of the solid figure about the origin. If it is a rotation, state the angle of rotation.

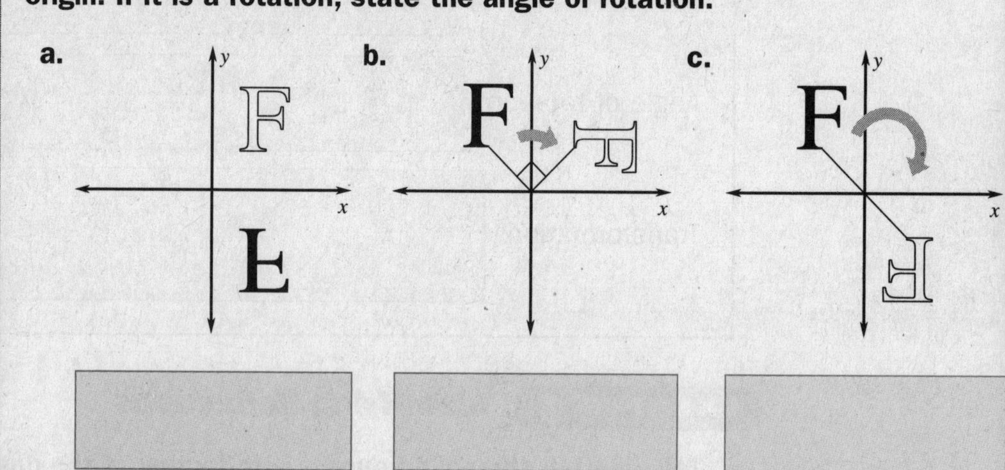

EXAMPLE 3 Identifying Transformations

Tell whether the transformation is a *translation*, a *reflection*, or a *rotation*.

You can use tracing paper to help you identify transformations. Trace the original figure, then try to slide, flip, or turn it to produce the image.

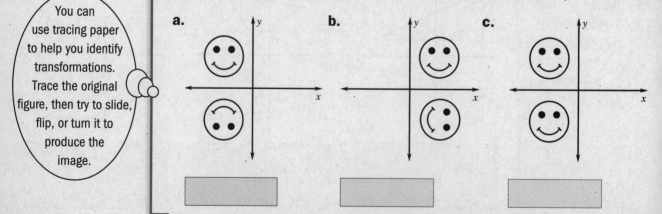

a.

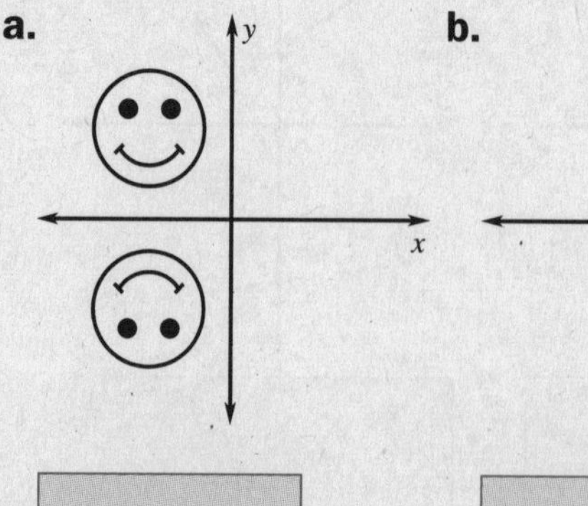

b.

c.

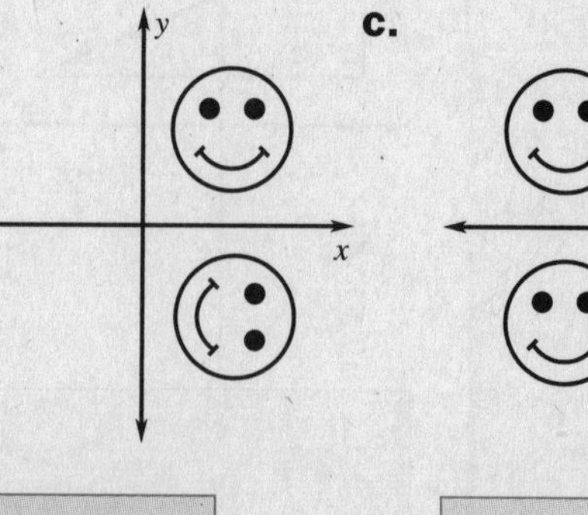

Words to Review

Give an example of the vocabulary word.

Integer

Positive integer

Negative integer

Opposites

Absolute value

Coordinate plane

Quadrant

Translation

Image

Reflection

Line of reflection

Rotation

Center of rotation

Angle of rotation

Transformation

Review your notes and Chapter 11 by using the Chapter Review on pages 576–577 of your textbook.

Writing Expressions and Equations

Goal: Write variable expressions and equations.

In your notebook, make a table of key words that can indicate addition, subtraction, multiplication, or division, like the one shown on page 583 of your textbook.

EXAMPLE 1 Expressions: Adding and Subtracting

Write the phrase as an expression. Let x represent the number.

Phrase	Expression
x cups of flour **increased by** 5 cups	
The **total** of 8 and a number	
A number **subtracted from** 14	
A number **decreased by** 3	

Your turn now **Write the phrase as a variable expression.**

1. A number m increased by 1	**2.** Seven less than a number t
3. The difference of 6 and a number v	**4.** Nine added to a number y
5. The sum of 11 and a number b	**6.** Fifteen fewer than a number n

WATCH OUT!
Order is important with subtraction and division. "The quotient of a number and 6" means $\frac{y}{6}$, not $\frac{6}{y}$.

EXAMPLE 2 Expressions: Multiplying and Dividing

Write the phrase as an expression. Let y represent the number.

Phrase	Expression
A number **multiplied by** 9	___ • ___, or ___
The product of a number and 22	___ • ___, or ___
12 **divided by** the number of feet	___ / ___
The quotient of a number and 17	___ / ___

EXAMPLE 3 Writing Simple Equations

Write the sentence as an equation.

Sentence	Equation
A number b added to 9 **is** 15.	___
The quotient of 25 and a number z **is** 50.	___

EXAMPLE 4 Modeling a Situation

Beach House A family is renting a beach house for a week-long summer vacation. The cost of renting the house is $110 per person per week and the total cost of the house for the week is $1320. Write a multiplication equation that you could use to find the number of people p that are going to the beach house.

Solution

The cost per person is ___ the number of people to get the total cost.

___ • ___ = ___

___ • ___ = ___

Your turn now **In Exercises 7–10, write the sentence as an equation.**

7. The difference of 7 and a number *a* is 2.	**8.** A number *w* times 20 is 160.
9. A number *p* increased by 4 is 10.	**10.** The quotient of a number *c* and 3 is 17.

11. You bought a young tree that is 9 inches tall. According to the label on the tree, the tree will reach a height of 48 inches. Let *g* be the number of inches the tree will grow. Write an addition equation you could use to find *g*.

Solving Addition Equations

Goal: Solve one-step addition equations.

EXAMPLE 1 Solving Equations Using Algebra Tiles

Use algebra tiles to solve $x + 3 = 4$.

1. Represent the equation using algebra tiles. =
2. Take away ___ 1-tiles from each side. =
3. The remaining tiles show that the value of x is ___. =

Answer: The solution is ___.

Your turn now **Use algebra tiles to solve the equation.**

1. $x + 4 = 7$	**2.** $5 + x = 6$
3. $x + 3 = 3$	**4.** $8 + x = 10$

Solving Addition Equations

To solve an addition equation, ___ the same number from each side so that the ___ is by itself on one side.

EXAMPLE 2 Solving an Addition Equation

Solve the equation $z + 46 = 130$.

$z + 46 = 130$ Write the original equation.

______ from each side.

Simplify.

After solving an equation, you should always check your solution.

✓ Check $z + 46 = 130$ Write the original equation.

$\_\_\_ + 46 \stackrel{?}{=} 130$ Substitute ___ for z.

$\_\_\_ = \_\_\_$ ✓ Solution checks.

EXAMPLE 3 Using an Addition Equation

Working You work at your job in 8 hour shifts. Today, you've worked 3.5 hours so far. How many hours h do you have left to work?

Need help with writing a verbal model? See pages 41 and 42 of your textbook.

Solution

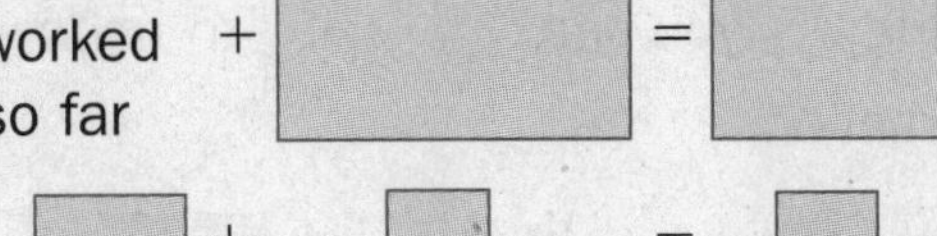

Hours worked so far + ___ = ___ Write a verbal model.

___ + ___ = ___ Write an equation.

______ from each side.

___ = ___ Simplify.

Answer: You have ___ hours left to work.

Your turn now **Solve the equation. Then check the solution.**

5. $c + 35 = 96$	**6.** $28 + m = 150$	**7.** $v + 47 = 83$
8. $z + 3.6 = 12.9$	**9.** $14.85 + b = 36.95$	**10.** $x + 2.25 = 60$

Solving Subtraction Equations

Goal: Solve one-step subtraction equations.

> You can also solve the equation in Example 1 by getting the variable by itself as you did in Lesson 12.2. Instead of subtracting a number from each side of the equation, you add a number to each side of the equation.

EXAMPLE 1 **Working Backward**

Shopping You went to a clothing store and bought a shirt for $25. When yo got home from the store you had $8 left in your wallet. How much money di you go to the store with? You can find the amount of money m you went to the store with by solving the equation $m - 25 = 8$.

Solution

One way to solve the equation to find the amount of money you went to the store with is to work backward.

After spending $25, you have $8 left. $m - 25 = 8$

To find the amount of money m you had before subtracting 25, you can ______ to *undo* the subtraction. ______ $= m$

Answer: You went to the store with $______.

✓ Check $m - 25 = 8$ Write original equation.

______ $- 25 \stackrel{?}{=} 8$ Substitute ______ for m.

______ $=$ ______ ✓ Solution checks.

Solving Subtraction Equations

To solve a subtraction equation, ______ the same number to each side so that the ______ is by itself on one side.

EXAMPLE 2 Solving Subtraction Equations

Solve the equation.

a. $17 = w - 9$ **b.** $a - 2.4 = 15.75$

Solution

a. In this equation, the variable is on the right side of the equation.

$17 = w - 9$ Write the original equation.

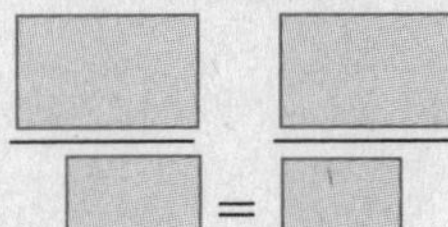

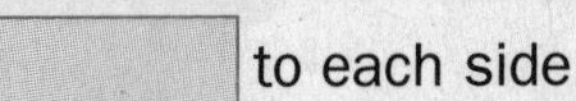 to each side.

Simplify.

b. $a - 2.4 = 15.75$ Write the original equation.

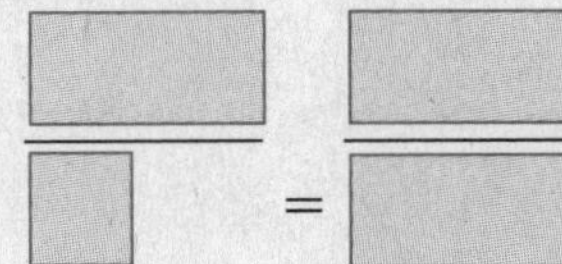

to each side.

Simplify.

WATCH OUT!

Line up decimal points correctly before adding decimals.

WRONG	RIGHT
11.95	11.95
3.1	+3.1
12.26	15.05

EXAMPLE 3 Using a Subtraction Equation

Weather According to a 5 o'clock news report, the temperature has dropped 6 degrees since noon to 19°F. What was the temperature at noon?

Solution

Let n represent the temperature at noon.

= 19 Write an equation.

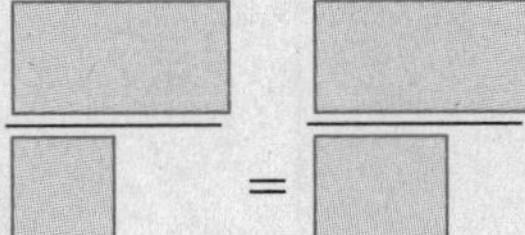

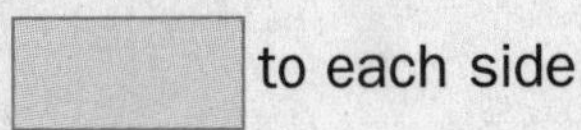 to each side.

Simplify.

Answer: The temperature was °F at noon.

Your turn now **Solve the equation. Then check the solution.**

1. $y - 8 = 5$	**2.** $32 = d - 14$	**3.** $7.8 = m - 4.9$

Solving Multiplication and Division Equations

Goal: Solve multiplication and division equations.

EXAMPLE 1 **Solving a Multiplication Equation**

Solve the equation $7x = 63$.

$7x = 63$ Write the original equation.

____ = ____ ____ each side by ____.

____ = ____ Simplify.

Your turn now **Solve the equation. Then check the solution.**

1. $6m = 42$	**2.** $4y = 60$
3. $27 = 3c$	**4.** $88 = 8p$

Solving Multiplication and Division Equations

You can use multiplication and division to undo each other when trying to get the variable by itself on one side of an equation.

Multiplication Equations To solve a multiplication equation, ____ each side by the number the ____ is multiplied by.

Division Equations To solve a division equation, ____ each side by the ____.

EXAMPLE 2 Solving a Division Equation

Check your solution to Example 2 by dividing your answer by 6. The result should be 10.

Solve the equation $\frac{x}{6} = 10$.

$\frac{x}{6} = 10$ Write the original equation.

= each side by .

= Simplify.

EXAMPLE 3 Using an Equation

Balloons A bag of 75 balloons is split up into bunches of balloons. Each bunch is made up of three balloons. Write and solve a multiplication equation to find b, the number of bunches of balloons.

Solution

= Write an equation.

= 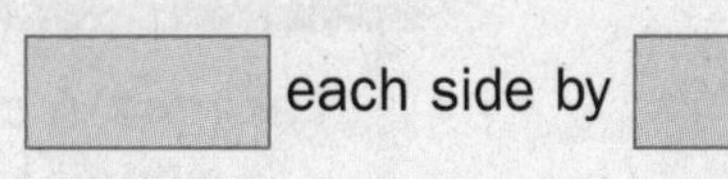

$= b$ Simplify.

Answer: There are bunches.

Your turn now **Solve the equation. Then check the solution.**

5. $\frac{m}{3} = 12$	**6.** $\frac{d}{8} = 5$
7. $24 = \frac{v}{4}$	**8.** $15 = \frac{y}{6}$

Functions

Goal: Evaluate functions and write function rules.

Vocabulary

Function:

Input:

Output:

EXAMPLE 1 Evaluating a Function

Lasagna A cook at a school cafeteria is making pans of lasagna. To make one pan of lasagna, the cook uses 12 ounces of tomato paste. How many ounces of tomato paste does the cook need for 2 pans? for 3 pans? for 4 pans?

Solution

To solve the problem, you can make an *input-output table*. Use the function rule $t = 12p$, where p is the number of pans (input) and t is the number of ounces of tomato paste (output).

Input Pans, p	Substitute in the function $t = 12p$	Output Ounces tomato paste, t
1	$t = 12(1)$	12
2	$t =$	
3	$t =$	
4	$t =$	

Answer: The cook needs ____ ounces of tomato paste for 2 pans, ____ ounces for 3 pans, and ____ ounces for 4 pans.

Your turn now **Make an input-output table using the function rule and the input values $x = 0, 1, 2, 3, 4,$ and 5.**

1. $y = x + 2$	**2.** $y = 5 - x$
3. $y = 4x$	**4.** $y = 2x + 1$

EXAMPLE 2 Using a Table to Write a Rule

A function rule is written so that it tells you what to do to the input to get the output.

Write a function rule for the input-output table.

a.

Input, x	Output, y
10	13
11	14
12	15
13	16

b.

Input, m	Output, n
0	0
4	1
8	2
12	3

Solution

a. Each output y is ________.

A function rule is ________.

b. Each output n is ________.

A function rule is ________.

EXAMPLE 3 Making A Table to Write a Rule

It can be helpful to choose letters that remind you of what the variables stand for. Example 3 uses s and a, the first letters of the words *squares* and *area*.

Pattern Make an input-output table using the number of squares s in the figure as the input and the area a of the figure as the output. Then write a function rule that relates s and a. Each square has a side length of two units.

1 2 3 4

Solution

Each output value is ______ the input value. The area is ______ the number of squares in the figure.

Squares, s	Area, a (square units)

Answer: A function rule for this pattern is ______.

Your turn now **Write a function rule for the relationship.**

5. First make an input-output table. Use the number of dots n in the bottor row as the input and the total number of dots t as the output.

6. Use the input-output table shown.

Input, x	0	8	16	24	32	40
Output, y	0	1	2	3	4	5

Graphing Functions

Goal: Graph linear functions in a coordinate plane.

Vocabulary

Linear function:

EXAMPLE 1 Graphing a Function

Costumes You are purchasing fabric at a store so that you can make costumes for a school play. You find fabric that costs \$3 per yard. The number of yards x of fabric you buy and the amount y you spend on fabric are related by the rule $y = 3x$. Graph the function $y = 3x$.

Solution

1. Make an input-output table for the function $y = 3x$.

Input, x	Output, y
1	
2	
3	
4	

2. Write the input and output values as ordered pairs: (input, output).

(,), (,),
(,), (,)

3. Graph the ordered pairs. Notice that the points all lie along a straight line. If you chose other input values for your table, the points you would graph would also lie along that same line.

4. Draw a line through the points. That line represents the complete graph of the function $y = 3x$.

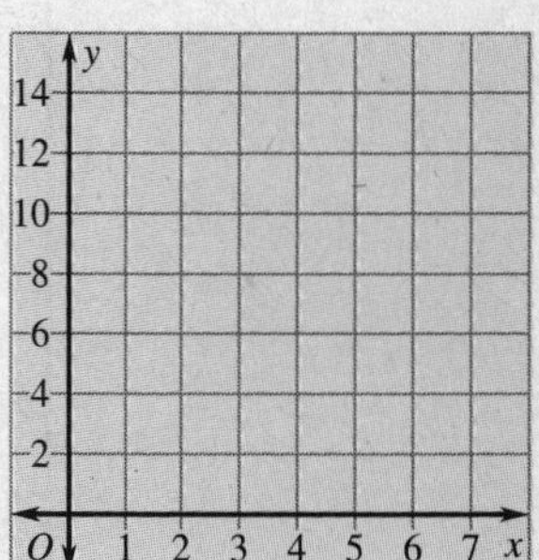

Your turn now **Evaluate the function from Example 1, for the given inpu[t]. Graph the ordered pair to check whether the point is on the line.**

1. $x = 5$

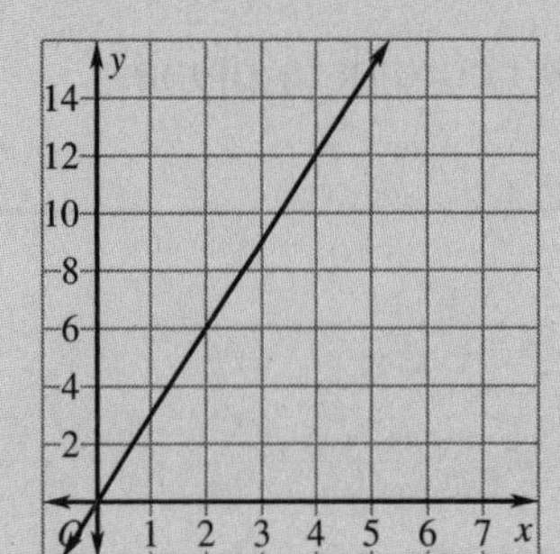

2. $x = 4.5$

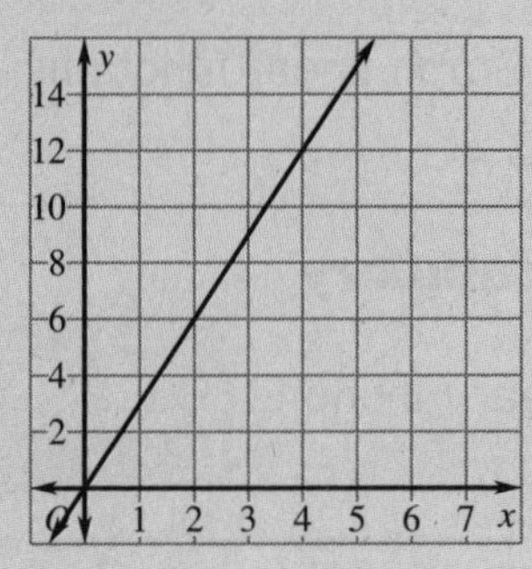

3. $x = \frac{1}{4}$

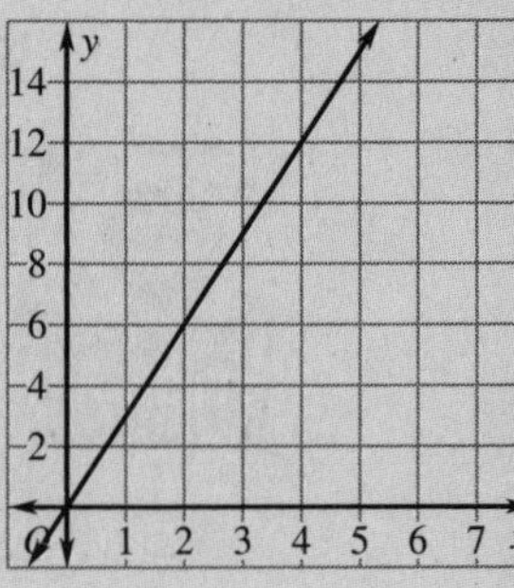

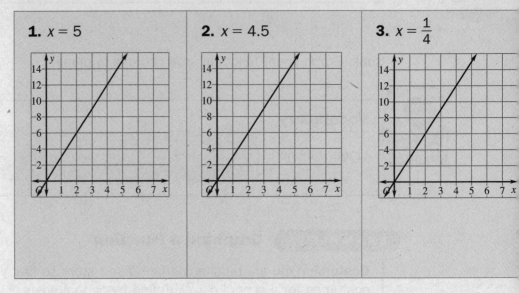

Representing Functions

There are many ways to represent the same function.

Words A number is the difference of another number and two.

Algebra $y =$ ______

Ordered Pairs $(-2,$ ______$)$, $(-1,$ ______$)$, $(0,$ ______$)$, $(1,$ ______$)$, $(2,$ ______$)$

Input-Output Table

Input, *x*	Output, *y*
−2	
−1	
0	
1	
2	

Graph

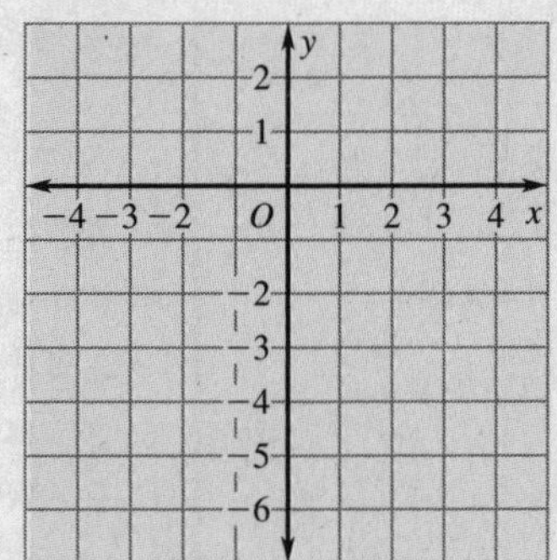

EXAMPLE 2 Identifying Linear Functions

It may be helpful to include a flow chart in your notes on identifying linear functions. Your flow chart should include steps for graphing ordered pairs, as in Example 1, and a step for deciding whether you can draw a line through the points.

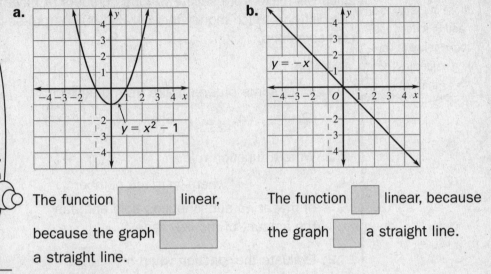

Tell whether the function is *linear* or *not linear*. Explain.

a.

$y = x^2 - 1$

The function ____ linear, because the graph ____ a straight line.

b.

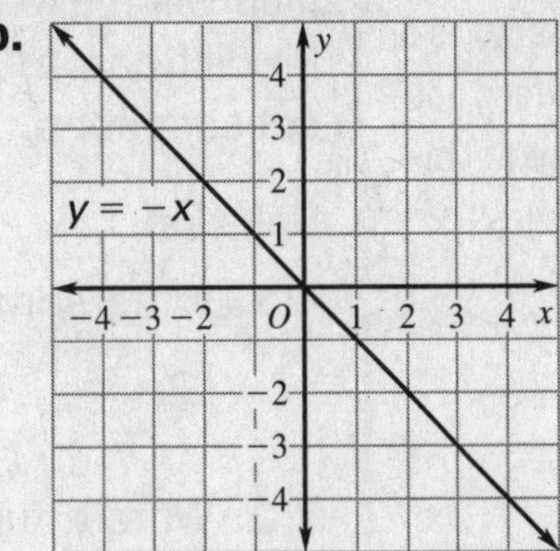

The function ____ linear, because the graph ____ a straight line.

Your turn now **Graph the function using the input values $x = -2, -1, 0, 1$, and 2. Tell whether the function is *linear* or *not linear*. Explain.**

4. $y = x + 2$

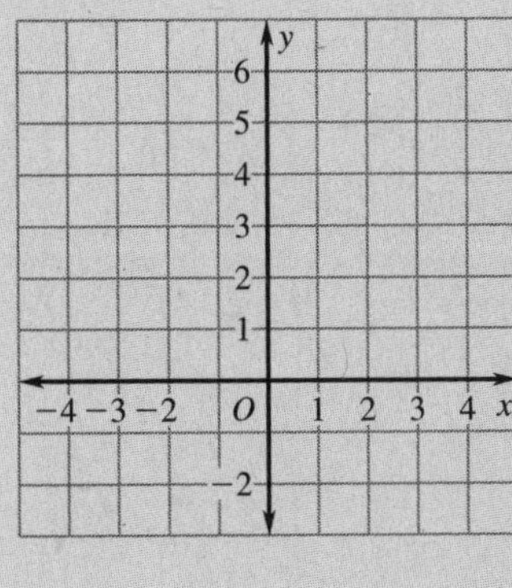

5. $y = 2 - x$

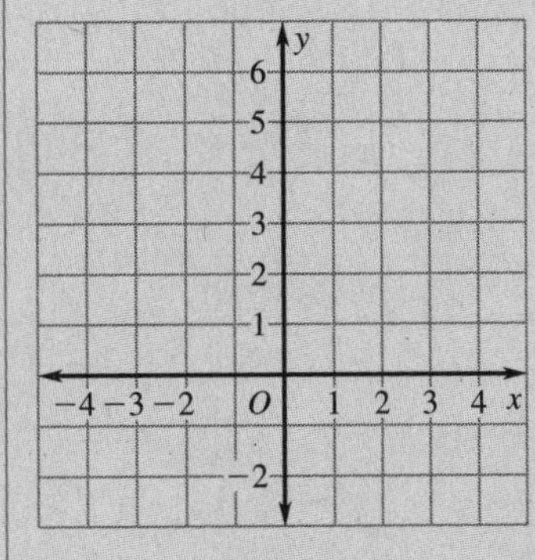

6. $y = 3x + 1$

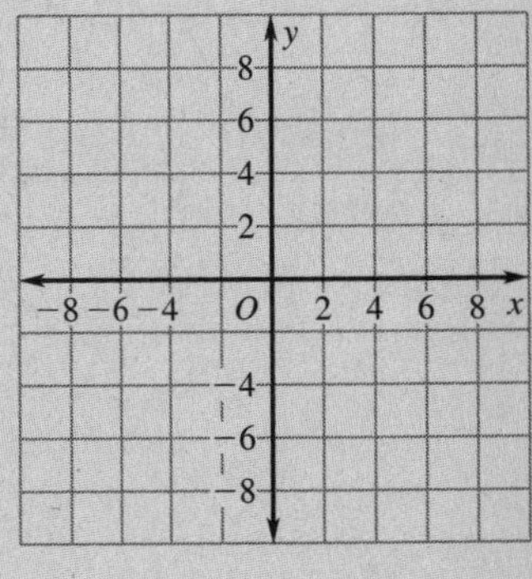

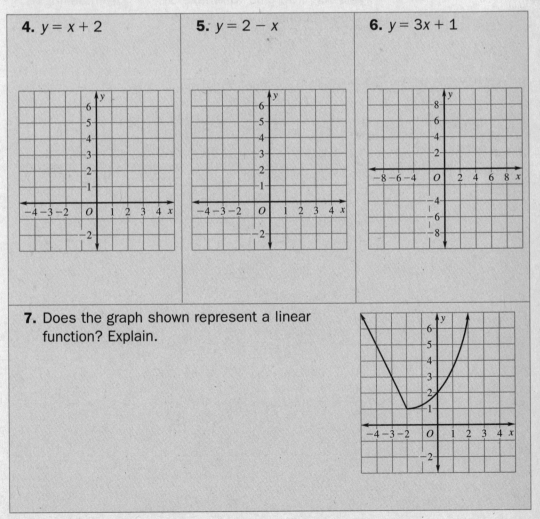

7. Does the graph shown represent a linear function? Explain.

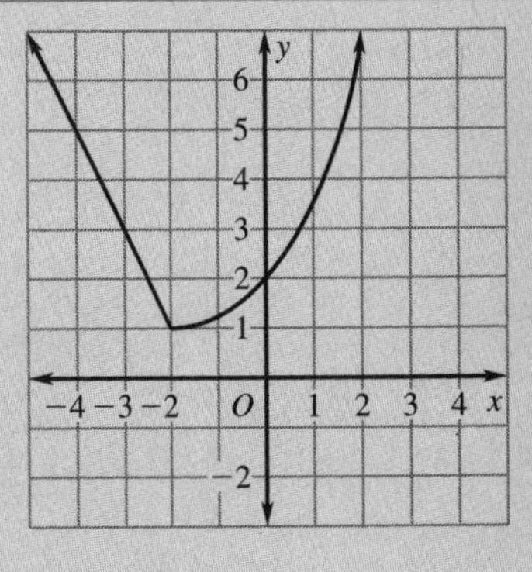

In many situations, including those in Examples 1 and 3, it does not make sense to have values less than 0.

EXAMPLE 3 Looking for a Pattern

Magazine Subscriptions The graph shows the amount of money a school club will make from selling various numbers of magazine subscriptions. Predict how much money the club will make from selling 50 magazine subscriptions.

Solution

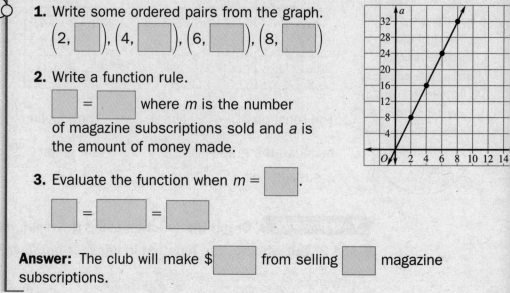

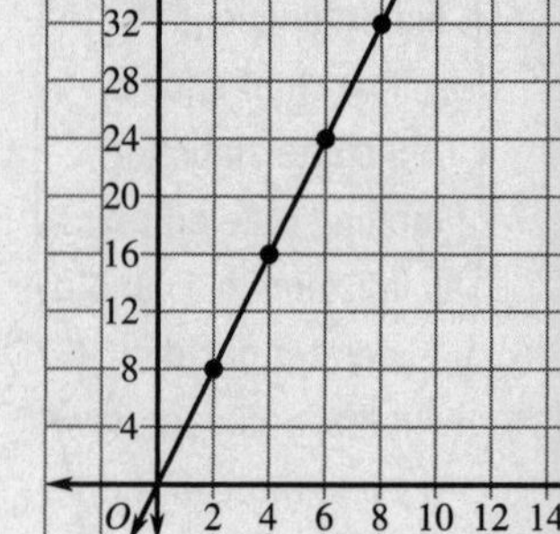

1. Write some ordered pairs from the graph.

(2, ____), (4, ____), (6, ____), (8, ____)

2. Write a function rule.

____ = ____ where *m* is the number of magazine subscriptions sold and *a* is the amount of money made.

3. Evaluate the function when $m =$ ____.

____ = ____ = ____

Answer: The club will make $____ from selling ____ magazine subscriptions.

Words to Review

Give an example of the vocabulary word.

Function

Input

Output

Linear function

Review your notes and Chapter 12 by using the Chapter Review on pages 620–621 of your textbook.

Introduction to Probability

Goal: Write probabilities.

For Your Notebook

Vocabulary

Outcome:

Event:

Favorable outcomes:

Probability:

Complementary events:

Finding Probabilities

The **probability** that an event will occur when all outcomes of an experiment are equally likely is as follows.

Probability of event = $\dfrac{\text{Number of}\ \_\_\_\_}{\text{Number of}\ \_\_\_\_}$

EXAMPLE 1 Finding a Probability

Board Game A board game has the spinner shown that is used to determin your next move. How likely is it that you will spin the spinner and land on "Move forward 2 spaces?"

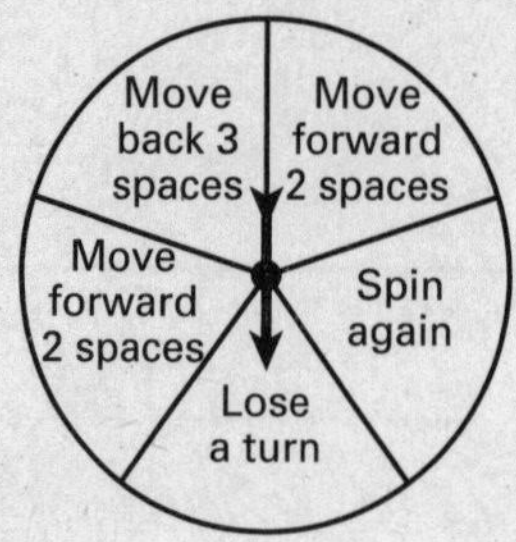

Solution

There are ___ favorable outcomes, which are ___. The ___ possible outcomes are ___

Probability of landing on "Move forward 2 spaces" = $\frac{\text{Number of \_\_\_ outcomes}}{\text{Number of \_\_\_ outcomes}}$

$= \frac{\_\_\_}{\_\_\_}$

Answer: You are ___ likely to land on "Move forward 2 spaces" than to not.

EXAMPLE 2 Describing Probabilities

You randomly choose a tile from a bag of lettered tiles. The tiles are shown below. Find and describe the probability of the event.

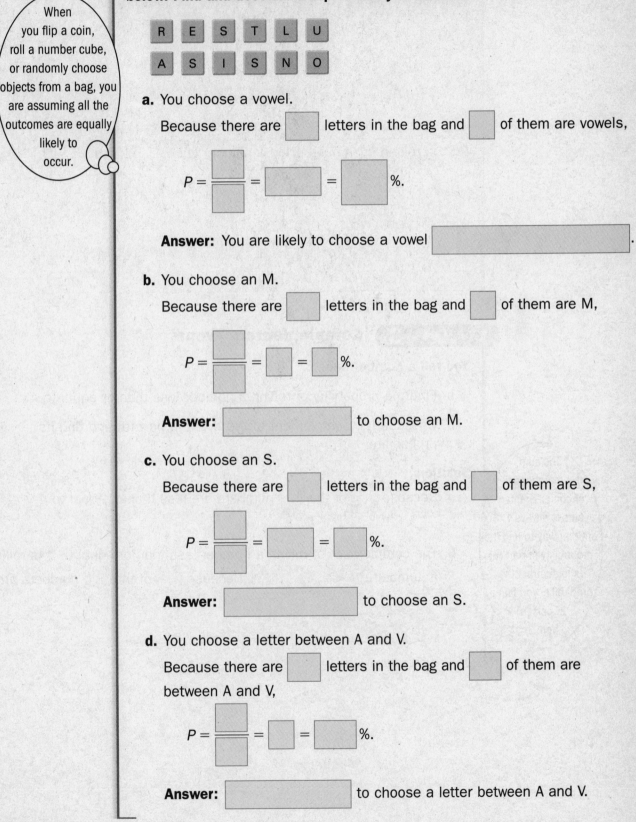

When you flip a coin, roll a number cube, or randomly choose objects from a bag, you are assuming all the outcomes are equally likely to occur.

R E S T L U

A S I S N O

a. You choose a vowel.

Because there are ___ letters in the bag and ___ of them are vowels,

$P = \frac{\square}{\square} = \square = \square\%$.

Answer: You are likely to choose a vowel ___.

b. You choose an M.

Because there are ___ letters in the bag and ___ of them are M,

$P = \frac{\square}{\square} = \square = \square\%$.

Answer: ___ to choose an M.

c. You choose an S.

Because there are ___ letters in the bag and ___ of them are S,

$P = \frac{\square}{\square} = \square = \square\%$.

Answer: ___ to choose an S.

d. You choose a letter between A and V.

Because there are ___ letters in the bag and ___ of them are between A and V,

$P = \frac{\square}{\square} = \square = \square\%$.

Answer: ___ to choose a letter between A and V.

Your turn now **Find the probability of the event.**

1. Each of the letters in the word CINCINNATI is placed on a separate piece of paper in a bag. You randomly choose a vowel.

2. You roll an even number on a number cube.

EXAMPLE 3 **Complementary Events**

You roll a number cube.

a. Find the probability of rolling a number less than or equal to 4.

b. Describe the complement of the event in part (a) and find its probability.

The sum of the probabilities of complementary events is always 1. So another way to find the probability in part (b) is to subtract the probability you found in part (a) from 1.

Solution

a. Because ___ of the ___ numbers are less than or equal to 4, $P = \frac{\square}{\square}$.

b. The complement of rolling a number less than or equal to 4 is rolling a number ______. Because ___ of the ___ numbers are ______, $P = \frac{\square}{\square}$.

Finding Outcomes

Goal: Use diagrams, tables, and lists to find outcomes.

For Your Notebook

Vocabulary

Tree diagram:

Combination:

Permutation:

EXAMPLE 1 Using Tree Diagrams

Rugs You are choosing a rug for the floor of your room. You can choose a square rug or a rectangular rug that can be made of wool or cotton. The rug can either have a pattern or be a solid color. What are the different kinds of rugs you can choose?

Solution

To find all possible outcomes, use a tree diagram.

1. List the rug shapes.
2. For each shape, list the material.
3. For each material, list the appearance.

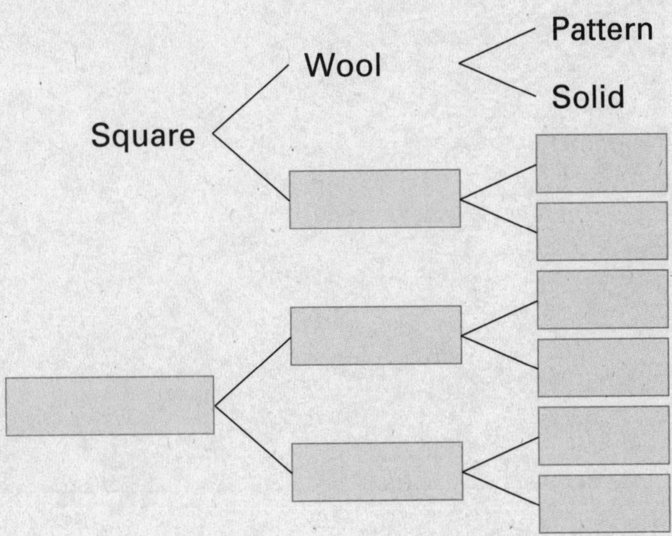

4. Find the outcomes.

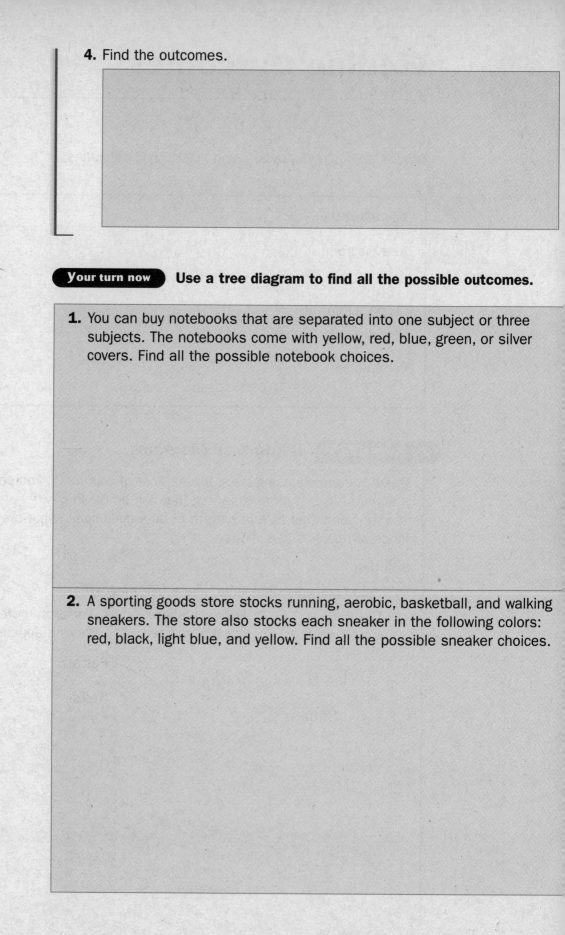

Your turn now **Use a tree diagram to find all the possible outcomes.**

1. You can buy notebooks that are separated into one subject or three subjects. The notebooks come with yellow, red, blue, green, or silver covers. Find all the possible notebook choices.

2. A sporting goods store stocks running, aerobic, basketball, and walking sneakers. The store also stocks each sneaker in the following colors: red, black, light blue, and yellow. Find all the possible sneaker choices.

EXAMPLE 2 Finding Combinations

Music You can choose 2 CDs from a list of 5 CDs. Find all the possible pairs of CDs.

Solution

Each outcome is a combination because it doesn't matter which CD you chose first. Use a table to show all the possible pairs of CDs.

CD 1	CD 2	CD 3	CD 4	CD 5	Outcome

If you prefer, you could use a tree diagram instead of a table to answer Example 2.

EXAMPLE 3 **Finding Permutations**

> **WATCH OUT!**
> Always read the problem statement carefully. In Example 3, all of the letters must be different, but other problems may allow for letters (or other items) to be reused.

Find all the ways three letters can be arranged using three different letters from A, B, T, E, and S.

Solution

Each outcome is a permutation because the order of the letters matters. Yo can use an organized list to arrange all the possible outcomes.

Starts with A:

Starts with B:

Starts with T:

Starts with E:

Starts with S:

Your turn now **Find all the possible outcomes.**

3. At a restaurant, you can choose two side dishes from the following: French fries, vegetables, applesauce, soup, and tossed salad. Find all the possible different pairs of side dishes.

4. You are scheduling your classes for the upcoming school year. You will be taking English, math, history, and science. Find all the possible ways you can order your classes.

Probability of Independent Events

Goal: Find the probability of two independent events.

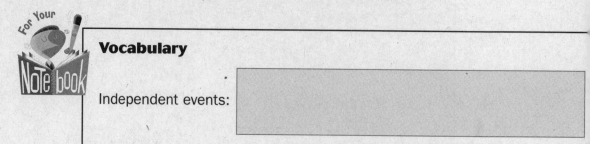

For Your Notebook

Vocabulary

Independent events:

EXAMPLE 1 Two Independent Events

Book Store You and your brother like science fiction, mystery, and biography books. At the bookstore you each buy a book. Assuming that you both will choose one of the three book types and that each of you are equally likely to choose each type, what is the probability that you both choose mystery?

Solution

To answer the question, make a tree diagram of the possible outcomes. Note that your choice does not affect your brother's choice.

Your choice **Brother's choice** **Outcome**

[ ] of the [ ] outcomes is favorable.

Answer: The probability that both of you choose mystery is $\frac{\square}{\square}$.

Your turn now **Use the situation in Example 1.**

1. What is the probability that you both choose the same kind of book?

2. What is the probability that at least one of you chooses science fiction?

EXAMPLE 2 Probability of a Sum

Another way to state the problem is to say "Find the probabillity that the sum is less than or equal to 6."

You randomly choose a tile from each bag shown below. Find the probability that the sum of the tiles is at most 6.

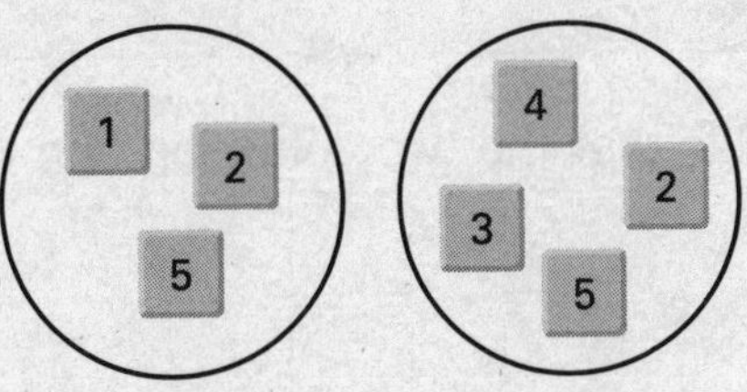

Solution

You can use a table of sums to list all the possible outcomes.

	2	3	4	5
1				
2				
5				

☐ of the ☐ sums are at most 6.

Answer: The probability that the sum is at most 6 is $\frac{\square}{\square}$.

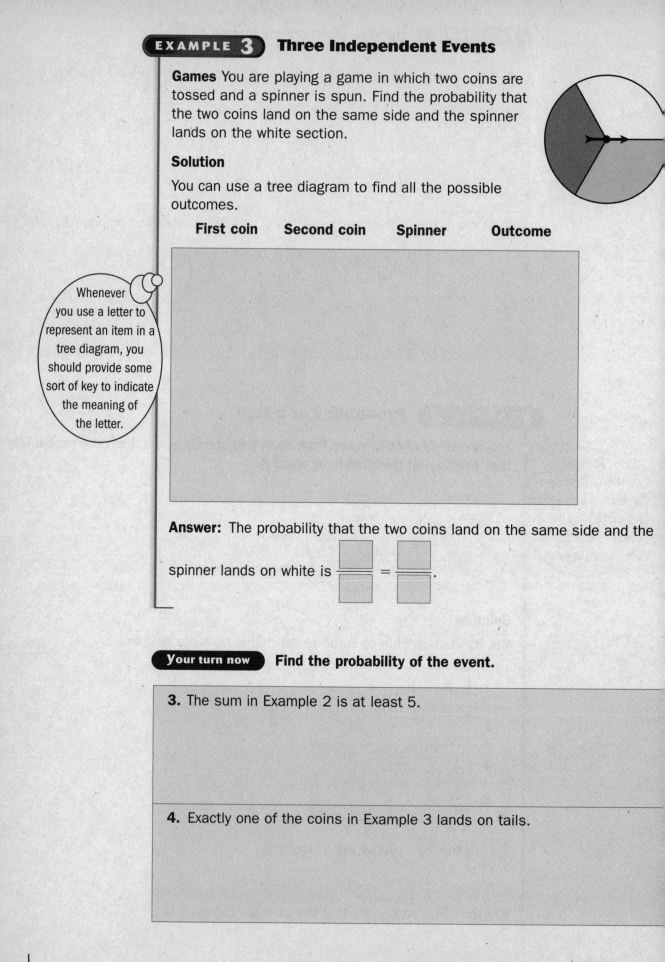

EXAMPLE 3 Three Independent Events

Games You are playing a game in which two coins are tossed and a spinner is spun. Find the probability that the two coins land on the same side and the spinner lands on the white section.

Solution

You can use a tree diagram to find all the possible outcomes.

First coin **Second coin** **Spinner** **Outcome**

Whenever you use a letter to represent an item in a tree diagram, you should provide some sort of key to indicate the meaning of the letter.

Answer: The probability that the two coins land on the same side and the spinner lands on white is $\frac{\square}{\square} = \frac{\square}{\square}$.

Your turn now **Find the probability of the event.**

3. The sum in Example 2 is at least 5.

4. Exactly one of the coins in Example 3 lands on tails.

Misleading Statistics

Goal: Recognize how statistics can be misleading.

EXAMPLE 1 Potentially Misleading Graphs

Lakes The bar graph shows the areas of three of the five Great Lakes. Without using the scale, about how many times greater does the area of Lake Superior appear to be than the area of Lake Michigan? Then compare the areas using the scale.

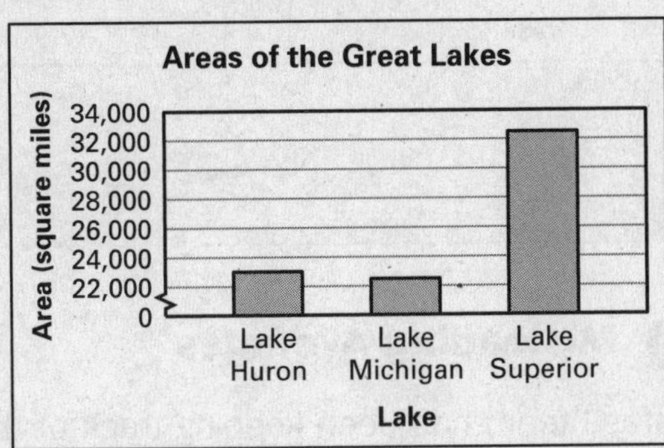

Solution

The area of Lake Superior appears to be about ________ the area of Lake Michigan, because the bar for Lake Superior is about ________ as high as the bar for Lake Michigan.

The area of Lake Superior is actually about ____% of the area of Lake Michigan, because

area of Lake Superior ÷ area of Lake Michigan = ________ ÷ ________

≈ ____%.

The break in the scale distorts the ________ of the bars.

Your turn now **Solve the problem below.**

1. Tell which line graph makes the population of Akron, Ohio appear to decrease more dramatically. Explain.

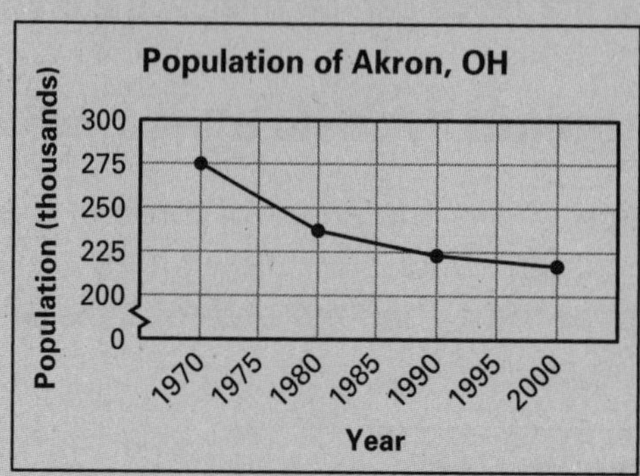

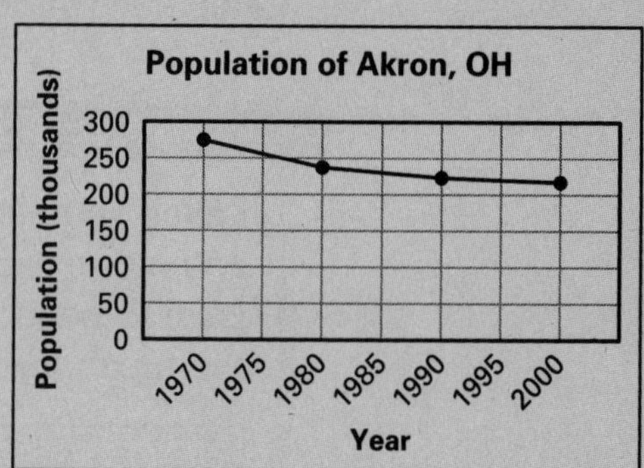

EXAMPLE 2 Misleading Averages

Football A football team has been keeping track of the differences in the numbers of points scored by each team. The differences in the numbers of points for the games the team has won is shown.

3, 21, 3, 2, 2, 14, 1, 2

Does 6 points describe well the differences in the points for the games won? Why might a team use this number?

Need help with finding the mean, median, and mode? See page 93 of your textbook.

Solution

Mean: $\frac{\boxed{}}{\boxed{}} = \frac{\boxed{}}{\boxed{}} = \boxed{}$

Median: $\boxed{} = \boxed{} = \boxed{}$

Mode: $\boxed{}$

If one data value is very small or very large compared to the other data values, then the mean could be distorted.

The ______, 6, ______ describe the data well because it is ______ the numbers. A team might use this number to convince people that ______.

Your turn now **The numbers of hours students in your class spent watching television in one week are listed below. Use this data in Exercises 2 and 3.**

23, 12, 22, 24, 13, 25, 21, 12

2. Does 12 describe the numbers of hours well? Why or why not?

3. Why might a student use 12 as the average number of hours of television watched?

Stem-and-Leaf Plots

Goal: Organize data using stem-and-leaf plots.

For Your Notebook

Vocabulary

Stem-and-leaf plot:

Leaf:

Stem:

EXAMPLE 1 Making a Stem-and-Leaf Plot

Computer Printers You are shopping for black and white laser printers. The prices of the models you are looking at are listed below. Organize the prices in a stem-and-leaf plot.

\$699, \$644, \$699, \$678, \$619, \$687, \$657,
\$632, \$699, \$668, \$647, \$660, \$639, \$618

Solution

WATCH OUT!
Be sure to include all of the stems between the least and greatest. In Example 1, 62 is a stem even though none of the data values have a 6 in the hundreds' place and a 2 in the tens' place.

1. Order the stems from least to greatest.

2. Write the leaves next to their stems.

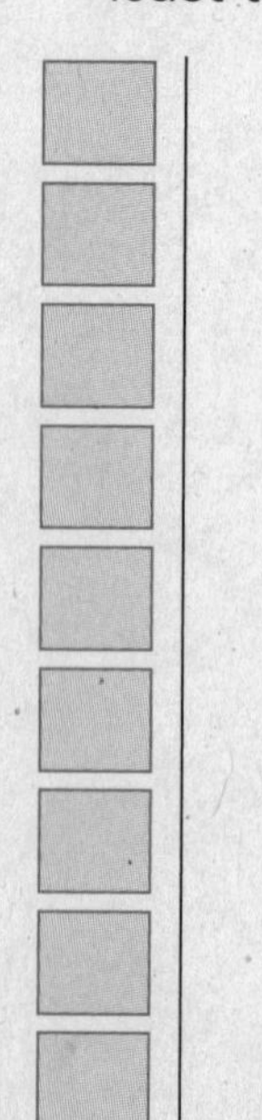

Key: 61 | 9 = 619

3. Order the leaves from least to greatest.

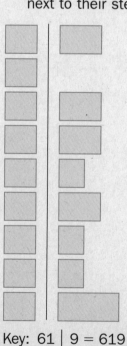

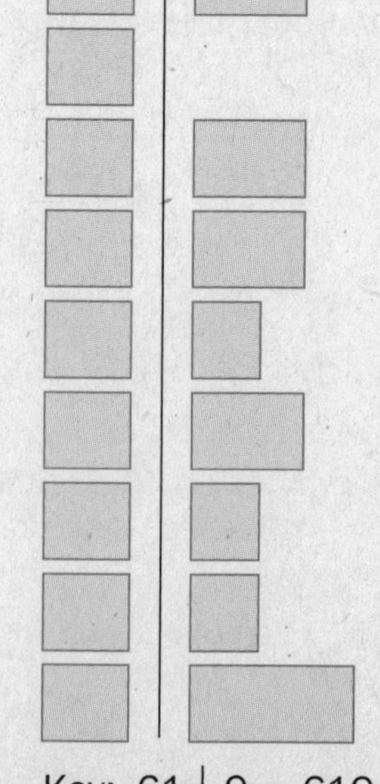

Key: 61 | 9 = 619

Your turn now **Make a stem-and-leaf plot of the data.**

1. 56, 38, 44, 62, 50, 48, 65, 39, 56, 34, 69, 50, 47

EXAMPLE 2 **Interpreting Stem-and-Leaf Plots**

Pumpkins The stem-and-leaf plot shows the weights, in pounds, of pumpkins at a grocery store.

1	3 5 6 7
2	0 5 6 8 9
3	5 6 8
4	2 5 7 8

Key: 1 | 3 = 1.3

a. What is the range of the weights?

b. Describe the weight group with the least number of pumpkins.

Solution

a. The lightest pumpkin weighs ____ pounds, because the least data value is ____. The heaviest pumpkin weighs ____ pounds, because the greatest data value is ____. The range is ____ pounds, because ____ = ____.

b. The least number of pumpkins is between ____ and ____ pounds, because the stem of ____ has the least number of data values.

WATCH OUT!

Read the key in a stem-and-leaf plot carefully. In Example 1, the key indicates that the data are whole numbers. In Example 2, the key indicates that the data are decimals.

EXAMPLE 3 Finding the Mean, Median, and Mode

Use the stem-and-leaf plot.

a. Find the mean.

b. Find the median.

c. Find the mode.

1	5 7
2	0 5
3	2 3 3

Key: 2 | 5 = 25

Solution

Make an ordered list of the ______ values in the stem-and-leaf plot.

______, ______, ______, ______, ______, ______, ______

a. Mean: $\frac{\_\_\_\_\_\_}{\_\_\_\_\_\_} = \frac{\_\_\_}{\_\_\_} = \_\_\_$

b. The median is ______, because ______________.

c. The mode is ______, because ______________.

Your turn now **Use the stem-and-leaf plot in Example 2.**

2. Describe the weights of the pumpkins that are in the most common weight group.

3. Find the mean, median, and mode(s) of the data.

Box-and-Whisker Plots

Goal: Represent data using box-and-whisker plots.

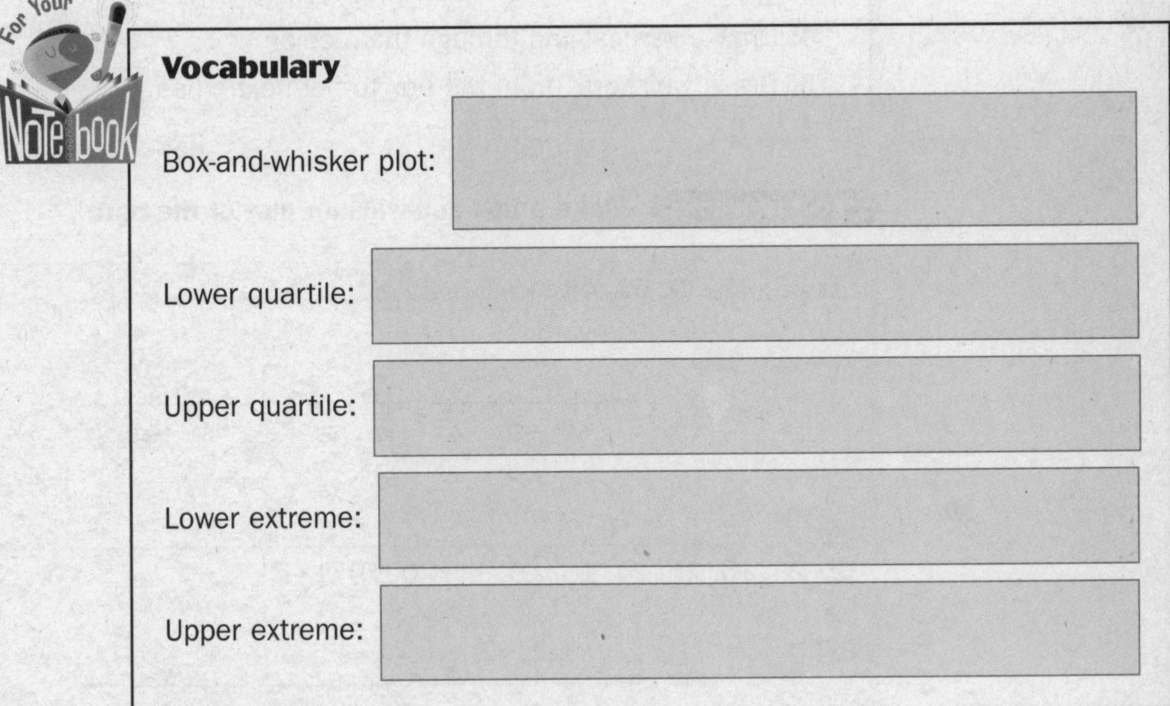

Vocabulary

Box-and-whisker plot:

Lower quartile:

Upper quartile:

Lower extreme:

Upper extreme:

EXAMPLE 1 Making a Box-and-Whisker Plot

Volleyball The heights, in inches, of players on a volleyball team are shown below. Make a box-and-whisker plot of the data.

70, 65, 68, 72, 69, 72, 68, 70, 71, 74

Solution

If a data set has an odd number of data values, then the median is not included in either half of the data.

1. Order the data to find the median, the quartiles, and the extremes.

Lower half | Upper half

☐ ☐ ☐ ☐ ☐ | ☐ ☐ ☐ ☐ ☐

The median is (☐ + ☐) ÷ ☐ = ☐, the lower quartile is ☐, the upper quartile is ☐, the lower extreme is ☐, and the upper extreme is ☐.

2. Plot the five values below a number line.

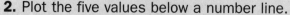

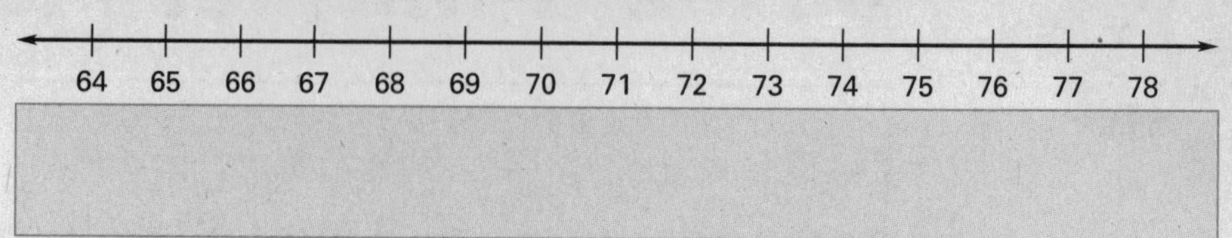

3. Draw a box with sides at both quartiles.
4. Draw a vertical line through the median.
5. Draw "whiskers" from the box to both extremes.

Your turn now **Make a box-and-whisker plot of the data.**

1. 46, 37, 39, 52, 48, 45, 57, 32, 61

2. 28, 15, 21, 24, 16, 19, 11, 20, 29, 13

EXAMPLE 2 Reading a Box-and-Whisker Plot

Identify the median, the lower and upper quartiles, and the lower and upper extremes in the box-and-whisker plot below.

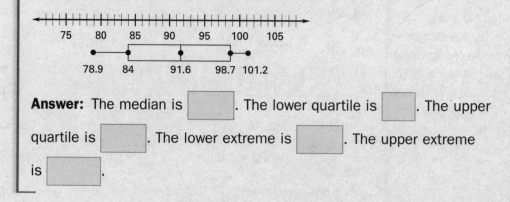

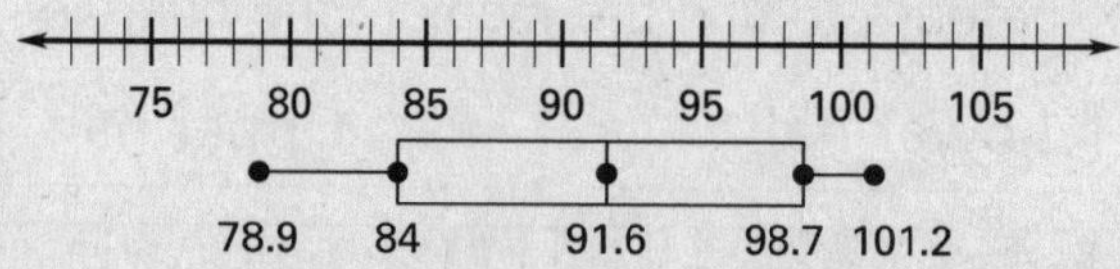

Answer: The median is ______. The lower quartile is ______. The upper quartile is ______. The lower extreme is ______. The upper extreme is ______.

EXAMPLE 3 Interpreting Box-and-Whisker Plots

Horses The box-and-whisker plots below represent the heights, in inches, of two different breeds of horses at a horse farm.

a. Find the ranges of the heights.

b. Compare the heights of the two breeds of horses.

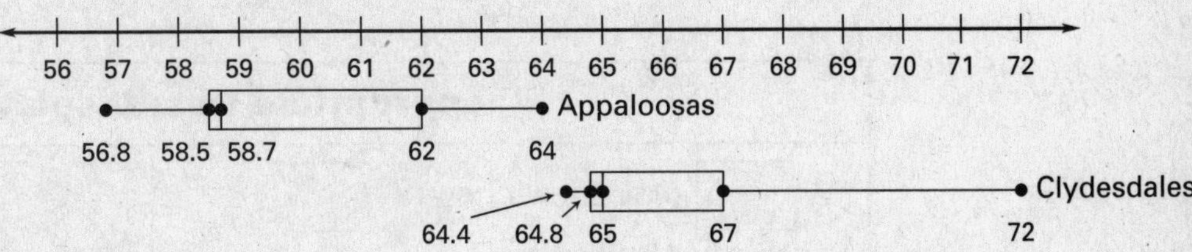

Solution

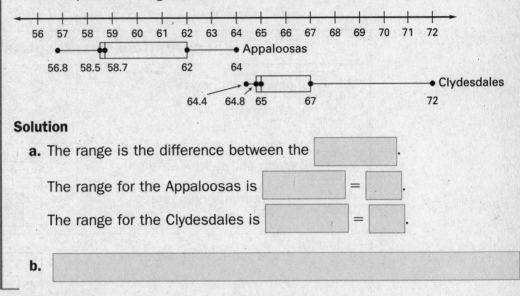

a. The range is the difference between the ______.

The range for the Appaloosas is ______ = ______.

The range for the Clydesdales is ______ = ______.

b. ______

Your turn now **Use the box-and-whisker plots in Examples 2 and 3.**

3. Find the range of the data in Example 2.

4. Identify the median, the lower and upper quartiles, and the lower and upper extremes for the heights of the Appaloosas in Example 3.

Choosing an Appropriate Data Display

Goal: Choose appropriate data displays.

<table>
<tr><th colspan="2">Appropriate Data Displays</th></tr>
<tr><td>A ____ plot shows how ____ each number occurs.</td><td></td></tr>
<tr><td>A ____ graph shows how different ____ of data compare.</td><td></td></tr>
<tr><td>A ____ graph represents data that change over ____.</td><td></td></tr>
<tr><td>A ____ graph represents data as ____.</td><td></td></tr>
<tr><td>A ____ plot displays ____ the data values and orders the data from ____ to ____.</td><td>1 | 3 5 6 7
2 | 0 5 6 8 9
3 | 5 6 8
4 | 2 5 7 8 Key: 1 | 3 = 1</td></tr>
<tr><td>A ____ plot shows the ____ of data using the ____, the ____, and the ____.</td><td></td></tr>
</table>

EXAMPLE 1 Choosing Between Two Displays

You can use either graph to find the median of the data in Example 1. The question is, in which graph is it easier to find the median?

CDs Which plot makes it easier to find the median number of CDs bought by a group of people in a month?

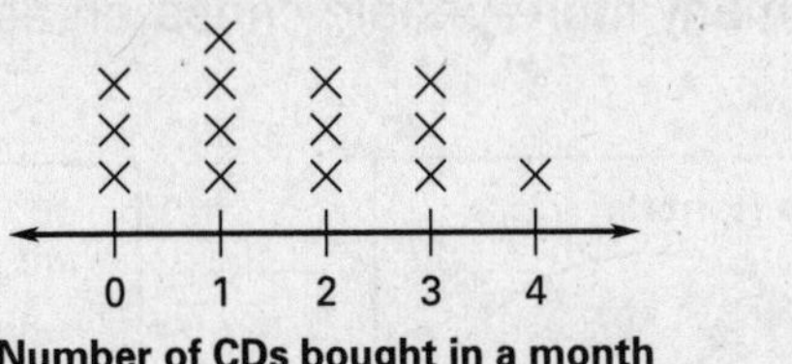

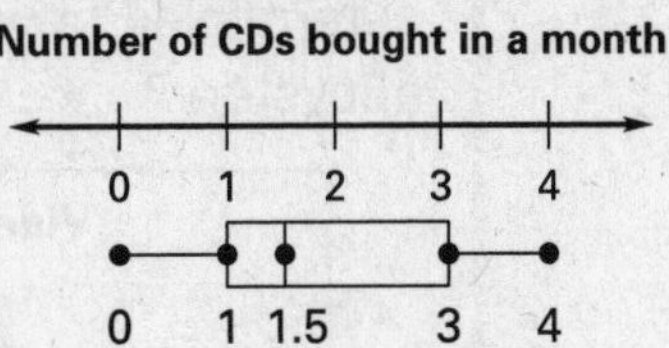

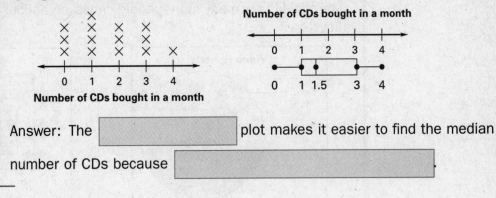

Answer: The ________ plot makes it easier to find the median number of CDs because ________.

EXAMPLE 2 Making an Appropriate Display

Bus Ride You ask 15 people on a bus how long their ride is to their destination. The list below shows their responses, in minutes. Make a data display that shows all of the data values.

15, 12, 12, 5, 8, 19, 10, 20, 18, 5, 17, 24, 6, 5, 15

Solution

You can use a ________ or a ________ to show all of the data values.

EXAMPLE 3 Choosing the Appropriate Display

Videos The data displays show the kinds of videos rented by people in a video store during a recent weekday. Which display is appropriate for determining how many more people chose an action/adventure movie than a mystery?

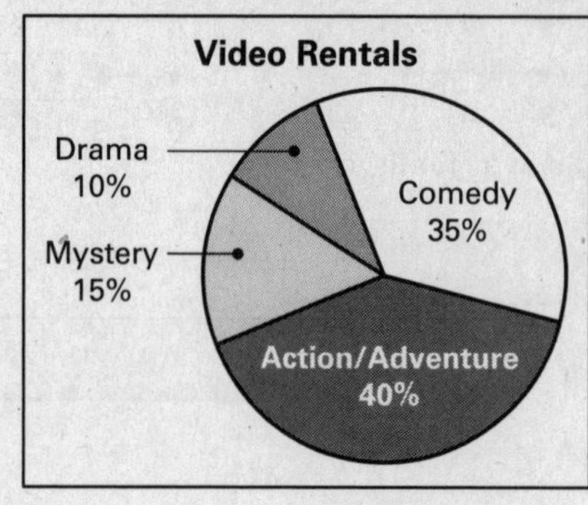

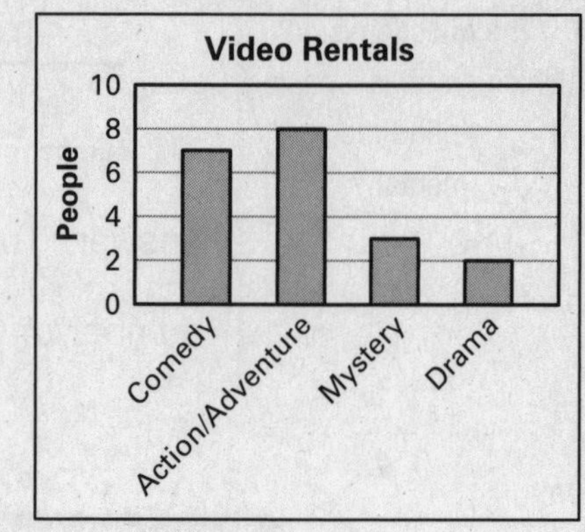

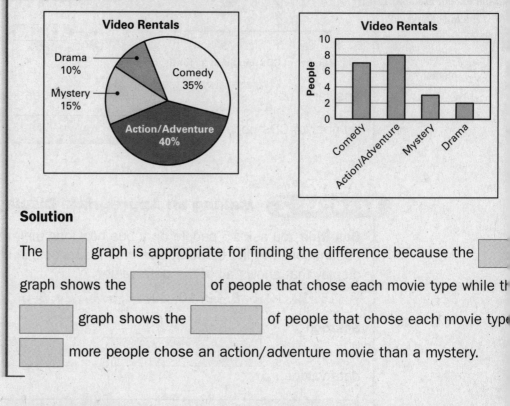

Solution

The ______ graph is appropriate for finding the difference because the ______ graph shows the ______ of people that chose each movie type while the ______ graph shows the ______ of people that chose each movie type. ______ more people chose an action/adventure movie than a mystery.

Your turn now **Choose an appropriate display for the given situation.**

For each type of data display you studied in you textbook, you may want to include an example in your notebook along with a summary of the information that you can read from the display.

1. You record the height, in inches, of a plant every day at 4:00 P.M. for a week. The data are listed below. Which data display would you use to show how the height changed during that time?

0.5 in. 0.8 in. 1.5 in. 1.7 in. 2.4 in. 2.8 in. 3.1 in.

Words to Review

Give an example of the vocabulary word.

Outcome

Event

Favorable outcomes

Probability

Complementary events

Tree diagram

Combination

Permutation

Independent events

Stem-and-leaf plot

Leaf

Stem

Box-and-whisker plot

Lower quartile

Upper quartile

Lower extreme

Upper extreme

Review your notes and Chapter 13 by using the Chapter Review on pages 668–669 of your textbook.